WHEN I GROW UP I WANT TO BE A CAT

WHEN I GROW UP I WANT TO BE A CAT

Surviving the education system
with Asperger's

MADELEINE LEVY

CAVALCADE BOOKS

First published in the United Kingdom in 2021

by Cavalcade Books
www.cavalcadebooks.com

ISBN 978-1-8381490-0-0 (paperback)
ISBN 978-1-8381490-3-1 (e-book)

Cover cat illustration by Nina Taylor
Chapter title page illustrations and illustrations on pages 25, 80, 94, 97, 99, 100,
158 and 161 by Matthew Recardo
Illustrations on pages 12 and 13 by Sam Kilpatrick

"I'm not crazy. My reality is just different than yours."

Lewis Carroll, *Alice in Wonderland*

CONTENTS

FOREWORD

by Richard Hayhow

It is a great pleasure to write the foreword for this book. I have known the author, Madeleine, for many years now, from the time we were brought together in the context of the Creative Minds conference steering group in Birmingham back in 2017. The conference was co-organised by Open Theatre, the company I am Director of, and aimed to discuss creativity and give disabled artists access to the arts. I remember thinking that it was a fairly random way to work together. At that time, I certainly puzzled a bit about how we might relate together and whether we could indeed work together.

In time what I realised about Madeleine was that, the woman who I thought was at times awkward and sometimes a bit "in your face" and certainly not someone at ease with themselves, was in fact a person trying to make sense of and manage the experiences discussed in this book. When we first met I felt that Madeleine was presenting in a very different way to who she really was – as a form of self-protection and of wariness about how the next person who came into her life would treat her.

As we both relaxed in each other's company, I began to realise what a remarkable person Madeleine is – and how much I enjoyed working with her and learning from her. As opposed to the person I first saw as shut off and awkward I discovered that Madeleine was full of life, articulate and intelligent, and open to exploring new ways of working and being in the world. The impact of the way other people had treated Madeleine could not be clearer. We began to make connections between her experience of the world and our experience as a company working with young people with a learning disability, autism or both. One of our company's five values is "joy" and the joy Madeleine and I found in working together was clearly the major catalyst in transforming the way we could work together: in Madeleine's words it enabled her to "show the world who I actually am without any façade".

Open Theatre has a non-verbal physical theatre practice that we use both to release the creativity of young people in special schools but also to support their learning and development through effective communication beyond words. Our practice fills the gaps where language is lacking to describe experiences feelings or events. Our practice places every individual at the heart of how we engage with them. We have come to realise the power of non-verbal communication as a means to enable a young person to express themselves and explore the world through and discover who they are. Our strapline is "Doing Difference Differently", reflecting the fact that we need to work with everyone as the unique individual they are and not use any pre-set formulas as to how to go about the work we do. In essence we work to discover what any young person can do, not what they can't do.

We work long-term in a wide range of special schools across the West Midlands, supporting teaching staff to develop a richer understanding of ways of engaging and communicating with young people in those schools. Times have moved on since Madeleine was at school and there is considerably more expectation and support for what young people in these schools can achieve. However, even if we can help increase the confidence and abilities of those young people through our work with special schools, the world outside school is still stacked heavily against them. This is not just in terms of being included in what the rest of us regard as our right to be involved in as adults – but also in terms of valuing what these young people can contribute to the way we go about our adult lives.

As a company we have also begun to understand the importance of a long-term commitment to the young people we work with. Through our engagement with young people in schools we build long-lasting relationships with them and an understanding of how their needs change over time. In this way we aim to promote both their inclusion in but also their contribution to society and clearly brings home the message that there is the need for this long-term creative support for so many young people. I know that this something Madeleine has appreciated personally in the way we have engaged with her over time and is keen to articulate in her book.

What is remarkable about the book is that Madeleine has captured a one-off experience, her time in school, with a clarity that gives us a unique insight into her life experience. This is clearly a particular individual's experience but at the same time is one that helps us draw out some basic principles about what we as a society are getting wrong in the way we think we should go about educating our young people. It is to Madeleine's credit that she has acknowledged that her experience is her experience, and that the experience of others will necessarily differ. By including the thoughts of others in the book the readers are invited to draw out similarities, but more importantly recognise and validate differences in experience. Equally for those young people for whom words are not an effective means of communication, Madeleine's book acts as a voice for them too, articulating the need for their individualised support plans and care, bespoke to them and responsive to changes in those needs throughout their lives. Not only this but this book is a beacon of hope for young people on the autism spectrum, their parents and carers. Madeleine lives independently, has two degrees and is about to complete a third. This book gives a very positive message that if given the right environment autistic people can, do and are achieving great things. If they are given a supportive environment and plenty of encouragement who knows what they will do next?

It is in this journey that we take as readers of Madeleine's book that our understanding will grow: through an acknowledgement and acceptance of differences more than similarities in the ways we impact each other's worlds. Madeleine is keen that her book is seen as a working document that can be used to unravel other young people's experiences and to discover better ways in which we can all support each other through life and take responsibility for moving out of our comfort zones and habits to embrace difference more fully. We all still have a lot to learn.

Richard Hayhow
Director of Open Theatre Company, Birmingham and Coventry

A THANK YOU

Huge thanks go to all the following people.

To all the individuals on the spectrum who allowed me to interview them as part of this project. You are truly wonderful people who make life lots more interesting.

To Arts Council England for providing me with a Covid 19 emergency response package. The money was used to support the publication of this book.

To Open Theatre Company Birmingham for supporting me throughout my working adult life and supporting me to gain a career in the arts.

To my parents and sisters for experiencing life's journey alongside me, and to my closest friends for loving me as I am.

They say that in life people either appear as blessings or lessons, but I believe that often a person can be a blessing and a lesson or each one individually. So, to this end I want to thank the individuals who have appeared in my life, either briefly or for a long while, as lessons to support, shape, teach or educate me: firstly, my teachers in primary school who understood me – Mrs Nash, Mrs Corn and Mrs Egan my primary school support worker; the teachers at my secondary school who were part of the special needs unit – Kate Wixon and Miss Vines; my support staff at my first university – David Walmsley and Caroline Lear for supporting me with getting this idea off the ground; Dr Bridget Escolme and Dr Tamara Atkin; Lee Burden from Autism West Midlands who supported me at the start of my career; Dr Tanya Rhitman, Dr Annette Rouebuck, Ann Jones, Emma Rose and finally Joanne Holmes, Estelle Seymour, Jane Manton, Eric Morgan, Matt King, Mel Daly and Richard

Hayhow who, not only do I consider personal mentors but have become firm friends, without whom I could not have achieved most of what I have done in my adult life.

To Allen Barker, Steven Osbourne, John Muriel Shepard, David Byrne, Robert Kidney, Christopher Matthew King, Jake Ikin, Ben Gallant, John Heaton and Charlie Gallant. You are all masters of occupational adaptation, even if you are unaware of the term.

To my partner for continually supporting and loving me no matter what I choose to do and anyone else who has experienced being an autistic obsession of mine.

Thank you all, your support means more than can be described in words.

INTRODUCTION

This is a book about my life growing up and about the education system as I experienced it. I have written it for a number of reasons. My first intent was to write a book that genuinely gives the perspective from someone on the autistic spectrum. So often the spectrum is written about by practitioners or academics who have no direct experience of the condition yet still describe themselves as experts in the field. How can you be an expert when you do not live with the symptoms every day? Most research and text currently available is aimed at psychiatrists, teachers, parents and other healthcare professionals to aid understanding about the spectrum. Whilst I believe this work is valid and valuable, not much writing addresses people on the spectrum themselves and the tone these texts are written in is often harmful to the individuals on the spectrum. I wish to change the way the autism world is written about by writing a guide for youngsters with Asperger's syndrome that supports them through the education system.

I want young people on the spectrum to know that they are not alone, that there are others like them and it is not their fault that they have a disability. I want friends of people with Asperger's and autism to be able to understand what makes us behave the way we do and how to work with us. I also want them to know how much we love them even though we sometimes find it difficult to express appropriately.

The book doesn't just give me a voice but gives a voice to other individuals who are on the autistic spectrum. However, I want to stress that my views are my own and I do not claim to represent anyone from the autistic community. If my words ring true for you, then that is great, but my views are there to raise awareness of issues and concerns faced by many I know. The book includes interviews with nine individuals on the spectrum who talk about their own experiences and struggles with the education system. There are a few issues that I believe contributed to their struggles in education.

Firstly, the educators were not provided with enough information about Asperger's to support the children who struggled. I feel that autism-awareness training should be mandatory for all teachers both in special schools and mainstream schools, and for supply staff.

Secondly, the *Diagnostic and Statistical Manual of Mental Disorders* (DSM), an American diagnostic reference for health professionals in the United States, listed autism spectrum as an umbrella of various disorders including pervasive developmental disorder in their latest edition in 2013. The manual clumped together a range of types of autism, such as Asperger's syndrome and autistic disorder. This is because often there will be similar behaviours which are presented in groups of young people. For example, if you should continue reading this book, you will see that many of us struggle with sensory difficulties and form special interests. What this meant was that because the DSM was an influential reference point used by many health professionals in England as well as the States, the way that Asperger's was dealt with in British schools – yes, I will say dealt with rather than supported – became standardised. For example, there will be a special learning unit in each mainstream school to house the children with learning differences and separate them from the mainstream children. How can the needs of someone with autistic disorder be the same as the needs of a student with Asperger's syndrome? How can teachers successfully support all of the school's special needs children in a confined space without trying to integrate them with mainstream children?

Thirdly, school systems are designed to support able-bodied people, that is, individuals who do not have a learning difference or a physical health need, and so individuals with those concerns are automatically at a disadvantage. School books are designed for people with neurotypical brains to understand; classroom layouts are not designed with wheelchairs in mind unless it is a special school, which automatically segregates individuals with learning difference and makes them seem other – why should there be a separate school for them? Why can't mainstream schools adapt their practice to include individuals with learning differences, rather than having them segregated into special units? Positive attitudes towards people with learning differences should be taught at school because those children grow into adults and if they are not punished for bullying individuals with learning differences then they will grow into adults who believe that people with learning differences are not of value in society. The school system needs to change!

Finally, school was made difficult because whilst there was support available, as I mentioned earlier, it was standardised support. A lot of people say to me, well you've had loads of support throughout your life think how unlucky others are who don't have that support and to them I say this: standardised support means that it was support offered to all children with a learning difference and was delivered in the same way rather than tailored to each individual. It was support that the professionals believed I needed rather than encouraging me and empowering me to think about what I needed for myself, and that was why I grew to resent, challenge and deny the support throughout my teenage years. This was to my own detriment, but I could not accept something which I saw as being designed to restrict or ostracise me.

This book aims to demonstrate that every individual on the spectrum is different and bangs the drum for individualised care and timetable planning in schools based on the interests and needs of the aforementioned individual. I believe that individualised care should be in place no matter who the child is, whether or not they have any disorders at all. This will make for a better and more fruitful education for all.

The interviews throughout the book demonstrate that although many of us exhibit similar symptoms, we are not all the same – and consequently we should not all be treated in the same way. This brings me to the principal reason for writing my book: to highlight the need for change in the education system. A one-size-fits-all model simply does not work when caring for individuals on the spectrum; individualised care is what is needed. All young people should have individualised education plans based on abilities and interests and all children should be supported and collaborated with to understand what their needs are. The education system is not designed to support the likes of spectrum individuals. Not enough individualised support is in place for individuals on the spectrum and many teachers do not understand how to work with an individual on the spectrum. Not only this but schools are so focused on teaching children the national curriculum, obtaining positive Ofsted reports and high exam scores that they forget to teach children basic kindness, respect and awareness of the differences of others – thus making the lives of individuals in minority groups difficult at best. This then continues on into adulthood, university and the workplace. Further, children are being denied creativity due to having such heavy focus on passing exams rather than exploring play and creative needs; therefore change is definitely needed and it is needed now.

This book is important in modern society because there is still loads of research to be done to support spectrum individuals. People from the Asperger community feel that there is still a gap in the care they receive and a lack of understanding in the way they are being treated by professionals and society, despite the fact that there is Autism Awareness Month in April and International Disability Awareness Day, there is still a spread of public ignorance which, I will argue, is the real epidemic rather than the increase in autism diagnosis.

My book is also a memoir, a story of my personal life and experiences – but importantly I also want and intend it to be a guide to help others: young people on the spectrum going through the education system and their parents, carers, siblings and friends, teachers and anyone else in society who wishes to understand how to interact with somebody on the spectrum. It's a guide that deals with many issues that any young person with high-functioning autism may face throughout their education. It includes lots of advice that I wish I'd been able to give myself at the time I was going through all the things I've been through.

I appreciate that my experience will not be the same as every child with autism or Asperger's. It is true what they say: once you have met one person with autism you really have just met one person with autism. We are all individuals, and in particular I cannot claim to understand how to support individuals with severe learning disabilities; nor do I represent any particular group or person. I can only speak from my own experience and use the information that I have gathered through speaking to others on what gets called the "high functioning" end of the spectrum.

I hope speaking with you about my experiences of the education system will help you through difficult times. I wish to support parents, to help you minimise the attempts at finding something that works for your child – I have taught myself through trial and error and I wish to be your support to help you minimise your attempts at finding an appropriate collaboration which empowers and involves your child in their own care.

For young people with Asperger's, I wish to be your friend. I wish to offer you advice when you are alone and I want to tell you how amazing you are and how amazing the gifts that you possess are. I want to tell you that you will succeed if you want to and not to let society grind you down. Children with Asperger's syndrome can grow up to accomplish great things and survive in this harsh and difficult world. They can go to university and flourish in high-powered careers. Perceptions and stereotypes that people have about the Asperger's community can and should be challenged.

My book carries the message that acceptance of oneself is what brings true happiness. This is a lesson that it took me a long time to learn. My Asperger's is a part of who I am, and not something to be ashamed of or embarrassed by. I and others on the spectrum are all as valid and capable as neurotypical individuals are and our opinions are just as worthy. Just because we are on the spectrum, it does not somehow invalidate our opinions or beliefs. People on the spectrum can achieve great things if given the right encouragement and a supportive environment to figure out life in. We have our own strengths and weaknesses, like everybody else, and can and should regard our differences as a gift – not a problem to be cured.

The book is divided into four chapters. They are big chapters, but I've used plenty of subheadings throughout to identify all the different topics I talk about. In the first chapter I introduce myself and talk about autism, both in general terms and about what it means to me. The next three chapters cover the three main stages of my education up to the age of 21: nursery and primary school in Chapter 2, secondary school and sixth-form college in Chapter 3 and university in Chapter 4. Of course, a lot of the things I talk about don't neatly fall into these distinct time periods. For example, I started having sensory issues as a young child, but they still affect me as an adult. So, there is some crossover and I haven't presented everything in a strictly chronological manner. For example, I talk about sensory issues in Chapter 2 because that's when they began to affect me, but I talk about them not only in terms of how they affected me then but also in terms of how they affected me later and how they affect me now as an adult.

I've tried to keep my writing as accessible as possible, and not be too academic or technical about any of the topics I talk about. Whilst I understand that some of the language used here is mildly academic, I do not wish to insult the intelligence of people on the spectrum by assuming that they will not understand my words. I would also hope that if people on the spectrum do not understand my words that they can be supported to read them by family members, carers or friends. I want my work to be accessible to everyone. If anyone has any suggestions on how to make my work more accessible, I've included my contact details at the end of the book and I'd be happy to hear from you. I always welcome ideas on how to make my work more accessible.

Finally in this introduction, I should include a brief warning. This book discusses difficult issues such as mental health, attempted suicide and depression, bullying, divorce, body awareness, sexuality and gender identity. If you do not wish to read these sections, then please feel free to skip them, but I feel that they are important and need to be discussed by society for a safer and happier population.

CHAPTER 1

ABOUT ME: MY VIEWS ON ASPERGER'S AND AUTISM

CHAPTER 1

ABOUT ME: MY VIEWS ON ASPERGER'S AND AUTISM

INTRODUCING MYSELF

APPLICANT SECTION

Position applied for: **Author of "When I Grow Up I Want to Be a Cat."**

Personal details

Given name: Madeleine | Family name: Levy

Preferred name: Maddy or Maddie depending on how you wish to spell it

Age: 31

Career:

Artistic Director of Alternative Voices Theatre Company. Final year Occupational Therapy student.

Favourite colours:

Royal blue, black, dark greens, purples, reds

Gender and sexuality: Bi-gender and bi-sexual

Religion: Eclectic Pagan

Allergies:

Mild tree-nut allergy, and food that is too spicy makes me ill.

Irrational fears:

Birds – I don't like the sound of their wings flapping – mainly geese and chickens, because geese tried to pull me into the lake at Cannon Hill Park when I was young, and chickens because they terrified me when I was on a farm when I was little.

Touching or eating bananas – I really hate the texture and taste of them.

Flying in aeroplanes – I don't like the sound or feel of take-off, landing and turbulence, and I don't like the idea that my life is in the hands of someone I don't know.

Also: being abandoned, MRI scans or going to hospital, dying or the idea of it, snakes, heights, losing items I am attached to, 3D-films and feet without shoes on. I hate feet being on tables or being touched by feet or having to touch feet. Ugh!

Special interests:

Historical re-enactment, theatre, acting, watching shows, cats, interesting people with nice personalities.

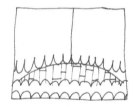

Sensory issues:

Hypersensitive to sound – loud piercing sounds hurt my ears. Difficulties with certain textures such as food which explodes in the mouth, and I don't like anything in between my fingers such as paint or making bread etc...

Dear lord, I was beginning to sound like an equal opportunities form there. Let's try again…

Hello there, I like routines, I don't like to be late.
I am constantly posting Facebook updates.
I get very anxious and I don't like change,
In fact lots of folks think I am strange.

I like rock music and history too,
I am finding it difficult talking to you.
I make strange noises and meow like a cat,
I think I ought to explain about that.

I wanted no profession or career,
I wasn't like my other peers,
The only thing that I wanted to be,
Was a brown and white cat, you see?

The reason for this is simple so,
I shall explain just so you know.
Cats only eat and sleep all day
They never work they only play.

They are well loved and looked after by their owners
They never listen to backstabbers or moaners,
They meow and they cry until they are fed,
And when they've had enough fuss they go back to bed.

Whenever I read a book, I always think to myself who am I actually listening to? Who is writing the words on this page? Why do their words mean anything to me and what credibility do they have to say it? I thought you might feel this way whilst exploring my words, so I thought I would start the book by introducing myself.

I wanted to make this book interesting by adding poetry to the beginning of the chapters. I want to highlight to professionals that it is true what they say: once you have met one person with autism you really have just met one person with autism.

I am in my early 30s and I have Asperger's syndrome. Until recently I worked in a care home, supporting elder adults with complex conditions such as dementia and palliative care needs, alongside my current job, writing blogs for Open Theatre Company's marketing team. I am a final year Occupational Therapy student and I have two other degrees. Moving on to more personal stuff, I have some problematic health behaviours, such as an energy-drink addiction – namely to Red Bull. I gained my addiction studying my first degree as I found it difficult to keep up with the fast-paced London life, and I have been trying to give it up on- and-off, unsuccessfully for several years. Psychologically, I often suffer from mental ill health due to depression. This is partly to do with the way I view the world. I have a tendency to view things in extremes, so either everything is very good, or it is terrible. There usually aren't any shades of grey, although my current job role has taught me to change my perspective somewhat. I also have a rigid need for routines and organisation. For example, I have a morning routine for getting to work. I get up at 6am and I have a bath and dry myself. I then clean my teeth and go into the bedroom to put on my uniform and dry my hair. I then have breakfast (which until recently was always scrambled eggs and cracker breads) and then I walk to work. I get upset and anxious if my routine is changed in any way and it can have a negative impact on the way I do my job once I get into work.

I am hyper-aware of how society views people on the spectrum and the fact that the world is often "ablest" – meaning that the world is designed to favour people who are able-bodied. An example of this is when lifts are too small to fit wheelchairs in or when people claim that I do not have a disability because they cannot see anything different about me. This sometimes adds to my depression. In life, I believe that you get what life gives you and you deal with it, but sometimes negative thoughts about my self-worth and sense of inadequacy go through my head when I am not tuned in to higher self-thinking. (The concept of higher self-thinking is basically about tuning into positive thoughts and being aware of the things you are thankful for in life – something I try to do every day). When I am thinking negative thoughts, however, I get frustrated because I tend to look at what I haven't got in life rather than appreciating what I do have. People often say that I've done well to get this far and that I have achieved a lot by even having a job at all. This frustrates me because I believe that I should be doing these things anyway to function in "normal" society.

When I was asked by my teacher in nursery school what my ideal job would be, I stated that I would like to be a cat. Most of the children wanted to be doctors, lawyers or vets, but I wanted to be a cat. My logic was this: I could be fat, lazy, have lots of attention, sit by the fire and never have to do any real work. I would still like to apply this logic apart from the fact that being a house cat doesn't really pay the bills. This anecdote contributed to the creation of the title and cover for this book.

I'll talk more about nursery school and about being diagnosed with autism in the next chapter, but my family had already noticed my difficulties with language as early as 1992, when I was two years old. One of my earliest memories is of my sister, who was then just a baby, and me playing in the garden. (In fact, it may be I only remember it because my dad videoed it and I remember the video or the video reinforced the memory.) I was playing nicely with my sister or so I thought. I was playing "Row your boat". You remember the one? "Row, row, row your boat, gently down the stream, if you see a crocodile don't forget to scream." Mum told me not to be rough with my sister, and Dad laughed because I got the words of the song wrong. "Life is but a dweam." In the video I also ran around after the camera screaming in a high-pitched voice, "Take one of me!" I also called our lovely city of Birmingham

"Birminghamsham". For a long time, I refused to call Birmingham by its proper name even though I knew it and that was when I realised that I became upset if things weren't exactly the way I wanted them.

For years, I've been told I have autism or Asperger's, but looking back, I think until I came to write this book I never really understood those terms, or what they meant to me, or to anyone else for that matter. I decided it was time to find out. I sat in a library in London at the National Autistic Society to do some research and embarked on what became a long and sometimes painful journey. Writing this book has meant that I have fully accepted myself as having a diagnosis.

I really think Rudy Simone had it right when she stated that there are seven steps that women with Asperger's syndrome go through in order to make peace with the idea that they have Asperger's:

1. *Awareness: We find out about Asperger's and the information speaks to us but hasn't hit home yet. We might experience some resistance or denial.*
2. *Knowing: The irreversible understanding that you have Asperger's. The realisation clicks.*
3. *Validation: Asperger's explains so much in life that often seems to have had no rhyme nor reason. This is not one moment but a series of moments that will continue for years if not forever.*
4. *Relief: I can finally, as the song says, "lay my burdens down." We don't know what our burden is until we're diagnosed but we can tell other people seem to be carrying it.*
5. *Worry: What does this mean for my future and my potential?*
6. *Anger: for all the blame and misdiagnoses that may have been laid upon by ourselves or others. Hopefully we then get to the next phase of our lives ....*
7. *Acceptance/thriving: we become keenly aware of our gifts and deficits and use what we have wisely.*

Rudy Simone, *Aspergirls* (2010, p.16)

I believe that my book demonstrates this process as I speak with you about my experiences of the education system and to try to help you through difficult times.

Writing this book meant recalling painful memories, and it means letting you in on thoughts and feelings that belong to me and others who have cared for and supported me. This is a hard thing to do, and it made me feel anxious when I first began my creative journey – a journey to find out who I really am.

AUTISM

The term autism was first used in its modern sense in the 1940s. Both the Ukranian-American psychologist Leo Kanner and the Austrian paediatrician Hans Asperger used the term to describe a condition they identified in children. Kanner described specific traits of what he called "early infantile autism" including "a powerful desire for aloneness" and "an obsessive insistence on persistent sameness". What Kanner called "early infantile autism", we today – 75-plus years of research later – more accurately call "autism spectrum disorder" or ASD.

Autism spectrum disorder (ASD) is a complex developmental disability. Signs typically appear during early childhood and can affect a person's ability to communicate and interact with others. ASD is defined by a certain set of behaviours and is a "spectrum condition" that affects individuals differently and to varying degrees. This means that autism is a complicated disability which affects children particularly as they are growing up. Autism is found in adults as well but is commonly written about in younger children.

Autism is not rare, as Kanner thought it to be, and nor does it only affect children. Autism is a lifelong developmental disability, and it is estimated that there are around 700,000 adults and children with autism in the UK alone.

As autism is a spectrum condition it affects people in different ways. At one end of the spectrum it includes those with severe learning disability; at the other end of the spectrum it can include those with above average IQs and exceptional ability in some areas.

Autism spectrum disorder is a complex condition, and rather than try and talk of a set of defining symptoms, it is better to think in terms of a list of challenges people with autism may face. The National Autistic Society provide such a list on their website, which goes as follows.

People with autism may experience:

- Social communication challenges
- Social interaction challenges
- Repetitive and restrictive behaviour
- Over- or under-sensitivity to light, sound, taste or touch
- Highly focused interests or hobbies
- Extreme anxiety
- Meltdowns and shutdowns

Social communication challenges might include taking things literally or not understanding sarcasm or abstract concepts.

Social interaction challenges might include behaving in ways thought to be socially inappropriate or appearing to be insensitive.

Repetitive behaviours might include body rocking, arm flapping, clapping or repeating certain sounds or phrases.

Restrictive behaviours might arise when a person with autism resists changes to their routine.

Sensory over-sensitivity might mean that a person with autism is unable to block out background noises in the way that a neurotypical individual might.

Many people with autism develop highly focused interests from a young age. This can be a positive thing, but it can also be problematic if it leads to other areas of their life being neglected.

Many people with autism suffer difficulties with mental health and are prone to extreme anxiety, often related to social situations or facing change.

When everything becomes too much for a person with autism, they can have a meltdown or go into shutdown. A meltdown is a complete loss of behavioural control, and can be verbal (e.g. with uncontrollable crying or screaming) or physical (e.g. with kicking or attacking themselves or others) or both. A shutdown, as the word suggests, involves "switching off" – just completely closing down and becoming non-verbal or staring blankly at a wall.

As you read on, you'll be able to see the greater or lesser extent to which the difficulties in the list above have affected me. In whatever way they have affected you, it's ok. This is our normal. If you have autism, welcome to our community. You are not alone on your journey.

Some of the items on the above list are key in the diagnosis of autism. I have mixed feelings about the issue of diagnosis; it can in some ways be positive thing and in other ways a negative thing – I'll talk more about this later, and you'll also get to hear others' opinions on the matter too.

A lot is still unknown about the spectrum and that is why I find it so interesting. For example, autism appears to be more common in males than females, but the reason for this is unknown. There have been and continue to be many theories about the causes of autism: that it comes from high levels of testosterone, that it is genetic or hereditary, that it is innate, that it is neurological, that it is caused by a failure in early attachments etc. Some have been disproved and others remain current. Those that have been disproved include the theories that the MMR vaccination or that having strict and cold parents cause autism. The National Autistic Society believe that autism is caused by a variety of factors which are physical and affect brain development. Our brains are wired differently from others in society and we have a different way of connecting with the world – and I will argue that this should be celebrated rather than ridiculed.

Seventy-plus years after Kanner, lots of research is being conducted and autism falls under a diagnostic category of mental health disorders. The emphasis placed on diagnosis and the surge in diagnosing individuals with autism in the 1990s led to people making sweeping statements such as autism becoming an epidemic and there being an "autistic crisis". I believe that neurodiversity is neither a crisis nor an epidemic and we should be exploring how to better support individuals to give them a better quality of life. Further, I believe that autism and autism spectrum behaviours have been around since the beginning of time and only since having the means of expression through writing has society been able to communicate and discuss openly about how to support such individuals.

ASPERGER'S SYNDROME

Asperger's syndrome (or Asperger syndrome, or Asperger's[*]), with which I have been diagnosed, is an autism spectrum disorder, but it differs from other ASDs by relatively unimpaired language and intelligence.

This means that if you are reading this and have Asperger's you are probably wanting some clarification and guidance as I don't know about you but words all sound meaningless if you repeat them often

---

[*] Pronouncing it with a hard "g" is ok as the name is Austrian, but try not to say "Asburgers" as some people like to pronounce it – there are no burgers here!

enough and you have probably heard this one thousand times since you were diagnosed. Or maybe you haven't been diagnosed yet and want to understand some of your non-conventional behaviours? This is fine. Basically all the previous statement means is that your brain is wired differently from others in society and you have a different way of connecting with the world. You have probably heard the term "neurodiverse" used; well, this is what that term means. It means our brains are different from other people and that should be celebrated rather than ridiculed.

Asperger's can be characterised by significant challenges with social interaction. For example, many of us often tell the truth as we see it and this can be perceived as bluntness or rudeness by others. Non-verbal communication: many of us are often non-verbal and use other systems of speech such as sign language or Makaton, along with restricted and repetitive patterns of behaviour and interests. For example, many people on the spectrum need sameness and stability like always eating lunch at 12pm regardless of what situation they are in. They also form special interests and can be very obsessed with a topic they are interested in. For example, I love historical re-enactment and am known for dropping it into any conversation at any given moment.

Although not mentioned in standard diagnostic criteria, physical clumsiness and atypical use of language are also common in those with Asperger's. (The former is probably the reason why I fall over when walking or walk into poles or fall on my head on dancefloors in clubs.)

Although the term Asperger's syndrome is well established, it is possible that in the future people will no longer be diagnosed with it as opposed to being diagnosed as on the autism spectrum. The reason for this is that the current edition of the influential American diagnostic manual *Diagnostic and Statistical Manual of Mental Disorders* (also known as DSM-5 and published in 2013) removed diagnosis of Asperger's as a distinct condition. If the lead of DSM-5 is followed by the World Health Organization's *International Classification of Diseases* (the diagnostic manual most commonly used in the UK), then ultimately Asperger's may no longer be diagnosed in the UK. (At the time of writing the issue is open as the latest edition of the *International Classification of Diseases* is at the draft stage.)

Personally, I believe that DSM-5 did the community a disservice when they decided to remove diagnoses of Asperger's. I believe that Asperger's should be a separate condition to autism, as whilst there are similarities between the two, studies have found that there are definite differences in the brains of people with Asperger's syndrome to those with autism[*], and the two groups of people need different support and different education and training due to those distinct neurological differences. I am continuing to use the term Asperger's because that is what I have been diagnosed with. I have heard recently that the community do not wish to use the term anymore because Hans Asperger potentially had dealings with Nazis. Whether that is the case or not is, in my opinion, beside the point as Asperger's was the name of the condition at the time I was diagnosed. It may be called something else going forward and that remains to be seen.

OTHER TERMINOLOGY

You'll also probably have heard the terms "high functioning" and "low functioning" used in connection with autism. They're used to refer to an assessment of an individual's level of functionality. I try and avoid the use of these terms for two reasons: firstly, because they are heavily derived from the medical model which views disability as a dysfunctional problem which needs solving[†], and

---

[*] See *Autism and Asperger Syndrome* by Uta Frith (Cambridge University Press 1992)

[†] See "Rethinking disability: the social model of disability and chronic disease" by Sara Goering in *Curr Rev Musculoskelet Med.* June 2015

secondly, due to the fact that the individuals I have met function differently from day to day. For example, in public I might appear high functioning. I get out of bed every day. I attend to my personal care. I have goals and make plans for the future. But some days I cannot get out of bed due to depression and pain, and I choose not to wash that day. Does this make me low functioning or am I just having a bad day? Is someone low functioning because they need support with personal care or do they just have a condition which makes doing so difficult? Once they are up and dressed they function like the rest of society, so I will leave that one for readers to ponder. I believe we desperately need more specific terms which are tailored to suit individuals and view each person as a human being.

Further, care professionals and the public at large do not seem to understand that the body does not work in isolation. It all works together. What I mean by that is that we all have mental health and we all have physical health and each one affects the other. For example, if you have a stomach ache, you are sweating and your leg is bouncing up and down, it probably means you are very anxious. You are not just physically unwell; you have anxiety. This means that often other conditions such as depression and anxiety are missed in young people with Asperger's as the symptoms of those conditions are dismissed as being "part of their autism". This was detrimental to me and meant that I did not receive help for my anxiety until early adulthood.

A further term that is widely used within the autistic community which I dislike is "Aspie". It came into existence in approximately 2010 to describe people with Asperger's syndrome. It was created by the community themselves due to a wish to make the diagnostic term their own and more accessible to them. Television programs such as *Community* and *The Big Bang Theory*, which are both American television shows, began to popularise the term and now it has become common speech. In both shows characters who potentially had a diagnosis of Asperger's became popular and the term Aspie was seen by the community as reclaiming the diagnosis and making it a cool description rather than something oppressive.

As someone in their early 30s with Asperger's I was rather surprised when a youngster at a conference at Autism West Midlands introduced herself to me as an Aspie before even telling me her name. The trouble for me is that I believe identity is multifaceted and is more about what you do and what you believe than about what diagnosis you might have. So, personally, I will never introduce myself as an Aspie but rather a human being who likes theatre and history. I can't stop young people from calling themselves that if that's what they wish to do, but I'd never condone it myself.

WHAT IS THE AUTISM SPECTRUM?

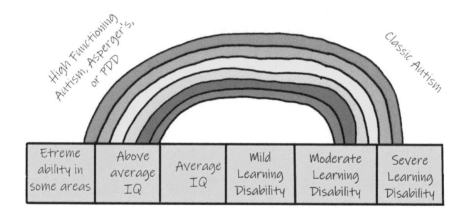

Etreme ability in some areas	Above average IQ	Average IQ	Mild Learning Disability	Moderate Learning Disability	Severe Learning Disability

By this point I cannot even count how many times I have written the term "autism spectrum" without offering a detailed explanation. The autism spectrum consists of the various types of autism. As mentioned earlier, autism is considered a "spectrum disorder" – an umbrella, with a range of autistic syndromes at varying degrees of severities. The types of autism include autistic disorder – also known as classical autism, Asperger's syndrome, pervasive developmental disorder (otherwise known as PDD-NOS), Rett's syndrome (primarily a common type of autism in girls) and childhood disintegrative disorder (also referred to as CDD). All of these diagnoses make up the term autism spectrum disorder and I fall under the Asperger's part of the spectrum. From now on when I discuss being on the spectrum this is what I am referring to, and if you feel you need more guidance you can always do your own research but please do use the picture above as a point of reference.

SOME DEVASTATING STATISTICS

"People diagnosed with an autism spectrum disorder die at an average age of just 36. For the general population, life expectancy is 72."

"Injury mortality in people with autism",
American Journal of Public Health 2017

"In December 2018 4,302 deaths of people with learning disabilities were notified to the learning disability mortality review programme of Bristol University."

LeDeR, *Annual Report 2018*
by the University of Bristol

"Only 16% of autistic adults in the UK are in full-time paid employment, and only 32% are in some kind of paid work."

The National Autistic Society, 2016

Given, as I have said, there are around 700,000 people on the autism spectrum in the UK – which is more than 1 in 100 – I think it's fair of me to call the above statistics devastating. They suggest the life chances of individuals with autism and/or learning disabilities contrast very poorly with those of neurotypical individuals. I haven't included these statistics to deliberately upset or scare anyone but just to give a realistic picture of what life is like now and a reminder to all of us who struggle that existence is resistance. I have fought very hard throughout my life in order to avoid becoming a statistic, and I just want to say to others who are fighting the same fight I see you out there and you are valid. Keep fighting!

CURING AUTISM?

Dad: *If there was a magic wand that I could use to get rid of your Asperger's, I don't think I would do it. Autism is part of who you are and it's one of the nicest parts of who you are.*

Despite the fact that my father wouldn't change my Asperger's, there are some people in the field of research who believe that it is possible. For example, Bryan Jepson in his book *Changing the Course of Autism* tells us that "autism is a disease rather than a psychological problem". He believes that medical treatment will solve all our autistic problems. Even though each child has a unique biochemical make up, according to Jepson, and what works for one child could make another worse, so there is still no definite cure, he maintains one can use a multi-tiered treatment approach. This means that if you remove what the child is missing, remove what is causing the harm and break the inflammatory cycle, you could effectively cure autism. Diet changes should be the first thing you improve because correct nutrition helps metabolism, and Jepson believes that autism is a metabolic disease affecting multiple organ systems. If you treat the entire body, autism can be cured. According to Jepson, parents need to find a good doctor who specialises in treating the medical needs of autistic children. However, they should not start all treatment at once so that doctors can record what is causing what, and which treatment is helping etc.

This fantasy is all well and good, but if autism is neurological then dietary changes alone are not going to rewire the brain. However, let's pretend for a moment that autism could be cured; if I were to cure my Asperger's, I'd be very afraid. I guess I'd know that it'd help me with some things in the long run. I'd love to be able to understand some forms of speech, and I'd love not to take everything literally or have violent outbursts of emotion and depression when I am overwhelmed. I'd love to be able to be better at problem solving and have better motor skills so I could ride a bike and be good at sports, but if I cured my Asperger's would it change my personality? I think it would, and I quite like my personality. I am kind and loyal. If you were to cure autism, I think you'd have to rewire the brain and cure the body, and in that sense you'd change the person. I'd be terrified, and although I'm not 100% sure, I don't think I'd do it.

Self-care and support are what's needed, not talk of a cure. This is because a lot of people with Asperger's suffer from mood-related disorders such as depression, because they are aware of their social differences. People on the spectrum, you need to practise self-care every day – by this I mean looking after yourself and doing one thing that you enjoy each day. Try to reach out to people and get a strong network of supportive friends, even if you only talk with them online. Do not believe that you can't do things because you are on the spectrum. This simply isn't true. You can do anything that you put your mind to. Yes, it may be more frustrating and there may be limits to what you can do due to your disability; it may take you a little longer than your peers to do it, whatever it is. You just need to push yourself out of your daily routines and your safe space (or comfort zone) to do it. This might be scary and make you anxious, but you will learn from it and may even make new friends.

There are many ways that parents can help too. Tell your child that they are on the autism spectrum early on and tell them those facts that go with it, but don't treat them as if they are different or disabled. Your child could be exceptionally bright academically, and there is no need to stop them from doing what they want to do. By all means protect them and keep them safe, but do not wrap them up in cotton wool. What will they do when you aren't there and there is no one there to fight for them? I had a friend who didn't go into the town centre by herself until she was a young adult, because her parents believed her to be unable because she had a diagnosis. By doing this, your child on the spectrum will just believe themselves to be disabled and will use it as an excuse not to do things that they are very much capable of doing. My parents and I have been fighting my whole life to make the rest of the world accept me and be willing to help me. I am about to finish my third degree, all from prestigious universities. If I'd have thought I have a diagnosis so I will never amount to anything, I wouldn't be here now, and if my parents hadn't believed in me, I wouldn't be where I am today.

FAMOUS PEOPLE WITH AUTISM AND AUTISM IN THE PRESS

There are many famous people with the condition who have contributed to the wider society. A quick Google search on the topic took me to a website* with a list of 30 inspiring individuals considered to be or have been somewhere on the autistic spectrum. The list includes pioneering scientists (Albert Einstein, Isaac Newton and Charles Darwin), tech entrepreneurs (Bill Gates, Steve Jobs), film directors (Tim Burton, Stanley Kubrick), poets (Emily Dickinson, W.B. Yeats), writers (James Joyce, Lewis Carroll and William Shakespeare) as well as actors Darryl Hannah and Dan Aykroyd, and other famous names. Of course, most of the names on the list are all old enough to have escaped a diagnosis, as the diagnostic criteria came into being either after their lifetimes or after them becoming famous.

---

* www.appliedbehavioranalysisprograms.com

Yet despite such an impressive list, when the press does cover stories involving people with autism the coverage always seems to be negative. In 2002 Gary McKinnon, who has Asperger's syndrome, was nearly punished for hacking into US military and NASA computer systems. It took ten years' worth of legal proceedings until his extradition to the US was finally blocked. All Gary was trying to do was look for evidence of cover-ups of free energy solutions and UFO activity. He wasn't trying to compromise the US's defence systems. In 2018 a Bristol man with autism was shot by the police with a stun gun. Incidents like this appear in the media far too often, where the papers report on the most extreme of incidents and seem to imply that autism has caused the problem. This causes further stereotyping and radicalisation of people with the diagnosis who are just trying to live their lives.

People need to understand the effect of being on the spectrum on the individuals who have it, on their families and the impact the diagnosis has on their education and understanding of the world. If more research were done, then maybe such an argument affecting poor Gary's life would not have ensued. Not enough is known about autism to help individuals who might find life challenging in certain areas. I am going to shine a very bright limelight on that fact and talk to you all openly about what it is like to be on the autism spectrum.

COMMON MISCONCEPTIONS ABOUT AUTISM, ASPERGER'S AND DISABILITIES

The history of research into autism and the treatment of individuals on the spectrum has sometimes involved some terrible things. I recently came across the statement: "We learn about experimenters feeding LSD to children with autism or shocking them with electricity to change their behaviour." I don't know which upset me more, the content of the statement itself or the fact it was being used as part of the blurb to sell a book (*In a Different Key* by John Donvan and Caren Zucker). Whilst I accept that those things happened and should not be swept under the carpet, it does not change the fact that statements like those are often what makes us feel unhuman. People on the spectrum are not something for society to experiment on; we should be celebrated for our differences and our neurodiversity. The word autism comes with its own preconceived stereotypes, and often when people hear the word they are already forming opinions about the way a person may present or behave.

There are some common mistakes and assumptions that people consistently make about autism, Asperger's syndrome and disabilities generally. It really is unhelpful to think that all people who have Asperger's syndrome and/or autism will behave in the same way. It seems some members of the general public are happy to believe sweeping statements and generalisations such as:

- Autistic people all lack empathy.
- Autistic people are all violent.
- Autistic people are all mentally retarded.
- Autistic people all have behavioural problems.
- Autism is more or less the same thing as Down's syndrome (or dyspraxia or another disability).
- Autistic people do not really have a disability.

Let's consider these false generalisations in turn.

Just because people on the spectrum might struggle to express empathy using body language and tone of voice, it doesn't follow that all people with autism lack empathy. This first statement that all autistic people lack empathy comes from the fact that psychologists are speaking about empathy in a different way to its common usage. When psychologists speak about empathy they are speaking about seeing things from a different point of view. They mean that people on the spectrum might struggle to express empathy using body language and tone of voice which makes communicating empathy difficult. Commonly society experiences empathy as the ability to care about others, and so if as a parent you first hear from a doctor that your child might struggle with empathy if you think of the common meaning, you may be concerned by this news. Do not fear! Read on and I'll talk about instances that demonstrate I don't lack empathy.

The idea that all autistic people are violent undoubtedly stems from the fact that some individuals on the spectrum can become violent during anxiety attacks, otherwise known as meltdowns. They might try to hit themselves, others or hit walls and the media have often overdramatised this. (And if you're wondering if I am violent, I can assure you that I am not. Well, except at weekends when I train with my historical re-enactment group! When I was younger, I could have violent outbursts during meltdowns, particularly at university and when I was struggling to understand what was happening to my body. Now that I know what is going on I have things pretty much under control. But having a violent outburst such as hitting a wall is anyway a very different thing from being a violent person, I can guarantee.)

The idea that all autistic people are mentally retarded is actually so ridiculous (and offensive) as to hardly warrant being refuted. Suffice it to say, many people on the spectrum possess great abilities and above-average IQs.

The idea that all people with autism have behavioural problems stems from a lack of understanding. Autism affects different people in many different ways. Just because some individuals with autism at one end of the spectrum might have behavioural problems, it does not follow that all individuals with autism do.

Autism is not the same as other disabilities. Down's syndrome, for example, is a distinct condition caused by the presence of an extra chromosome. It is just laziness of thought and lack of understanding that causes people to lump distinct disabilities together in their minds. I certainly can't claim to be an expert on Down's syndrome – although I do know that people who have Down's syndrome can also achieve great things if given the right support and encouragement – but I do know very well that I don't have it. Of course, someone with autism or Asperger's might have other conditions too. I have dyspraxia and have suffered from scoliosis of the spine – both of which I'll talk more about later. But this does not make them any less the different and distinct conditions that they are.

The final false generalisation really makes me cross. Just because you're not in a wheelchair and autism can't be seen, it doesn't mean that it isn't a real disability. There are several types of disability and autism is one that is hidden. People on the spectrum are still entitled to disability benefits and to sit in the disabled seats at the front of the bus as much as the person in a wheelchair or the person that uses assistive walking aids.

This stereotype also feeds into when people say things like, "Oh you have autism, do you? You don't look like you have." What exactly is autism supposed to look like, Karen? I shall call out what people mean when they say this and address the elephant in the room. What they mean is: you don't look retarded or you are not in a wheelchair. Please educate yourselves.

Why do people think such things as the above false generalisations? Perhaps people just find it easier to think in terms of lazy stereotypes. I'm sure the media doesn't help matters, with programmes such as *The Undateables* where the underlying assumption is that people with disabilities struggle and are unworthy of forming meaningful romantic attachments.

People with autism come from all nationalities, cultures, social backgrounds and religions. And nor is autism something new. I believe that autism has been around since the beginning of time and only since having the means of expression through writing has society been able to communicate and discuss openly about how to support individuals on the spectrum.

There's one final generalisation that I want to mention that I find troubling. People sometimes say, "Well we are all a little bit on the spectrum, aren't we?" Well, no we are not actually because if we were we would all have a diagnosis and nobody would have access to the support they need. Yes, everyone experiences sensory processing and has senses which they like and dislike, which is where I believe this statement originates from. Yes, everyone may have one or two behaviours which their friends or colleagues find odd. However, I believe statements like that are very dangerous because the government could use them to take away the limited support that is desperately needed by a specific group of people. What makes someone who has one or two autistic traits different from someone who is on the spectrum is that their traits do not make it more difficult for them to live their life. It was living in a shared house at university that made me realise this; my male ex-housemate definitely had autistic traits – however, he's probably going to kill me for saying so.

In writing this section I hoped to clear up some of these misconceptions and beliefs that the public have. This section aims to give readers a better understanding of misconceptions about autism, Asperger's syndrome and dyspraxia. Just having a definition does not mean anything at all in the grand scheme of things, and still to this day I don't really understand why I act differently to everyone else; I just know that I do.

AUTISM AND THE EDUCATION SYSTEM

There is still loads of research to be done to support spectrum individuals in education and in life generally. People from the Asperger community feel that there is still a gap in the care they receive and a lack of understanding in the way they are being treated by professionals and society.

The report "Autism and education in England 2017" by the All Party Parliamentary Group on Autism suggests much still needs to be done to provide the appropriate support for children with autism and to embed understanding of autism in the education system – it is telling that the report includes numerous recommendations for government, local authorities and schools.

I will state again that not enough individualised support is in place for children on the spectrum and many teachers do not understand how to work with an individual on the spectrum. Not only this but schools are so focused on teaching children the national curriculum, obtaining positive Ofsted reports and high exam scores that they forget to teach children basic kindness, respect and awareness of the differences of others – thus making the lives of individuals in minority groups difficult at best. This then continues on into adulthood, university and the workplace. Further, children who are not on the spectrum are being denied creativity due to having such heavy focus on passing exams rather than exploring play and creative needs.

I know that in my direct experience the education system was difficult for me. Educators were not provided with enough information about Asperger's to support the children who struggled. It felt like we were there to be dealt with. I deliberately say dealt with rather than supported because there was a special learning unit to house children with learning differences and separate them from the mainstream children. How can the needs of someone with autistic disorder be the same as the needs of a student with Asperger's syndrome? How can teachers successfully support all of the school's special needs children in a confined space without trying to integrate them with mainstream children?

School systems are designed to support able-bodied people, that is individuals who do not have a learning difference or a physical health need, and so individuals with those concerns are automatically at a disadvantage. School corridors are not wide enough for wheelchairs to get through. Universities are designed with the disability department being on the top floor of a building with limited and restricted access. Individuals are automatically segregated into separate buildings or schools when we should be teaching positive attitudes towards people with learning differences as early as nursery school, because children grow into adults and if they are not taught to respect children with learning or physical differences, then they will grow into adults who believe that people with learning differences are not of value in society. The school system needs to change!

School was made more difficult than it needed to be for me because, whilst there was support available, it was standardised support. Standardised support means that it was support offered to all children with a learning difference and was delivered in the same way rather than tailored to each individual. It was support that the professionals believed I needed rather than encouraging me and empowering me to think about what I needed for myself, and that was why I grew to resent, challenge and deny the support throughout my teenage years. This was to my own detriment, but I could not accept something which I saw as being designed to restrict or ostracise me.

One of the things this book aims to do is to demonstrate that every individual on the spectrum is different, and it bangs the drum for individualised care and timetable planning in schools based on the interests and needs of the individual. I believe that individualised care should be in place no matter who the child is, whether or not they have any disorders at all. This will make for a better and more fruitful education for all. We are being offered the chance to start again. Instead of going back to the way things were, we need to be looking at the flaws in the education system and fixing them so that the adults of the future have a better chance of being able to sustain our society.

WHAT HAVING AUTISM MEANS TO ME

For me, being on the spectrum is a journey of self-discovery. It is a different way of viewing the world from that of a neurotypical person. For me, being on the spectrum is about accepting that trying to fit in or "masking" (hiding the fact that you are on the spectrum by forcing yourself to stop doing autistic behaviours) does not work and it is just about adapting my behaviour to fit social situations appropriately.

Most often I don't believe myself to have a disorder. It only comes into my mind when I do silly things like fall through an obviously broken chair and get stuck in it at a colleague from university's house as he watches in dismay. Then I laugh and think to myself I wouldn't be me without it. Or when I had to work extra hard to understand what one of my housemates was saying to me, because he possessed tremendous wit and I used to struggle to understand sarcasm and figures of speech. In adult life, I think being on the spectrum does affect me a little now that I think about it. For instance, I am distant with people because I can see cruelty in others easily. I used to get intense attacks of anxiety, which didn't stop me from doing everyday things, but it did mean that I was constantly in a state of worry.

I upset a housemate once when I said that I have no faith in humanity and that all people do things for selfish reasons. I often feel isolated, and when I was at university doing my first degree, I found it hard to introduce myself to people unless mass amounts of alcohol were involved. I am serious a lot of the time, and my ex-boyfriend used to like to make me laugh because he said it didn't happen very often, but I am happier now – although when I do seriously laugh it sounds like a cackle and it makes others laugh too. I appreciate toilet humour and I like literal comedians like Jimmy Carr and Lee Evans. I have difficulties in understanding figures of speech because I take things literally. For example, when my support worker told me to pull my socks up, meaning work harder, I would sit and pull my socks up.

Mum: Well, God lived inside Madeleine's little red play bus in our living room for years. Her Religious Studies teacher told her that God is everywhere; you know how they do in schools to religiously influence children? Well, my daughter's rationalisation was if he's everywhere he lives in her play bus. So, for an atheist it was very difficult for a couple of years, because I had God living in my living room. I couldn't argue with her logic. He had every right to live in a play bus ... why did he have to live in a church or in a cathedral? If he wanted to live in the play bus, it was a bit random but it was fine. He lived there for ages.

More recently at work my manager told me that I could have a gold star for my performance and I had been wondering for ages when she would produce my gold star until one of my colleagues explained to me that it was a figure of speech.

I feel that everyone should treat other people how they wish to be treated themselves and I don't trust people straight away. My worst fear about going to university was that people wouldn't like me. I envied how easily my ex-boyfriend knocked on the doors of my flatmates at the time and introduced himself, whilst I could only sit and wonder how I was ever going to approach them.

Once I do make friends with people, though, I am eternally loyal, unless you hurt me so badly that I cannot look at you. I like having Asperger's because it makes me feel unique. I am not like the thousands of people that pass me on the commute into Birmingham – secretly I'd say that it pleases me. A million people must pass me by on that journey, and they'd not notice that I have a hidden disability. They'd not see that I have something that they don't, which is to my credit and strength. They'd just think they saw a young woman who looked slightly lost or needed help finding her platform if the train is re-directed.

I would say that my main goal in life, as a young adult with Asperger's syndrome, is to find happiness, and I suggest that all children with Asperger's and their parents should embark on the same activity.

Some people have asked me: why are you writing this book? What could an idea like this possibly contribute to the wider literature on the subject? I know I'm certainly not the first person with autism to write a book, but I hope I've explained in the introduction enough of the reasons for doing so. Also, I believe it to be the first British book which covers university as part of the education process written from the perspective of a person with autism (who is bi-gender). In any event, it is a book written from the perspective of a person who themself is on the spectrum not a scientist or expert with no direct experience of the condition.

DYSPRAXIA

As I've mentioned, alongside my Asperger's I have dyspraxia, which I'll just say a few more words about before we go on to the next chapter. This means that I have a range of developmental disorders which affect the initiation, organisation and performance of actions – not really helping my clumsiness or handwriting in any way.

As the Dyspraxia Foundation explain it, dyspraxia is a "developmental coordination disorder ... affecting fine and/or gross motor coordination in children and adults" and is a "lifelong condition". It means, for example, that I find it difficult to do up buttons on clothes, and unless I write down which order to complete a task I can sometimes forget important steps. I also have difficulties catching balls and with visual spatial awareness. This means that I sometimes cannot tell how close I am to an object or how much space is between the object and my person, making driving a car extremely challenging, which I will discuss later on.

TO CONCLUDE CHAPTER 1

In conclusion, I have chosen to write a book which gives a voice to people on the autism spectrum, particularly people with Asperger's. The book also aims to highlight the need for change within the education system to support individuals who are on the spectrum. The book aims to give people on the spectrum information about the condition in an accessible way. Also, to support young people on the spectrum and to teach them that they have just as much value in the world as any other person. Next the book aims to show parents and carers of individuals on the spectrum how to support them. I have done this because I feel that there is a gap in our knowledge when it comes to caring for and supporting people on the spectrum and because I want the public to understand that there is a need for individualised care in schools as all people on the spectrum are different even though they may exhibit similar behaviours. I also want them to know that people on the autism spectrum can achieve great things and not to write us off. I have introduced myself to you and spoken about the way I view the world. I have highlighted some difficulties people with high-functioning Asperger's may have and have pointed out the differences between autism, Asperger's and dyspraxia. I have talked about whether or not it is possible to cure autism and I have spoken about some famous autistic people. Finally, I have also discussed some common misconceptions about autism, Asperger's and disabilities generally which I hope have cleared up any concerns you may have if you are a person with Asperger's or have been told you have a child who is on the autism spectrum. The next chapter will discuss my experiences with the education system from nursery school to primary and will point out the difficulties and frustrations that came with being on the autism spectrum, such as communicational difficulties and sensory issues.

CHAPTER 2

NURSERY AND PRIMARY SCHOOL

(AGES 4-10)

CHAPTER 2
NURSERY AND PRIMARY SCHOOL
(AGES 4-10)

A STATISTIC AND A POEM

"On average, parents had to wait three and a half years before their child got a confirmed diagnosis of ASD."

"How long does it take to get an autism diagnosis?"
theconversation.com 2015

I like to view things in extremes,
Everything is awesome or everything is bad,
There are no shades of grey,
But my single-mindedness got me where I am today.

I have a rigid need for routines and organisation,
Let me give you a demonstration,
I used to eat scrambled eggs for breakfast almost every day,
I take things literally, so you'd better mean what you say.

I have diaries dating back to 2001,
I get anxious if I can't get everything done,
I write lists of events that have occurred in my life,
I write lists of what I would want from a husband or wife.

I suffer from a deep sense of inadequacy,
It's taken many years of learning to like being me.
I feel like everything I do is not enough,
I have to work so hard all the time,
I hope that people can learn from all of my rhymes.

I work to achieve the same as neurotypical people do,
The ones who patronise and think they're better than you.
They think that they're "normal" and that I am strange,
Well let's make them seem odd for a change.

There is no such thing as "normal" at all,
Free beer and madness for one and all.
I am the one with the inspiration, foresight and determination,
I tune in to higher self-thinking and positive regard,
To help me through when times are hard.

I am thankful for what I have in life and all the negatives that
    people say,
Because in the end it's made me who I am today.

MY PRIMARY SCHOOL

My primary school was just like any other school except that it was
a Jewish school. Recently it has become a multi-faith school, but
when I went there back in 1995 it focused on the Jewish faith. I
went there because my father is a non-practising Jew and at the time
the family felt it was the best school in the area that was going to
support my needs. It was also reasonably close to where we lived.
Sometimes going to a Jewish school made me feel different from
other children. I felt singled out by the fact that I'd never sung or
performed in a nativity play, but I am proud of my father's Jewish
heritage. I am proud to say that I have Jewish ancestry, because it is
another thing that sets me apart from everyone else. My father is of
a Jewish family, but because my mother is not Jewish we are not
classed a Jewish family as the laws of Judaism state that the family is
only considered Jewish when the blood runs through the mother's
family line.

I remember the school playground the most clearly. It was a big
area of tarmac that had play equipment right at the very bottom.
There were games tables so that the children could play chess and
draughts. There were also things like snakes and ladders, and
hopscotch painted onto the floor. To the right, there were climbing
frames and, I think, a slide. I remember that we used to play cricket
and rounders on the tarmac at the front of the school building.

Behind the school there was a grassy area that the children called "the back field" where the older pupils would go to play football and rugby. Every morning we would line up and go into the building in order of year groups. We would have assembly at 9am where we would rise to greet the headmistress with "Good morning Misses Lesser," and sit down again to begin to sing the Hebrew hymns.

Every Friday we would celebrate Kiddush, a prayer which is recited over a cup of wine or grape juice to sanctify the Shabbat (Judaism's weekly day of rest – Saturday) and other holy days in the Jewish faith. We would set a table in the great hall and all the year groups would gather together for the prayer and afterwards would get to eat some tasty bread before going home. Our Kiddush was a mock ceremony, of course, because the real feast didn't start until the evening, but it meant that every child could take part in religious activity whether they practised Judaism at home or not. I loved all the prayers and songs. If our year were good, we'd be chosen to sit at the table in the middle of the hall in front of all the other years, although I never got to sit at the table until my last year in the school when I was due to leave. At the end of the ceremony the prefects would hand out the bread once we'd lined up in front of our classroom doors before home time. I think the bread was the best part for me because it tasted nice and the way it was handed out was something that was done in exactly the same fashion every week; it symbolised going home on a Friday afternoon. Then I'd get to go home to my mother and father where I wasn't treated as if I was different from everybody else. Home was a sanctuary for me. Home meant safety.

Our headmistress, who I didn't like much because she was strict, gods rest her soul, would sometimes tell us stories of a boy called Ka Ton Ton who was no bigger than the size of your thumb. She'd talk to us of the mischief he'd get up to, and there was always a moral to the story at the end. Those stories bored most of the children because they couldn't wait to go home at the end of the day, but I always listened intently because I was amazed at how a little boy could be so small but so full of life.

Students would either learn to read and write in Hebrew or they would learn to play music as their special subjects. I was hopeless at Hebrew and I often use it as an excuse for my appalling handwriting, as Jewish people read from right to left rather than left to right. I played the recorder in assembly with my best friend most mornings. She was better at it than I was and was often chosen to play the more complex solos. You'd have school dinners until you were in Year 5 and then you could have sandwiches if your parents gave you permission. The school used to let us have crisps at play time, but then they were banned because the parents became anxious that we'd get attacked by low-flying pigeons. I think the parents were just being neurotic.

This was the structure of my schooling until I was ten years old. We had the same routine and the same procedures every day for six years. I became used to it and perhaps it helped develop my need for structure and routines. I didn't even realise at the time that other children at different schools had different experiences, even though my sister who is younger than me went to a different school towards the end of her primary education. I am the oldest of three children. My two sisters are younger than me and will be referred to throughout the book as eldest and youngest sister; they wished to remain anonymous for the purpose of the book.

GAINING A DIAGNOSIS AND EARLY SIGNS

On the one hand, gaining a diagnosis can be very important to some individuals with autism. It can lead to getting support in school in the form of special learning assistants (and later on at university you can apply for equipment to help with educational needs such as recording devices to record lectures and laptops to help write notes). A diagnosis can also help individuals to understand their behaviours and sometimes give them a sense of validation.

On the other hand, if a diagnosis is not managed correctly it can lead to individuals on the spectrum feeling singled out or as if they are other. The label can also lead to bullying in schools if the school does not model a disability-positive attitude. If you decide to go down the diagnosis route, as parents it is important to support your child with building self-esteem. Support them to feel valued and equal to all members of your family. Gaining a diagnosis can often take a long time due to specialist waiting lists and the quality of the school's learning needs support system. I did not receive my diagnosis until the age of eight but there were early signs that my nursery school teacher and parents noticed.

My nursery school teacher recognised that I might need support because I was showing some early signs of autism:

1. I played alone and did not interact with other children.
2. I lined up my Thomas the Tank Engine trains in order according to the numbers painted on their sides and became upset if anyone disturbed the order.
3. I had language difficulties.

At home, my parents suspected I might have a learning difficulty because:

1. I only rolled one way as a baby and could not turn myself back round.
2. My physical development was delayed and I did not walk until I was two.
3. I only ate three types of food, which were cod fish, scrambled eggs and white bread.

4. I got very upset if anything changed and I refused to move on from Calpol, which was baby pain relief, to the pain relief for older children. This was because the pain relief for older children was orange flavour rather than strawberry and I was more familiar with the strawberry flavour. This meant that Mum had to give me a double dosage of the children's strawberry because I refused to take anything else.

5. I had language difficulties. For example, my mother would ask, "Do you want a biscuit?" meaning did I want a biscuit, and I would say, "You want a biscuit," because I had an under-developed concept of self. I also called my father "Daddy Darling" because I'd thought that was his name when Mum had told me, "Say goodnight to Daddy, darling," meaning that I was her darling, but I'd not understood.

6. I was late learning to read and could not read in my head until I was at least seven years old.

My parents initially sought help from the school, but they refused on the grounds that my cognitive ability was fine and I was not disruptive in class. The school was basically operating in a reactive fashion and was not willing to intervene until I was failing. One day a local politician knocked on the door of my family home and asked if he could rely on our support. My father railed him with concerns and finally things started to progress.

Dad: It was when Madeleine was first in the Reception Class that her teachers suspected that there might be some kind of issue. The main problem seemed to be her difficulty in tasks such as putting her coat on. She once came home with her coat on inside out and upside down!

The difficulty in trying to secure appropriate help from Birmingham Education Authority was that Madeleine was not exhibiting behavioural problems. Their attitude was that they would wait until she was failing before they were prepared to intervene. I was not prepared to accept this. Despite meetings with the school and telephone calls to the Education Authority I got nowhere... until a councillor who was up for re-election knocked on our door asking me if he could rely on my vote. I invited him in and bombarded him with my concerns about the lack of foresight being demonstrated by the Local Authority. As far as I can recollect, this councillor was on the education committee. Miraculously, after I spoke to him things began to move, and Madeleine finally began to receive the help that she needed.

Nevertheless, there were still battles and frustrations ahead. The educational psychologist was not particularly helpful, but the speech therapist and occupational therapists were great. A referral to a child clinical psychologist assisted in a diagnosis of Asperger's being made.

Even after the diagnosis was made, and help had been implemented, we still had to battle with ignorance in the education system. For example, Madeleine spent a whole holiday working on a biology project only to have her hard work rejected by her teacher, because she had not prepared quite what was asked for; there was no recognition of the good work she had done or the effort that she had made. I believe it was the same teacher who then wrote one of the only poor school reports that Madeleine ever received. All of her criticisms were about Madeleine's lack of skills in areas over which she had no control. The teacher's attitude made me feel incredibly angry and frustrated.

I believe that the education system is much better at recognising signs of autism these days. The events my father describes took place in the 1990s (I was eight in 1998) and modern understanding of autism was still in its relatively early years then. For example, it had taken until as late as 1980 for the American Psychiatric Association to distinguish autism from schizophrenia, and the genetic role in autism hadn't begun to be properly recognised until the 1980s.

My advice to any parents who notice signs and think their child may be autistic would be to think carefully about the type of support your child needs. If you feel that you can support them at home without a diagnosis, then by all means do so, but you have to truly be honest with yourself as to whether you can support your child in a way that they need. If not, then I believe a collaborative approach is useful. You may need to speak with dieticians for weight management and support with eating; personal trainers and physiotherapists for support with gait, strength and exercise; counsellors and therapists to work on self-esteem, anxiety and depression; and keeping the teachers in the loop as well can prevent bullying. If you do decide that a diagnosis is beneficial to your child because it leads to positive support, then seek diagnosis early because the waiting lists are long and the support is much needed. (Personally, I am only in favour of diagnosis if it opens a door for positive support to be accessed rather than giving an individual another label to be used against them.)

The first port of call for gaining a diagnosis is to go to your GP. They may then send other professionals to visit you at home such as speech and language therapists, psychiatrists and occupational therapists and then they will do an assessment. It is not usual for diagnosis to be made before the age of two.

There is a lot of support for families nowadays that did not exist when I was growing up. For example, Autism West Midlands are a charity based in Birmingham who can offer a range of in-house support once your child has a diagnosis, along with family fun days and informative lectures on varying topics surrounding autism. In London, the National Autistic Society does a similar job, and I applaud and highly recommend the work that both organisations are doing to support the autistic community.

However, not everybody receives their diagnosis early on. I will now interview someone on the spectrum who I met later on in life as part of Open Theatre Company. He gained his diagnosis a lot later on in life and I found the difference in the length of his responses in comparison to the girls I have interviewed simply fascinating.

INTERVIEW 1: MATTHEW

Can you introduce yourself?
I'm Matthew Recardo, aged 36.

Tell me about your diagnosis?
Asperger syndrome/high-functioning autism

What age were you when you got your diagnosis?
32

What are you studying at the moment?
I'm not studying anything.

Do you have any special interests?
Acting, pro wrestling, martial arts, film and theatre. Also plastic straws. I love to play with plastic straws (for stimming).

Do you have any sensory difficulties?
I am sensitive to high-pitched noises and bright flashing lights. Also, I cannot watch 3D films as I get sensory overload. I also find it hard to filter external noise when trying to focus on one sound.

What did you enjoy most about school?
Drama lessons

What did you find challenging about school?
Pretty much everything else: fitting in, bullying, learning the "one size fits all" way that mainstream schools teach etc.

> **What do you think schools could do to better support individuals on the spectrum?**
> Mandatory autism awareness training for all teachers, whether in Special schools or mainstream. Also, teach autism awareness to pupils in social studies.
>
> **What are you doing with your life presently?**
> Working as an actor, support worker and Drama facilitator.

Matt's responses demonstrate the diverse styles of communication that exist between people on the spectrum and also show how you can gain a diagnosis much later on in life. He subsequently told me that gaining a diagnosis has helped him to understand himself better.

CHALLENGING TEACHERS

If young people on the spectrum have challenging teachers, then life can be pretty tough. Remember earlier when my father mentioned my reception teacher who gave me a bad school report? Well, she also used to call me stubborn and lazy because I could not cut with right-handed scissors when I was left-handed. She even tied my left hand behind my back on one occasion, and she would not let me leave the table at lunch time to go out to play until I had cleared my plate. There were some school dinners that I did not like and this used to make me very upset until I came up with an agreement with one of the boys and he sat next to me so that I could give him my food when the teacher was not watching. I suppose he was happy because he got free extra food.

I also had a teacher in Year 3 who criticised me for not being able to read in my head and used to always make me stand to answer mental Maths problems in front of the class. In Year 3 I was seven years old and it was the first time I ever felt depressed. I was quite an overweight child and the girls used to pick on me and call me "fatty". I remember when I was in Year 6 I was accused of bullying another boy on the spectrum and it made me really angry because I was not bullying this child at all, I was telling him the truth about some of his behaviours and he was oversensitive about it and reported our group of friends. I remember writing that my learning support worker was a dickhead in my school book and getting told off for it by the teacher.

I am certainly very glad that I have always had parents willing to support me, but I do feel that I had to battle with prejudices in the education system. I think it is because schools are told they have to follow the national curriculum. Teachers are under so much pressure for their class to score this grade in this test and that grade in another test that any behaviour that they are uncertain about or find difficult to deal with either gets swept under the carpet and ignored so that the individual does not get any help or at worst the behaviour is punished or ridiculed.

I feel that the national curriculum does not allow for creativity. For example, all children must learn this set of things by key stage four and it does not take into account individuality or specific interests that a young person may have. I feel that it's time the education system introduced child-specific learning plans which take into account each child's needs and interests. I found certain lessons very challenging and the teachers did not do much to support me with those lessons.

MATHS

Now, I know some youngsters on the spectrum are wonderful with Maths and numbers. I don't know but I think you can either be brilliant at expression and creativity or brilliant with numbers and dates. I have never met anyone who is brilliant with both Maths and language. If you are not brilliant at either, do not worry. It does not mean that you are bad at being autistic. Some individuals have expressed feeling this way to me. I believe that it means that you have not discovered what your gifts are yet. If you believe it means that you are average, then average is just fine too. There is nothing wrong with being average. You are still a good person with your own unique qualities.

I used to hate mental Maths all the way through my school career. In the morning after assembly, if we were being taught Maths, we'd have to do mental arithmetic and I could always feel the class laughing when I scored something like two or three out of twenty. It was just humiliating. Hence the reason why I only have a Functional Skills Maths qualification. I will go back and do my Maths GCSE one day; I just need to find the time to do so. I know I need one but I just don't like it.

Things would only get worse with Maths classes in secondary school – which I'll talk about more in the next chapter. Another of my most disliked lessons was, of course, Physical Education.

PHYSICAL EDUCATION (P.E.) AND DYSPRAXIA

My dyspraxia means that I face potential difficulty in activities requiring coordination and movement. I've explained more about the condition in the opening chapter. I could not balance very well, and I have never learnt to ride a bike due to falling off too many times when I was younger. I also once wore a giant Dalmatian dog head to P.E. at primary school because we were celebrating Purim (a Hebrew festival of the saving of the Jewish people from King Haman, which is traditionally celebrated by public celebration, dressing in costume and eating certain types of food). I wanted to dress as a dog even though the other children were dressing as kings and queens, but I had dressed as a king for many years previously. My teacher had told me to take the head off, but I refused and played cricket with the dog head on. This was particularly difficult as it left me with limited vision, and now I am older I can appreciate why she asked me to take the head off, but the other children laughed at me, so I became more stubborn about it.

Then, when we were in Years 5 and 6, we had to go swimming, and I didn't like getting changed with the other children. I had trouble doing up my buttons and it took me longer than everyone else to get ready and I got blamed for holding up their lunch times.

Sports day was another common routine at my primary school that I didn't enjoy. None of the other children wanted me in their team because I was clumsy and I couldn't run very fast. I fell from the balance beams and had to start again; still to this day, I cannot climb rope. My Year 5 teacher was very competitive and always chose me last for the teams because she knew I wasn't any good.

Don't you just find that P.E. is another form of bullying? Autistic or not, many people experience being bullied during P.E. as a child, especially if you were overweight like I was. One hot sunny day in my secondary school when the teachers were making us run the track, I decided enough was enough. That was the day I decided never to go to P.E. again.

Young people on the spectrum, if you are being bullied in P.E., please tell someone about it. Do not keep it to yourself otherwise the problems will just continue. Find a teacher you trust or talk to your parents. If neither of those solutions work, then suggest that you drop P.E. for a subject that you need extra support in. Do not stop exercising altogether, though. Find an activity you enjoy and do that in your own time because you do need to stay healthy and active otherwise it will cause you health problems in your adult life.

Parents, please, if your child is being bullied in P.E., then don't make them continue with it. When I got to secondary school, I just used to skip P.E. and go to the park until I got a doctor's note much later on about my scoliosis. (I suffered from scoliosis of the spine when I was 15 years old. Scoliosis is a deformity of the spine which results in a curvature.) I also got my diagnosis of having dyspraxia due to my inability to do Physical Education, and I believe that there are other ways of helping your child exercise. For example, take them to the park to rollerblade or when they're older take them to the gym or find a physical activity they do enjoy and do that with them. You can avoid bullying altogether by doing this and I don't really see why P.E. is on the curriculum other than a need to make children exercise. Take the children swimming in their own time so that they avoid the embarrassment of being slow in front of other children in their class. Or if they have issues getting dressed like I did, they can avoid all of that social embarrassment. I'm sure the children can use the time they would have spent on P.E. doing something more productive like being helped with homework or mental arithmetic.

Young people on the autistic spectrum, if you're having problems, please don't get upset and lash out. It doesn't solve anything, and it automatically puts you in the wrong. Don't refuse or be rude to your teachers; instead, ask for help and if they won't listen then I'm sure your parents will. My parents did and I have many happy experiences from school not just the bad ones. I started to develop special interests in primary school as I was beginning to learn what lessons I liked.

LESSONS I LIKED AND POSITIVE EXPERIENCES

My childhood was not all doom and gloom, folks. In Year 4 my favourite lesson was literacy hour. I loved my literacy book; I loved to write and express my feelings. However, my handwriting was appalling. Soon I had to use handwriting packs that the teachers supplied for me to try and help me improve it. I know now they were only trying to help, but it made me feel different from the other children. I refused to do the work and got into many arguments with teachers and my mum, who cared about me. I remember having helpers who tried in vain to support me, but I found it incredibly difficult to let them. I saw it as a weakness as I did many other things at that time. It was then that I discovered how difficult Geography was for me, and many other subjects that were always going to be a struggle. I think now if I couldn't write and express myself, I'd be extremely unhappy. I wrote my first ever poem in Year 4 and it goes something like this:

My magic box

I will put in my box
A silk moon, shining silently over Saturn
A purple parrot perching politely on a palm tree
And a pink puppy dog's tail.

I will put in my box
A sad song, sung by sultans on sad Saturdays
A sour, silly, shouting teacher sitting on a sofa
And a black sun.

I will put in my box
A rock of an ancient mountain
Frozen water from St. Michael's cave
And a block of teeth from a fairy's castle.

I will put in my box
A tough, talking, tiny giant sitting on a tree
A firework from the forest frost-nay
And a wicked witch of the west.

I will put in my box
A soggy, sulking sausage sitting in a pan
A long, forever-lasting light of the moon
And a frost of fog flying over forever green.

I will put in my box
A flashing forest full of frogs
A spell spoken in Idalade
And a blue century called a millennium.

Alongside realising my love for writing and creativity, I also realised in Year 4 that I had no fear of embarrassment. My friend and I used to play our recorders in the playground to practise for concerts. I think this irritated the other children whilst they were trying to play their games, but we didn't care. I entered a competition at school every year called the Oratory Contest. This was where we had to prepare a speech about a certain topic to present it in front of the school. The winner won the Oratory Prize on prize day and read their speech out again in front of the parents. The speech could only be a certain length of time; I loved it. I never won, because only certain children ever won the competition, but it prepared me for speaking in front of large audiences and helped me realise my love for acting. When I spoke I could be me, but I could pretend to be someone else as well. I could pretend to be a more confident version of myself, and that's when I discovered a need for theatre and expression.

As I got older, though, I became increasingly nervous about public speaking. I threw up before giving a presentation at the beginning of my MPhil degree course. It's a shame because children are so energetic, so ready to take risks that I think adults should try to tap into that energy whenever they are about to perform or go for a job interview.

I loved the school plays. My first play was when I was in Year 2, so I'd only have been six or seven years old. I was the weather woman in our school's version of Noah's ark. Mum still has the video somewhere, and I hope to god she never shows it to any partners I might bring to meet her. I think she did show my ex-boyfriend it once, but I loved and trusted him enough for him not to judge me. He always said he loved me for who I was.

Other special memories include circle time in Year 1 with a very supportive teacher who looked after me for my mother after school, bringing in my Playmobil circus in Year 2, and having a teddy bears' picnic on the back field where we all brought in our favourite teddy. Mine was my teddy Ruxbin because he told me stories to help me sleep at night.

In Year 3 some Viking re-enactors came into the class and we built a Viking longboat on the back field and made authentic-looking coins, which event, I think, contributed to my becoming a historical re-enactor in adult life – alongside a trip to Bosworth Field with my dad. Every year we had a prize day where they rewarded effort in school and I loved it because the prizes were always new books. My friends and I had a food fight one day and a dinner lady that we didn't like slipped up in a fish cake. When we reminisce, we remember that to this day!

So, please understand that I'm not saying everything about school is bad. The negative experiences can tend to overshadow the positive ones, but if you look deeply enough you will find that you do have some positive school memories to share.

SCHOOL TRIPS

Some children on the spectrum can find going on school trips very difficult. They might have worries like: What will I eat? What time will I be home? and Where can I sit so that it's not too loud?

The place they're going to is new and the routine is nothing like their routine at home. Sometimes they can find the excitement or anxiety overwhelming, and they could experience sensory over-stimulation or have meltdowns. Schools may not even want such children to be offered places on trips and the Office of the Children's Commissioner's 2013 report on illegal exclusions, "Always Someone Else's Problem", found widespread evidence that children with special educational needs (SEN) were routinely excluded from school trips.

Such exclusion is wrong. I feel that it is important to include individuals on the spectrum in trips and extracurricular activities, no matter how hard and disruptive it may seem to the teachers or parents. Young people need to push themselves out of their comfort zones and they cannot do that if they stay in their bedrooms at home away from frightening and uncomfortable experiences. It's how you meet new people and experience new things and make great memories of the world.

There are ways that you can support someone on the spectrum to help them enjoy school trips or at least experience them. Take your child for a pre-visit separately to their peers so that they know what to expect. Give them a timetable so that they know what will happen on the day and ensure that there are quiet spaces for them to go if they need some time to themselves.

I know I enjoyed going on school trips because they got us out of the classroom environment. We went to places like Aston Hall and the Birmingham Museum and Art Gallery. We also went to Severn Trent's East Birmingham food waste digestion plant to learn the science behind cleaning water. Going on such trips always used to make me very anxious because each one was a new situation.

However, my biggest challenge with regard to trips was when I went on the school's residential.

My first residential trip was in Year 6 when I was 11 years old. We went for a week to a place called Bockleton Study Centre in Worcestershire. I remember it being a fun but rather difficult experience for me. Prior to going on the trip, I remember being very anxious and counting down the days. My main worries were to do with it being a rather physical trip with lots of walking and outdoor activities, but there were plenty of other challenges for me to face too: interacting appropriately with my peers, navigating the orienteering challenges, managing my money properly and having appropriate clothes for the activities. My mum had packed my bag so that I had clothes for each day.

She had packed the correct amount of clothes for the week, and laid each day's on top of the other so that each day I could just pick out those for the day and have a set of clean clothes. But as soon as I got in my room, I tipped my clothes on the floor and put them into the drawers in the room because I did not want to seem different from my friends or for them to know I needed extra support. Very quickly, I ended up forgetting to bring my coat for cold water activities and wearing several pairs of socks and not having enough by the end of the week.

We did a lot of walking and so the trip was physically tiring, and we also had to collect items around the centre for an orientation day. I found that really hard because I find it difficult to read maps and my sense of direction is very limited. As an adult, I still struggle to tell right from left and it took me many years to remember the route to get from my house to my secondary school, making travelling by bus difficult.

During the residential I also found it hard interacting with the other children in my class. My friends and I will never forget when I danced around a pole in the middle of the hall after dinner to try to impress the boys. All I achieved was shocking the teachers around me and getting people to laugh at me rather than with me. At the end of the week there was a disco and I just sat in the hall listening to the music, wondering how I was ever going to approach anyone. We went shopping in the village on the way home – that was fun, but I remember feeling glad when I was back at my parents' house. I was safe and away from anything new and challenging that I'd have to experience. I was back in a familiar environment with familiar routines around me.

ANXIETY AROUND CHANGE AND GENERAL ANXIETY

Have you ever been anxious that you are going to miss your train because you have an important job interview that you have to be on time for? If not, then imagine a time that you have been anxious. Imagine the feelings you get, the sick feeling in your stomach, the sweat on your face, the fear that you are going to be late or run into someone that you don't want to speak with. Now imagine feeling that fear every day.

Until very recently I was anxious every day. I was anxious about travelling on public transport because I don't like the sound of children crying and I don't like being late or sitting next to strangers. I was anxious when my rota changed at work because it meant I had to work with different people and hadn't been expecting to. I was anxious when I had to speak on the phone to strangers and I was anxious introducing strangers onto the ward I worked on. I was anxious when I had to speak about myself or whenever my routine changed, such as if we ran out of scrambled eggs.

Dealing with anxiety has been one of my biggest problems throughout my life, both as a child and as an adult as well. This is not uncommon; lots of children on the spectrum experience anxieties, especially around transitional periods in life – such as moving from nursery to big school or primary school to secondary school. (The same is true for adults, made worse by the fact that a lot of the support for young people with learning differences stops at the age they become an adult and so they are often left with no financial or educational support and they then struggle to find something to move on to after education.)

I know I certainly experienced great anxiety around the transitional periods in my childhood, and I'm grateful to my parents for helping me through them by offering encouragement each step of the way. The first change I remember as a child is transitioning from home to nursery school, and I remember not being able to sleep all night and lining all my picture books up in order on my bed to try to help me sleep. The biggest changes that little ones experience are with the move from the cot to the "big girl" bed, as it is sometimes called, and the transition from the potty to the toilet. Whilst I do not remember these, I do know that many of my anxiety dreams are often about falling; firstly, when I was younger it was about falling out of my cot, and now I dream about falling from the sky. I think it is important how these changes are managed when children are young and that parents offer plenty of praise and encouragement rather than becoming fixated on milestones. Your child will learn when they are ready and should not be forced to progress quicker than they are able. Milestones are a guideline not the be all and end all, and it does not mean your child is somehow abnormal or different if they do not walk until the age of three, for example. It just means their development is different to the societal norm.

Of course, everyone experiences anxiety in some form or another sometimes, be it a big job interview or having to deliver a lecture, but for me my anxiety was so intense and so strong and over things that a neurotypical person may not even consider as being anxiety-provoking, such as going to a party or talking to another person. I once went to a party when I was in primary school and I was so anxious about meeting people that I threw up all over the stairs. Mum did not take me to any parties after that, and although I did like to go to playgroup, I did not begin to socialise properly until I was at least ten years old.

Mum: *That party was a classic. I'd never met this child's mother before, and I had this feeling that Madeleine shouldn't avoid situations, that she should be helped to experience things, so I did make her go to playgroup, and I stayed with her longer than other parents did. I did make Madeleine go to other children's parties, but I asked if I could stay, but at the party she threw up all over me, on this woman's stairs, when I'd never met her before and I ended up scrubbing the stairs carpet, borrowing a top off this woman, and then thinking well perhaps I ought to take my daughter home, poor little thing. She's obviously so anxious that she's just been sick. That was the turning point, and after that if Madeleine didn't want to go to a party or didn't want to stay, instead of thinking that she ought to because it was helping her socialisation, I just thought nah it's not worth it if it makes her that anxious.*

Other examples of anxieties around change when I was younger included reading new books. My favourite books that Mum read to me were *The Very Hungry Caterpillar*, *Lucy and Tom's Christmas*, *Hairy Maclary from Donaldson's Dairy*, *Mog the Forgetful Cat*, and *Cat and Canary* by Michael Foreman. I'd make her read these books again and again. I wouldn't read anything else for about a year and I got upset when she suggested reading a bigger book. It made me feel anxious because it was a change. I think that Lucy Daniels' *Animal Ark* was the first series of books without pictures that she read to me. I didn't read myself until very late on in my childhood, and instead of reading the words I'd memorise what I'd remembered Mum saying to me to avoid embarrassment due to the fact I could not read well. I also memorised long paragraphs of text, so my vocabulary developed but I didn't understand the meanings of the words I was using. This pictorial memory is great for learning lines now when I perform plays.

Another anxiety-related behaviour was the way in which I played with my Thomas the Tank Engine train set. I loved Thomas the Tank Engine. I'd line up the trains in order of their numbers, and for those trains that didn't have numbers on them I'd put them in order of colour, primary and secondary etc. If you disrupted my train order, I'd get very upset. I'd give anything to have those trains back (and my Gargoyle collection). I gave them to my next-door neighbour's son and I wish I hadn't.

I was still playing with my Thomas the Tank Engine train set by the time most children would have begun to explore imaginary play such as having tea parties or playing schools, but I did not do that until much later on in my childhood and when I did it was in a very different way. When I was around seven years old, I began to use imaginary play as a way of processing what was happening in the world around me. I used to play with my eldest sister and we would pretend to be characters from television shows we had watched. She stopped doing it before she went into secondary school, but I never have. The characters I create have worlds that are much more horrendous than mine and usually have to cope with really difficult life situations such as gang crime and violence. As an adult, I still talk to myself and create characters to help me calm down if something has stressed or upset me. Most often nowadays the characters are based on musicians I idolise, such as Dani Filth from Cradle of Filth or Corey Taylor from Slipknot and Stone Sour, or from vampire films. I used to be embarrassed to admit this, but now I just call it processing and usually do it when I am at home on my own when my partner is at work. It just helps me calm down. Those musicians inspired me and helped me keep going through difficult times when I was younger. I know to others it may seem very odd, but to me it offers me a routine and structure and helps me feel safe. My imagination is then transferred into more traditional hobbies such as writing play scripts and playing Dungeons and Dragons with friends on a Thursday evening.

As a child, every time we went to the park I'd stand on top of the climbing frame singing religious songs because I always sang them at school. It'd make me anxious if I couldn't sing them. I think that a need for rigid structure and routine can be restricting, but it can also be rewarding if you find ways to adapt with it rather than let it hinder the opportunities that you have in daily life.

Mum: *There was a park which we called "the little park" on Howard Road, Madeleine would stand on the top of the climbing frame singing David Israel David Israel at the top of her voice all the way through. She mechanically learnt all of the Jewish songs and she just really liked to sing them. Maddy also sung them at Christmas because her uncle thought it was funny.*

I also got anxious when the other children changed the words of the Hebrew songs to humorous odes, singing "hi hi custard pie" instead of the actual lyrics, which I could sing to you even now. It was not correct to sing that, and so it made me anxious. Everything I did had to be done in a way that was correct to me. It may not have been correct to everybody else, but it was correct to me and so it had to be done.

I was always anxious about visiting new places and I often found I could not sleep the first night in a new situation. Only now in my early 30s do I feel I have mostly overcome my anxiety. I was asked to speak publicly at the Creative Minds Conference in Birmingham in October 2017 as one of the hosts for the conference, introducing ideas such as creative enabling and talking about bridging the gap between the arts and individuals with learning differences in the West Midlands. There were 250 people in attendance at that conference and I spoke to them all without fear as it was a subject I was passionate about. Since then, I've remembered my love of public speaking and can handle almost any situation I am presented with.

The anxieties around change were the reason for first starting to develop a need for routines and rituals that I still have to this very day. For example, as an adult if I am going on a big trip like a holiday or re-enactment weekend, I will pack and re-pack my bags to make sure I have everything. I will also make several lists and probably still end up leaving something behind. However, this does not hinder me as I have developed skills to cope in everyday life. I don't play with Thomas anymore, but there are still things which make me need to have stability and sameness.

It wasn't just the anxiety and need for sameness and routine that made me stand out as a child. I remember being in reception and I guess I was starting to be socially weird. I began to interact with other children in strange ways like picking their spots or fingernails, and it was also in that class that I did not have a very supportive teacher. By the time I was seven years old, I was starting to feel incredibly singled out.

I can remember what my reception classroom looked like. We had the carpet right up against the far wall and a black board above it. The tables were set so that we sat in groups of four and we could see the back field out of the classroom windows. There was a sink in the far corner for when we did activities like painting. Our uniforms were simple; in the summer the girls were made to wear chequered summer dresses, which made me look hideous, because of the fact that I was overweight. In the winter it was a grey skirt, a blue shirt and tie – but I could never tie mine, as I had difficulties putting on clothes properly, so I had an elastic one – and black shoes. I hated going into shoe shops and I had many fights with Mum because we could never find shoes that fitted me that I liked. I have one foot slightly bigger than the other, which made it incredibly difficult to buy shoes. I often have to wear insoles now because I have plantar facilitis, an inflammation of fibrous tissue along the bottom of the foot which connects the heel to the toes, caused by the arches in my feet collapsing. I am convinced this is due to stepping on a rock at re-enactment and wearing terrible authentic shoes, which have no grip, as others of my friends have complained of developing the same issues, but Mum says I have always had it.

Mum: *I remember having to carry Madeleine out of shoe shops whilst she was screaming and having to sit in the car trying to compose myself. There was a particular type of shoe she wanted, which were black shoes with a Disney princess that faded in the corner of the shoe. She wanted the shoes to be individual rather than wear plain black shoes like the other children. She had collapsed arches in her feet, which made buying shoes difficult, and the shop did not have any of that style of shoe that fitted her; she screamed and I had to carry her from the shop.*

On another occasion, we both recalled the previous attempt at buying shoes and had gotten ourselves worked up before we went. Thank god that now you can have mail order.

I had problems with other things, which still affect me to this day. I get attached to objects as well as people, and I experience strong emotional responses to the loss of objects that I am attached to. For example, I would feel a similar strength of emotion when losing a box set of DVDs that belonged to a colleague as I felt when my mum's nan died when I was young. I feel distraught at loss and cannot console myself for many hours or days, depending on what it is that I've lost. For example, I remember when my mum's nan died, and I sat on her bed in the hospital playing with my Thomas trains trying to get her to open her eyes, but to no avail, because I didn't know she was dying. I just knew I felt a sense of loss, and that I felt extremely sad.

I needed everything to be the way I thought it should be, which was not necessarily right for other people; I had a need for consistency which I struggled to maintain despite the needs of others around me. I repetitively watched the same videos and read the same books, sometimes over thirty times a week. I watched one favourite video so much that the man in the video shop gave me it to keep. That was *The Adventures of Milo and Otis*, a wonderful film about a cat and a dog who get lost and then find each other again.

I got very upset one Christmas when my grandmother, gods rest her soul, bought me a cheetah toy, which claimed to be original Disney, but wasn't because it wet itself. I was distraught, because in my mind that just wasn't right, and not how *The Lion King* story went. My father was annoyed because it appeared as if I was being ungrateful for my grandmother's gift. I collected Puppy in My Pockets, and I found a cat and a dog that looked exactly like Otis and Milo and carried them with me everywhere. I was happy when I was five years old when we finally got our own dog. She was a collie-lurcher cross which meant that she had a beautiful collie face and long lurcher legs. We named her Scruffy, because she jumped in the lake at Highbury Park. Scruffy didn't like baths very much and was an incredibly naughty dog. She'd jump over the fence and we'd have to catch her, which became an infamous excuse as to why we were always late for school. I loved Scruffy because I had always loved dogs, and when I needed somebody to tell my problems to she was there.

I was a very clumsy child because of my coordination difficulties, and I had irrational fears about it. I was continually afraid of falling over, and when I was left alone I felt I'd done something wrong to deserve it. I was also afraid of the dark until my father decided to leave the light off in my room one day so I'd have to get off my bed to switch the light back on.

The first incident of clumsiness that I remember happened when I was four years old. My sister and I used to play with soft toys on the stairs, and one day I tripped and fell all the way down. I don't know if my sister pushed me, but even now she gets upset if I suggest that she did, so I think I must have tripped on one of the teddies. Mum took me to watch *The Lion King* at the cinema to try and make me stop crying, because she hadn't realised my arm was broken. She also did not know of my sensory difficulties with going to the cinema.

My eldest sister: Madeleine fell down the stairs, I never pushed her, she slipped on the soft toys at the top of the stairs, and then she told everyone that she thought she could fly!

I do not remember saying that I thought I could fly, and forever after jokes were made about me thinking I could fly. I took everything literally and got upset because I knew I couldn't fly, so it must have been a ploy to laugh at me.

I was scared of going to the cinema until I was about seven years old. When I was six, Mum took me to see *The Hunchback of Notre Dame* and I cried all the way through it because the loud sounds, darkness and the branding of the opening credits of the film scared me. I did not know then that I was hypersensitive to sound. The first film that I wanted to see was the *Star Wars* re-release in 1997 and I had to get over my fear of the opening credits so that I could watch the film.

In 2011, relaxed, autism-friendly cinema screenings were introduced in London, and subsequently in many other cities too. With autism-friendly screenings, simple adjustments are made to reduce stress and sensory input, such as the lights are left on and the sound is lowered. I think this is a wonderful initiative, creating an environment where individuals can feel included and not judged for their diagnosis. However, it came a little late for my benefit; I had to struggle to get used to the loud sounds and queuing that is the cinema environment if I wanted to see a film when I was younger. I am now quite used to going to the cinema generally and so a relaxed screening wouldn't be much different for me now. I still won't go to watch 3D films, though, but that is because I hate things jumping out at me. It is too much for me and I get sensory overloads.

I also had the privilege of attending a relaxed performance of *Sleeping Beauty* at the Birmingham Hippodrome recently and I was thrilled to see that more of an effort is being made to include individuals on the spectrum at such events. However, I found myself becoming irritated by the fact that people were allowed to talk and move around throughout the performance; perhaps as an adult I am becoming more neurotypical?

Another time of high anxiety for me was when my youngest sister was born in December 1995. I was anxious because I believed that when she was born my family would stop loving me as they would have to give her all of their time and attention.

RELATIONSHIPS WITH MY SISTERS

A lot of people on the spectrum have difficult relationships with their siblings because they prefer to do things on their own terms and struggle to understand how to interact with their brothers or sisters properly.

I always got on with my eldest sister, though. I don't remember her not being there. I believed that she was Mum's favourite and I felt like I was Dad's favourite, so we were happy. That all changed when my youngest sister arrived. I don't remember being told that my little sister was going to be born. I do, however, remember the week she was born, in December 1995.

I remember when Mum went to hospital and my sister and I stayed in the house with Dad for a week. Dad did not cook often, so we had McDonald's most days. I was scared because I was beginning to think Mum was not coming back, even though Dad explained several times that she was.

It felt to me as if Mum had just disappeared and I was upset and anxious. I was the more irrational sibling and I thought that I must have done something to upset Mum and that was why she'd left. I think it would have helped if Mum would have told me all about hospitals and where she was going in a factual way; maybe she did and I just don't remember it.

When Dad was at work my sister and I had to stay with our next-door neighbour. I didn't like this because it was not my usual routine and I started to think that Mum wasn't coming back. After a few days Dad took us to the hospital that Mum was staying in. He bought us videos and teddies. I guess he was trying to make us feel comforted, but I was on edge. We came into the room after climbing lots of stairs. I hate hospitals, and this was one of my earliest memories of one.

Mum was sitting up in bed when we came in, and both my sister and I were ecstatic to see her. Then we saw a baby in her arms. The baby looked around the room and cried. I didn't like the crying sound. Later in life I discovered that I am hypersensitive to sound and so I cannot deal with loud unexpected noises as they are painful to me.

Mum had got us presents and said they were from our new sister. I got two action figures from the 1990s X-Men cartoon, which I loved, and I was very happy but I was still unsure how to behave around my new sister – who I soon realised was here to stay when she came home with Mum.

I was very selfish when I was five and I didn't think that I wanted a new sister. What was wrong with the one I had? I didn't want to share Mum's attention with two other people. Where would that leave me? I know that a child without autism might experience this reaction, but as I was constantly anxious and worried, my reaction was very extreme – even to the point of refusing to call my new sister by her name for three years and calling her "thing" or "it" instead. I was mean to her and I liked to make her cry, because it made me feel better about myself. Today, I feel very differently, and

I'm incredibly proud of everything my youngest sister has achieved and I strongly regret the way I treated her.

My eldest sister was the strongest sibling and one day a teacher once asked me, "Where did you get that bruise on your back?"

"My mum did it," I answered, too scared to tell them that my eldest sister had pushed me into a door (and threatened to do it again if I'd tell anyone). So, down to the school went my poor mother to sort out the matter.

Mum: *Madeleine nearly got taken off me because – I don't know what they were fighting about but – she got pushed into that door handle and she had a massive bruise on her back. When they asked who'd done it at school, Madeleine told them that her mother had done it because she didn't want to get her sister into trouble. She nearly ended up getting taken off me.*

I taught my youngest sister the swearing alphabet to get her into trouble at school, and when she was six the teachers asked her what the letter F stood for. She swore in class and Mum was called in. My youngest sister and I certainly get on better now, and whenever she is in Birmingham I try to spend time with her. We have a lot of similar interests and I believe she has autistic traits. Maybe that was why I didn't like her? She was too similar to me.

My youngest sister: When I was a child Maddy taught me the swearing alphabet to get me into trouble ... A is for Arsehole ... B is for Bollox etc.

Mum: *Well, that wasn't really anything to do with autism that was just childhood banter...*

My youngest sister: But it's funny because that was how I learnt the alphabet. Maddy would sit there and teach me all these swear words...

Mum: I didn't know this. It's quite interesting. I'm learning more myself, talking to you guys about this stuff.

My youngest sister: Well, I remember this one because I got in trouble because they asked me how I knew my alphabet.

W was for WaggaMuff or something because Maddy just could not think of anything.

I don't think autism should be diagnosed unless the person has a severe problem with it. For example, I don't think it's fair that I get detention for refusing to run track in a heatwave but Maddy gets away with throwing a chair at a teacher because she's autistic. It should not be used as an excuse for bad behaviour, but at the same time if she wasn't diagnosed then running away from someone because they caught her off guard does sound a little odd and would probably lose her a few friends. I have both an autistic and non-autistic sister and I relate more to the one with autism. I prefer life in black and white, and sometimes having someone live by that view is refreshing. I wouldn't say it makes life much harder, having an autistic sister. The only problem I see is that Maddy does not understand certain boundaries (I could have lived without seeing her write her diary stark-bollock naked). Some of the things that first stick out in my mind when I think of her as a child are: her tracksuit bottoms, which she wore almost every day except when Mum took them to wash them, her obsession with order and some of her unmentionable role-playing sessions which I shan't go into.

I'll never forget her sleepovers with all her friends whilst she was in secondary school, especially the one time we went on the trampoline and it was about 1am and everyone was making too much noise, so the neighbours hosed us, but she carried on anyway whereas most people would've apologised and gone in. I remember thinking that was cool at the time because she didn't care what people thought, but as I got older things like that seemed to stick out more and I began to realise what Asperger's was, but then, and even now, I don't see it as a problem. I see it as a different way of life and I sometimes think life would be better if everyone had autism because I don't know about autism on a whole but Mad is trustworthy, loyal, hard-working, determined and unable to lie, and if everyone was like that the world would spin a lot faster.

Mad and I get along better than most siblings, and over the years we've done a lot together. Some of what she does is strange and we don't always share the same view, but some of what I do is also strange and some of my views may stick out against others. Maddy does not have a problem with autism; she just has autism, and I think it's what makes her tick.

All in all, I have good relationships with my siblings and with my parents. However, nothing I can do can make it up to my youngest sister for the way that I treated her. I should just pray that she forgives me and understands how truly sorry I am and how cruel other children can be.

WHAT MIGHT HAVE HELPED

Here I don't want to blame my parents for anything with the benefit of hindsight; I just want to give readers an idea of what I think might have helped in this situation.

I wonder if it would have helped if my parents had have tried to encourage me to play with my new sister a bit more and to tried to get me to share my things. I appreciate that must have been a very difficult task, considering that even when I was at university I considered labelling my things with my name on them so that my housemates could not share them. I also think that my parents should have punished me more for the way I treated my youngest sister. I don't remember being told off much for the way I treated her.

DEALING WITH DEPRESSION

In 1997 when I was seven years old, I remember starting to feel depressed. I was overweight. The other children bullied me about it. One of the girls used to call me fat, and it may sound like a trivial thing, but for someone as sensitive as I was this was one of the most hurtful things I had ever heard. Also, our teacher used to make us do silent reading for fifteen minutes each day in the morning after assembly. I couldn't read in my head. She made me stay in at break time for it, because she said I needed to practise as I was disrupting the other children.

One day I went home to cry in the bathroom. Mum came up and found me crying on the toilet. She asked me, "What's wrong, little one?"

"I want to kill myself," I replied.

"But why would you want to do that when you're so young?"

"Because I'm fat and the other children don't like me." I sobbed and sobbed, and I think Mum cried too.

I used to hit my head repeatedly off walls, trying to kill myself, but Mum didn't know that. That's why I spent so much time on my own in my bedroom. I'd lock myself away, because I didn't want to make anyone else sad if they saw me weak and vulnerable. I still don't like to let people see me cry. I used to believe it was a sign of weakness. I'd rather hurt myself than other people even now. I started to develop coping mechanisms for feeling depressed, and I became good at writing poetry, and play scripts. I still use them now to deal with my feelings. In secondary school I started to keep my diaries.

I've suffered with low self-esteem and mild depression for many years, but I feel a lot better now because I have accepted that autism is a part of who I am. When I am well I feel that there is no need to feel inadequate anymore. Everyone who I care about loves me for being me. The people who don't are not worth my time or effort. With lots of support from family, friends and therapists I finally see that I am who I am, and I am learning to be happy that way.

It is not uncommon for individuals on the spectrum to develop depression as I did, perhaps as a consequence of general anxiety, being bullied, failings of the education system or struggling with communication and expression. (Difficulties with communication and language can lead to depression because it is very frustrating being unable to express yourself accurately, knowing what you want to say in your head and having it come out completely different when you are talking to others – or constantly being taken advantage of by others because you are vulnerable and loyal.)

If this is you, you may have noticed by this point that you are different from other children and may be being ostracised by the school or your neighbours or even your siblings for being different. Do not panic.

If you are a young person on the spectrum suffering with depression, please talk to someone. Don't keep it all locked inside you. If you have a good relationship with your parents, talk to them, or there are counsellors and your friends to talk to, or there are charities you can go to such as Autism West Midlands and the National Autistic Society.

The longer you keep it to yourself the longer it will hurt you. Please remember that all situations in life are temporary and whatever pain you are feeling now will not last forever – unless of course you also experience chronic pain or have other lifelong health conditions, then you will learn how to manage your pain as you get older so that you may experience relief or the pain will decrease. I am here with you for the moment. Be brave and fight through; your difference is a gift and it does not matter what others think of you, even your own family; all that matters is you stay within the law and stay true to yourself.

If it's your child or your friend having these difficulties, then try to be patient with them and offer them support. Parents, please listen to your children. You are there to support them and help them through difficult times, not make things harder by being unsupportive or dismissive. Don't shout at them if they cannot get a word right straight away, and do not take offence if they shout at you. They are probably angry and frustrated with themselves or their situation. Be there to listen to them. Don't read the newspaper if you are uninterested in what they are saying; no matter how repetitive or monotonous it may be, you never know when you may miss something interesting or useful. Don't tell them, "I'll be with you in a minute once I've finished my paperwork," because a minute may be too long. Don't tell them whatever the problem is will feel better when they're older because it may not. There will be noticeable signs if your child is suffering from depression. For example, do they spend a lot of time in their bedroom? Do they go out to play with their friends at all? Are they eating massive amounts of food or not eating at all? If the answer is yes to questions one and three, then you may want to try to talk to them; see if they're ok. Equally they may not wish to speak with you, but if you continue to worry then you should try approaching a teacher who you know your child trusts. Tell your child that you are worried and that is what you're going to do. You don't want to break their trust by going behind their back. It could be that they're afraid of what will happen if any adults are aware of the problems.

SEGREGATION

The trouble with any school is that, in my experience, they do not prepare for how to support young people with needs that are outside of their norm. I had a classroom assistant all the way through school, but I didn't actually get a statement until I left primary school when I was 12. I did not go to a special school and I struggled in mainstream school because the teachers there did not know how to support me.

I had to have lots of time out of school for assessments in Park View clinic, and although I liked getting the McDonald's for lunch and missing lessons it made me feel different from the other children. They'd ask me where I'd been sometimes, and I didn't know how to answer them. I don't remember being told about autism or being told I had it. I wish someone would have sat with me to explain everything factually and scientifically.

I was taken out of classes to sit in the corridor with other children who needed learning support. I was made to do handwriting packs and mental Maths. I hated being taken out of classes, because it made me feel different from the other children. The corridor was cold and sometimes the teachers left us alone with a Maths book or a handwriting pack because there was not enough staff to support us and the mainstream children. I didn't realise the handwriting pack was supposed to help me and it felt like a punishment for being different. I'd refuse to do my handwriting homework. I don't blame Mum and Dad for not sitting down and telling me factually.

They never wanted to make me feel different. They always wanted me to feel like the other children, but because of the autistic label that just wasn't possible. Another thing that made me feel different was having a support worker at all. This was because she sat with me in classes and I did not view any other children having an adult sit with them all of the time. All of these things contributed to my depression but having a support worker was invaluable and I would not have done as well on my exams without her support.

LEARNING SUPPORT

I received learning support when I was in Year 4 because my diagnosis had finally been made. This meant I had a support worker, but having one made me feel different from the other children. This was because she sat with me in classes and I did not see any other children having an adult sit with them all of the time. Despite me pushing against her and not always doing what I was told, I developed a good relationship with my support worker, and this was what she said about me.

Support worker: *My first impression of Madeleine was that she was a cheerful girl, and always willing to learn, and do what she was asked to do. Some things took her a little longer to think about. For example, if she was planning to write a story, she would often spend more time planning it than writing it. I used to have to remind her to start writing!*

Madeleine always asked for help if she was stuck with anything or didn't understand anything. I remember helping her to climb the wall in P.E. because she didn't like to go too high. I was always usually right behind her, giving her plenty of encouragement. When she was writing anything in her book or if she was doing any art work, I can always remember, she would press very hard with her pencil and there was often an imprint on several pages following where she had written!

Madeleine would always take everything I said very literally. If I said, "Come on Maddy, pull your socks up," meaning work a bit faster, she would always pull her [actual] socks up. She didn't like working in Year 4 when we were in the classroom in the upstairs part of the school, because it was quite close to the kitchens. She didn't like the smell of the food cooking for lunch. Once or twice, she said it made her feel quite sick.

I am not quite sure whether autism should be diagnosed. If someone is diagnosed with autism and they benefit from extra support in school or support at home, I am in favour of it. I am not in favour of a diagnosis if it means that a child becomes "labelled" and stands out from everybody else. All children are different with different needs, and it is a shame if they are all labelled as autistic.

So, although I remember feeling very resentful at the time because having her sit with me in lessons made me stand out, my learning support worker was a lovely woman who, with hindsight, I can see helped me greatly in primary school so that I was ready to move on to secondary school when the time came. When I was younger my parents were told that I would "probably never go to university and I would be lucky if I had a job stacking shelves for a living". It is thanks to people like my support worker that I am where I am today and I do not stack shelves for a living, thank you very much! There is certainly nothing wrong with stacking shelves if that is what you want to do but I was told that it was all I could hope to aspire to and as someone with great ambition I found that comment very hurtful and restrictive to my potential.

When I was in secondary school, I did not have a direct support worker because I was in the special learning centre at my school. I hated that too because they decided that it would be a good idea to put seven students from each year who needed learning support into the centre and expected that we would all get on and support each other. No ways! I got a taxi free in the morning to pick me up from my house and take me to school, but again it made me feel different, so when I was 12 I started to learn to take the bus to school.

In university I got a learning support mentor who I could arrange meetings with at my own convenience, and it was then that I started to value the support I was being given. It was because of him that I began to plan writing this book back in 2009. I also got free equipment from the Disabled Students Allowance (DSA) such as a Dictaphone to record my lectures, a free laptop and an office chair to support my back when I was writing my dissertation. (This is why I stated that a diagnosis was sometimes useful later on in life.)

When I went on to do my master's degree, I continued to see a learning support mentor and she helped me to edit this book for the first time in 2011. She also supported me with the challenge that was finding a job.

Young people on the spectrum, you may feel that learning support is a waste of time or that your support worker makes you stand out from other children in your class. But they are really useful in the long run and you need to make them work for you – not meaning that you are their boss but meaning that if you build a good relationship with them, then they can support you with what you are struggling with and will become useful for you. Tell them what lessons you find hard and work together with them. Tell them about your problems and you will find that they are one of the best things that you could have. I still write to my support worker from primary school occasionally now and I am an adult. I don't see her anymore, but she helped me so much that I value her and we keep in touch.

Parents, I do believe that learning support is useful, but I feel that it is important to combat your child's feelings of otherness; help them to see that this support is to help them rather than to punish them. Help them to know that other children are cruel and the ones who are commenting about their differences are the ones who are not worth their time. Help them to see that their Asperger's is a gift rather than something to be ashamed of or embarrassed by.

INTERVIEW 2: A PRIMARY SCHOOL TEACHER WHO IS ON THE AUTISM SPECTRUM

I will now introduce the perspective of a young woman on the spectrum. I interviewed her about her experiences growing up on the spectrum; she was also one of the students who I supported when I worked as a mentor during my second year of university. Support is invaluable and helps you to become a better version of yourself if it is the correct support. The interviewee wished to remain anonymous for the purpose of this interview, but her answers to the questions provide valuable insight into the difficulties that she faced whilst growing up and the support she received.

Introduce yourself

I am 31 years old and I was diagnosed with Asperger's syndrome at the age of seven. The symptoms were very apparent when I was in the Early Years Foundation Stage (Reception and Nursery). I was very socially awkward. I had no spatial awareness. My concentration was extremely poor and my mind would flit from one thought to the next. I couldn't maintain a conversation as I wouldn't respond appropriately to what was said or answer a question properly. Nor was I able to stick to the subject of conversation without deviating to a topic that I was interested in. I didn't keep eye-contact and I was very fidgety, and at the time teachers didn't make an effort to keep me focused on the learning on the carpet as we might do now as educators. Routine was crucial for me; if there was a sudden change, like a change of teacher or if I didn't know what was going on, I would be very stressed out, even hysterical sometimes. I had social skills and communication interventions with children who were also on the spectrum like me. When I moved up to Year 1 and went into formal learning, where I had structured lessons at tables and learnt out of books and wrote on paper, I did a lot better at school. School found I was doing well academically, so I was supported with the social skills side of my disability.

When I was in Year 6 suddenly everything clicked. I grew up and matured. I was motivated to do well academically and I knew what socially accepted behaviour was and how to act in a neurotypical manner. As a result, I fared well at high school, although doing exams such as my GCSEs and A-levels were tough. Because I was obsessed with studies, I could never switch off when I was in higher education and have a proper work/life balance. As I was also busy with extracurricular activities like music and drama, I had very little time for myself.

It was upsetting not being able to do as well as others. I came from a family where my cousins got ten A*s and four As and studied medicine, but I was more creatively inclined. Unlike typical Aspies, I had a gift for English Literature. I was able to understand metaphors and infer from text and empathise with characters, so I found it easy to conceal my condition during high school and live an ordinary life. I was bullied, however. For being me. For having an eloquent way of speaking. For being religious. For not indulging in alcohol, cigarettes and drugs. And for being a virgin – most of which I thought was a virtue, but it turned out to be social suicide growing up.

Tell me about your diagnosis

Sorry I've rambled on about my introduction. I think I've answered questions 1, 2, 3 and 7!

When did you gain your diagnosis?

When I was seven years old.

Tell me about your job?

I am a primary school teacher. It is challenging because of all the ridiculous demands that the curriculum makes on the children. They are aware of the diversity of needs for children. There isn't enough additional adult support, even though the children come up needier and lower than ever. But senior leadership insist on results being produced.

As an Asperger's the stress is insurmountable. I am constantly worried about work. Constantly planning, differentiating and adapting my lessons to meet the learning needs of children. The paperwork and amount of assessment and deadlines for data are overwhelming. I keep on top of it by working systematically. Completing tasks weekly on specific days.

I struggle with staying tough, though. You need to be thick-skinned. There is a lot of politics and it is difficult for me to put up and shut up when I can see that there is so much wrong with the system. The government, the head teacher, the senior leaders and everyone are expected to comply; compliance is key, so the only way to cope is taking it day by day, week by week and counting down every day until half term.

Did your culture have an impact on the way you were treated when you were younger? If so, tell me about it?

Culture. Well, wow! What can I say? Being bicultural and from an Asian background can be a curse. Culturally people are often in denial when their children have needs. Only my mother, as an educated professional nurse, understood that I had needs and ensured that I got the help that I was entitled to. She ensured I never got behind with my education. Sent me to extracurricular clubs and activities to socialise. Took me to the library so I had access to reading and books.

I come from a culture that stigmatises people who are different. Doctors, lawyers, accountants and engineers, mathematicians and scientists are brainy; everyone else is stupid. *So*, you can imagine what people thought when I was interested in English, History, R.E., Drama, Sociology and Spanish. What was she going to do? How is she going to make a living? How will she have enough money to pay back her student loan, get a house and be married with three children by 25 at this rate? Why can't she stick to the status quo? Fortunately, they didn't know about the Asperger's; if they knew, they wouldn't understand.

What did you enjoy most about primary school?

I enjoyed plays and performances at primary school. Acting was my strong point. It was a time I could be a completely different person. I had a good voice. People admired me as I was talented at it and I felt like someone worthwhile.

I also enjoyed Year 6, when everything came together and I was a high-functioning student. I understood the routines of the classroom. I could concentrate on learning and work independently and produce high standards of work. I had a good relationship with friends and teachers.

What did you find challenging about primary school?

In my introduction I told you a lot about the challenging parts of primary school. But between Years 3 to 5 there was a time when teachers didn't understand my diagnosis. I was a middle-ability child, not stupid but not ridiculously bright either. And when my Asperger's affected my cognition and understanding, teachers didn't get why I didn't understand something. They thought I wasn't listening or I was lazy because I didn't get it first time round. And even though I was able to hold a conversation then, I still couldn't articulate my needs. Teachers would make fun of me. Say condescending things under their breath, which I didn't get at the time as I didn't understand sarcasm. My parents didn't get it either. At that time what the teacher said was absolute and final. It's the other way round these days. Parents blame teachers for everything, condone their children's wild behaviour and do nothing to support their children at home (a challenge in my profession which is infuriating). As a result, when I got home and I was fed up of behaving appropriately and putting up pretences, the smallest thing a family member could say would trigger an explosion of upset and anger. I was violent towards myself. I would hit my head against a wall, scream and cry because there was no other way to express my frustration and agony.

What do you think the education system could improve in order to better support youngsters on the spectrum in primary school?

Fortunately, there is a lot more knowledge and acceptance of autism and teachers are well trained on how to support children. The problem is, with funding being cut, it is very difficult to get an education health care plan to support a special educational needs child (SEN). You need a mountain of evidence and when initial concern forms are filled out they are often ignored as there are already *so* many children with needs that the SEN co-ordinator doesn't have the time nor the energy nor the support herself to accommodate new children with difficulties. Children need to be a danger to themselves and others before additional adult support is provided – which is sad. Really sad.

Do you have any sensory difficulties?

I am sensitive with sounds and touch. Unexpected loud piercing noises shake me up a bit. I don't mind physical contact, but there are times when I just don't want to be touched and hugged and my mother chooses to do it anyway, which results in me shouting, "Fuck off you stupid bitch!" because she doesn't get it when I say, "No, please stop." I sometimes hate being prodded or tickled or slapped out of jest, depending on who it is. If I have a close relationship with the person, it is different, but I am picky about who can and cannot do that.

How do you deal with them as an adult?

Well honestly? I struggle. And I don't always cope. I am on anti-depressants. I get anxious very easily. I am always on edge. I have self-harmed and attempted suicide in the past. I used to have a very supportive line manager and at work people understood my need. The new senior leader is a cold fish who is very black and white and just has an agenda and a job to do – which [makes things] difficult. I suppose having me-time at the weekends and holidays to switch off entirely from work helps. I find it hard to maintain constant contact with my family. I don't have the time nor the energy to call them every day and make small talk. It is pointless, a waste of time and sometimes talking just doesn't help after a long hard day at work.

I am lucky in the sense that I have a husband who loves me. He doesn't really get the Asperger's and depression, but he isn't insensitive. I can talk to him if I need to. At school when I have a problem, I used to be able to say to my old line manager: I have a problem, this is what's wrong and together we can make steps, do this this and this to make it right and move on. As my line manager isn't as supportive now, I guess I have to talk to my team and work it out with friends in teaching and sometimes on my own – which isn't a problem, but it will take slightly longer. Fortunately, depression doesn't affect me in a way that I lose myself into an abyss and refuse to get out of bed. If I did that, I don't think I'd ever get out. Sometimes it is difficult to take care of myself. I always wash regularly, but little things like cleansing, toning and moisturising my face – which is something every woman ought to do daily – can be a struggle at times. When I'm more relaxed I tend to get back into it. I don't know how I cope as an adult. I am taking it day by day. I don't know how many more dark times will be ahead but for now... my story isn't over yet.

SENSORY ISSUES

I don't like alarm sounds as they hurt my ears,
I dislike large crowds and their shouts and jeers.
Food should not touch (it was a texture thing)
I like to feel comfortable in the clothes that I'm in.

I like to wear a big coat I am sensitive to touch,
I never used to like hugs very much.
I have a low pain threshold and sensitive teeth,
My parents couldn't get me to brush for weeks.

I was scared of the cinema for a long time,
The loud noises petrified me and it felt like a crime,
That I did not enjoy it or think it was fun,
And I had to sit through till the movie was done.
3D movies are even worse
I don't like when things jump out at me in bursts.

If I have a sensory overload I just shut down,
That happens if there is too much stimulation around.
I sit on the floor, hold my ears and rock,
I constantly like to wear odd socks (that isn't autism I just like
    them).
I like attending rock music shows
"But how if it hurts your ears when you go?"
The sound is controlled and I am expecting it then
It is not the same as when,
A police car drives by you really fast
Or a pigeon takes off nearby like a pain in the arse.

Let me explain more to you about sensory things,
As there are many challenges and difficulties it brings.

When I was a child I had many sensory issues, some of which I have as an adult. I am not alone in this; the National Autistic Society states that, "Many spectrum individuals struggle with processing day to day sensory information such as sounds, sights and smells. This is usually called having sensory integration difficulties, or sensory sensitivity. It can have a significant effect on the way a person lives their life." Some of my sensory difficulties have certainly affected my life greatly.

TASTE

When I was a child I didn't wean easily and for a long time would only eat white foods, and the foods couldn't be touching each other. I had a very limited range of foods, and as soon as my mum introduced a new food to me I dropped one of the other ones. It had to be specific types of food because my taste buds were so acute that I could even tell the difference between brands of butter. I knew, for example, if my mum had used butter from Tesco's rather than Sainsbury's.

I also refused to change to adult toothpaste because the children's strawberry one tasted nicer than mint and was part of my routine. This led to problems with my teeth because I simply refused to brush them for many months. These type of behaviours are still present in my adult life, just in a less extreme fashion. I've learnt to cope with foods touching. I am better with it now because it's just rather embarrassing when you like pasta and you like potato but you won't eat a meal your friend has cooked for you because the two foods are touching one another. Also, I have learnt that it really does not matter which supermarket your butter is from.

Once I realised that these difficulties were behavioural, I developed ways to cope with them. Now I ask myself, "What is the worst thing that would happen if your food was touching?" or I separate the different foods on the plate myself rather than throwing a tantrum or refusing to eat. I guess my coping strategy is cognitive reconditioning. Cognitive reconditioning is a therapeutic process of learning to identify and argue against irrational or unhelpful thoughts. When I was a student, I realised that the irrational thought was that I thought something bad would happen if my butter was not from Sainsbury's, and so once I recognised that, I reasoned with myself like this: if I don't eat this different type of butter I shall starve, and starving is a negative thing; therefore, I will learn to eat different types of butter because I do not wish to starve. I realised that the butter being different was not an issue.

My eating habits nearly split up my parents on a family holiday because I wouldn't eat and I was becoming difficult to look after.

Mum: *Autistic people don't like change, so to cope with that they try and keep things the same. We spent one holiday in Spain where my husband and [other] daughter went out for day trips and I stayed in the hotel room with Madeleine doing schoolwork from her primary school, because it was somewhere different, but doing schoolwork with her mother was familiar enough so that she was not anxious.*

Eating, eating was a massive problem. I mean, now Madeleine's got older her range of food has expanded massively, but when she was little it was a nightmare. The first time I had an argument with her father was about her not eating, because as the hotel was all inclusive he didn't want to pay for extra food. There was a reasonable range of food, but it didn't include Madeleine's kind of food and she saw a McDonald's on international drive and he wanted to force her to eat what was available. Madeleine made herself ill on holiday in Jamaica because she refused to eat, and a man even cooked fish especially for her, but because it wasn't cod she wouldn't eat it and we were in despair.

95

Dad: One of the most difficult challenges was Madeleine's extremely restricted diet. At one time she would ONLY eat cod and scrambled egg. This made holidays or eating out extremely difficult. When we could not find anywhere that sold cod, we would buy alternative types of fish and tell her that this was cod. This usually worked! However, there were occasions on holiday when we were seriously worried because Madeleine was not eating at all, because we could not obtain the foods that she would eat. For example, we had to travel to Gibraltar on one holiday to Spain because that was the only place where we could buy Ribena. This was the only drink that she would consume.

Madeleine would only eat bread from Sainsbury's; she could tell the difference between bread from different supermarkets. Although there is evidence to suggest that children with autistic disorders do have oral sensitivity to food, I have always believed that there was a behavioural aspect to her fussy eating as well. When she was older Madeleine succumbed to peer pressure and vastly expanded her range of foods, although there are still some common items that she will not touch. For example, she will hardly eat any vegetables.

I would say that for a parent it must be incredibly tough to see that your child has troubles with eating and not know what to do about this, but all you can do is try new tactics, advise and hope that they will educate themselves. A dietician who I visited did tell me that if you try a food for seven days consistently that you will learn to like it, and that is also one of the strategies that worked for me.

If you are a young person with Asperger's experiencing difficulties around food and taste, my main advice would be to just try the food. Now, I know that may not be what you want to hear because it is scary or outside of your routine, but you are missing out on so many different great tastes by not trying stuff. Like did you know that, and this is my opinion by the way, Italian ice cream is some of the best in the world? How will you know it is the best unless you try it? How will you know if you refuse to eat it because it is not the brand you are used to at home? Trust me, sometimes some fear and some risk are good things.

My advice to parents, carers or friends would be to create a positive and calming environment for your child to eat in. Create a mealtime routine and help your child or friend to see the consequences of not eating the food, but not in a threatening way or in a way that could be anxiety-provoking, such as shouting or getting frustrated. For example, teach them about eating vegetables by showing them a healthy food plate. Role model positive eating behaviours by eating vegetables yourself. Reward children with small gifts or behaviour charts. All of these are positive ways to support children to try new food, but please do not force them or shout at them as it may cause them sensorial pain and distress if you do.

TOUCH

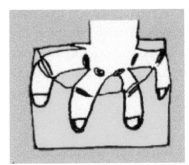

Just as I did not like foods to touch each other, I did not always used to like to be touched myself. I didn't like being hugged. I did not like hugs right up until I went to university and one of my housemates was crying and she came into my room needing comfort. She sat on my bed and sobbed, and I didn't know what to do until eventually I decided that I might be able to put my arm around her.

Now I like hugs, and my partner can most often hug me whenever he wants because I am used to him now. However, I still prefer a warning when it is going to happen so I can prepare myself for it psychologically.

This is because I am sensitive to touch; as such I have a moderate pain threshold and some sensations hurt me. Examples of sensations that hurt me include that I can only use certain types of hairbrushes because the spiky ones hurt my head and that I used to only wear trainers because wearing high heels hurts my feet and disables my balance.

When I went home from university after the first month or so, because by then I'd realised exactly how much she did for me, I gave my mother a hug, and it was probably one of the first times I had done this because when I was younger I wasn't very tactile at all, and she thanked me for the hug. I think she may have even cried a little, but she's said she does not remember this when we have talked about it subsequently.

I have difficulties with certain textures and am afraid of bananas because I cannot stand the texture of the peel; also, my mum fed me lots of bananas when I was younger, so I generally just abhor them now. I also dislike latex gloves for the texture reason. It makes me feel physically ill when I put them on, and I have to wash my hands immediately after wearing them. When I worked in a care home this was incredibly difficult and I was constantly washing my hands. As a child, I disliked finger painting because I did not like the texture, and to this day I cannot stand the feel of anything between my fingers; this makes cooking desserts an interesting experience!

Children on the spectrum, if you do not like certain textures that is absolutely fine. Do not let others force you to use them. I ask my partner to knead the dough if we ever make bread because I cannot stand the texture, similarly if we make anything using breadcrumbs. If people care about you, they should not force you to use textures you do not like.

Parents, if you find that your child does not like having their fingers or face painted, try to introduce them to paint and art in another way, such as painting pictures on walls or building models with playdough. This will help them have similar experiences to others, but they will not be forced to interact with textures that they find uncomfortable.

SOUND

I am hypersensitive to sound. This means that some sounds hurt my ears because sounds are magnified so I hear them very loudly and distinctly. For example, in my old flat I hated the sound of the refrigerator whirring, and I could hear people having conversations outside. I can sometimes hear what music is playing in my next-door neighbour's house and when they cough. Alarm sounds hurt my ears immensely and I often put my hands over my ears when I hear them. I am afraid of birds because the flapping of their wings hurts my ears. Train stations are some of the loudest most abhorrent places on earth, so I have taken to playing my own music to drown it out or to wearing noise-cancelling headphones, sometimes called ear defenders, to block out the sound.

SIGHT

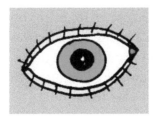

I was less troubled by the senses of sight and of smell than I was by the senses of taste, touch and sound. There are many sights I love. I love to watch bright colours. I love fireworks and I love those calming bubbles that you can sometimes see in sensory rooms. I love reflective lights and I love circles of light on ceilings or floors such as you may see at a disco. I get excited about Lego because it is brightly coloured.

SMELL

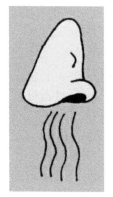

The only sense that I did not really experience challenges with as a child was smell. My sense of smell was under-developed, and so smells had to be really strong to register with me right up until I had my second round of corrective surgery for my spine in my late 20s. I think that was a good thing because it meant that I could not smell most unpleasant things at work or if I was clearing out the bins at home, so I did not see it as a problem.

Now though, however, my sense of smell has been heightened since the surgery and certain smells make me feel really sick, such as really strong cheese or going into a perfume shop such as Lush.

DEALING WITH SENSORY SENSITIVITY

My advice to young people on the spectrum is to seek out sensory stimulus you enjoy. Maybe you enjoy sitting on soft carpets or wearing soft clothes? Maybe you enjoy hard surfaces and wearing thick heavy clothes? Maybe you like fidget spinners, chewing pens or you like coloured lights? Whatever you like, use it to help you calm down and keep you happier. If you don't know what senses you enjoy, try out different things until you find something you like. You can make a comfort box filled with nice sensory stimulus such as soft gloves or brightly coloured beads to help you calm down.

My partner has recently installed coloured lights in our house and I find that different colours affect my mood in different ways. I love the green and blue lights because they are calming for me. As an adult I currently use a fidget spinner, which I spin to calm me when I am anxious. This was bought for me by one of the members of

Open Theatre Company and I love it because it also reminds me that I am accepted and cared for.

I also use noise-cancelling headphones when sounds are too loud for me. I like them because they do not make me stand out from others; I just look like I am wearing big, good quality headphones.

In the 1950s an occupational therapist called Ayers began to work on sensory integration theory, which was used to understand which underlying sensory issues affected performance in children. Subsequently there have been many sensory therapies which have developed, including sensory and relaxation rooms. There are also sensory toys and items such as the aforementioned noise-cancelling headphones which have been created to support people on the spectrum. When I was a child, however, not many of these things existed or were too expensive for the family to buy, so I did without, apart from to have my blanket, which I loved because it was soft, and all of my favourite teddies which were a comfort to me.

For me, the sounds that calm me down are church bells, choral music and the sound of the sea. Smells that I like are the smell of freshly cut bread, fresh doughnuts, freshly cut grass or paint or new plastic, also leather. The touches that I like are long hugs from someone I know and big heavy blankets or clothes or bean bags. The sights that I like are those I've just mentioned, disco lights on the floor and so on. The point is that you can find sensory things that you do like and that is what sensory integration therapies aim to help you do.

Organisations such as Autism West Midlands have sensory rooms, which are specially created environments designed to provide an immersive sensory experience for people on the spectrum and reduce anxiety.

You might seek out your nearest sensory room, or parents or friends with a child with autism might do so. It is very advantageous as it often calms children and/or adults down and gives them something to focus on.

Sensory processing sometimes works in the opposite way, though, and causes a sensory overload, otherwise known as a meltdown. I shall give an example. In my adult life I am a historical re-enactor. I travel the country performing different battles for the public. I was first involved in re-enacting the Battle of Hastings at Battle Abbey in 2011, and there was a parade for the public which involved us walking through the town, stopping to have little one-on-one combat slots and marching on again. We were required to hold burning torches for the aesthetic pleasure of the crowd. See if you can spot the sensory stimuli?

So, I had the crowd clapping and the sounds of the swords clashing against each other. I also had the sound of drums being banged and the sounds of children crying or screeching, as they often do. I had the heat of the flames against my face and the cold weather that surrounded the rest of me (the battle was in October). I had the texture of my armour, which is very heavy, surrounding my body, and I had lots of colourful things to look at, such as various costume designs and fireworks that were happening around us. I could also smell the sea as we were quite close to the water, and I could smell a mixture of foods that the public were eating, such as hot dogs and burgers etc.

How did I react to this? Well, I sat down in the middle of the parade and I covered my ears and I rocked back and forth, and it was only because a supportive colleague saw my predicament and helped me to stand that I finished the parade, leaning against him to support the weight of my armour.

Young people on the spectrum, if you experience a sensory overload, or meltdown, try not to panic. Escape to somewhere quieter if you can and try not to lash out at others. Stay calm; if you panic you will stay in a heightened negative state for longer. The situation will not last forever and there should be somewhere quieter for you to escape to if you need. Try to tell someone you know what is wrong so that they can help you.

Parents, teachers or friends, if your child or friend does experience a sensory overload, just listen to what they need. If they are non-verbal, offer them things to help them and they will accept or refuse as they will. For example, you could turn off the light and if your child cries you know to put the light back on again.

UNDERSTAND HOW YOUR BRAIN WORKS: MAKE SCIENCE YOUR FRIEND

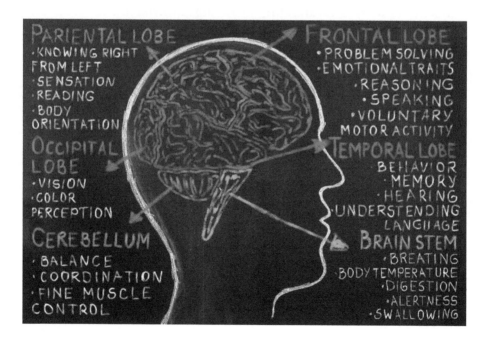

At school, if somebody had said to me "now you are going to study science" I might have jumped out of the nearest window; but now I find it fascinating because it has helped me to discover how my brain works. I will let you in on a few sensory secrets that not many people know unless they study Anatomy because the doctors will speak to you in difficult words and jargon that only a mastermind would ever hope to understand; trust me, when I learnt this I felt like I was just being spoken to in gibberish.

Recently, doctors discovered that different parts of the brain have developed differently between autistic and neurotypical individuals. The part of the brain that controls emotions (the limbic system) has developed differently in autistic people. This means that autistic people will process emotion differently from neurotypical peers.

The above image shows you that somebody with Asperger's syndrome will struggle with altered wiring of their frontal lobes which causes difficulties with the way social information is understood, as well as affecting grouping information together and interests. People with Asperger's syndrome may experience differences with their somatosensory cortex, which is the area of the brain which deals with sensory inputs, stimuli and coping mechanisms; and difficulties in other areas of the brain which are shown in the diagram. I am not writing this to dramatise differences or point out that you are somehow abnormal or odd. I am writing this to help you understand how your brain works so that you may effectively deal with the sensory difficulties that you might have and find something which works for you to help you deal with stress or overload.

INTERVIEW 3: ANNIE

When someone is on the autistic spectrum, they can also have other conditions alongside this and their sensory difficulties so sometimes some of their needs are missed by professionals as they do not always understand that no part of the body works in isolation. Everything works together and so, for example, a child with Asperger's syndrome, anxiety and depression may never be diagnosed with anxiety or depression until much later in life, or not at all as sometimes it might be dismissed as part of the autism as I mentioned in the introduction. I was not diagnosed with anxiety disorder until my late 20s, and I have never had an official diagnosis of depression, even though I have been prescribed anti-depressants and have self-harmed and attempted suicide in the past. The reason I mention this is to encourage individuals on the spectrum, and their parents, to look at the whole of themselves and do not miss anything that might be vital to their health in later life. The next interviewee's experience is interesting here as she had other conditions alongside her Asperger's syndrome.

Introduce yourself

Hi, I'm Marianne (Annie) Amelia Cassandra Partridge, a transwoman and blind student of History at York University.

Tell me about your diagnosis? What is it?

My diagnosis is of Asperger's syndrome, high functioning.

When did you receive your diagnosis?

I received my diagnosis at the age of eight, due to the tests offered by my childhood psychologist.

Do you have any sensory difficulties?

I feel textures very intensely. I also smell and hear and taste things very strongly, so if textures are too rough or feel unpleasant in another way I cannot wear clothes made of them, and I can only eat food which smells pleasant – food with even a whiff of the unfamiliar or unpleasant means I cannot eat it. I can't be in a room with a too strong smell either, or in a room with loud and frequent sounds which disorientate me greatly.

How do you cope with them as an adult?

As an adult, I just ensure I avoid crowds and areas which might aggravate my sensory sensitivities, like food courts, clubs or large shopping centres. I only wear clothes of soft wool, cotton or [with] silk in them as synthetic fibres are especially unpleasant, and I only buy clothes from stores which I have used before.

What did you find challenging about school?

I faced many challenges throughout my time in the educational system, mainly issues with behaviour or interactions with peers or staff. Taking things literally has often been seen as cheekiness or rudeness by teachers (which was never my intent) or stupidity by other students. I have often misinterpreted social situations, which has led to bullying; in such scenarios I have often been told by teachers that I was in the wrong and that "If you were a little bit more normal, this wouldn't happen." In the classroom, teachers have often become impatient with me needing to clarify things which were not black and white but instead sounded ambiguous, or if I argued with them because their own views did not fit into my worldview on the spectrum. Teachers have frequently misinterpreted my unwillingness to do new things or to adapt to their individual teaching methods as criticism and recalcitrance.

Were your family supportive?

In short, my family have not been especially supportive. My parents have refused to truly acknowledge my diagnosis unless it suited them, for instance getting the teachers to apologise after incidents in school or getting a more friendly studying environment for me. Mum has always wanted me to "be normal" and raised me without any real recognition of my AS at home, disciplining me harshly for incidents which humiliated her in public. My father has long held the belief that AS is curable and has hoped that I will "grow out of it" in adulthood. My sister has long referred to me as "retarded" and bullied me for being different, often playing on my obsessions and other tendencies of the condition to tease and taunt me. The family have always disregarded my opinions as simply parroted from the opinions of non-spectrum people or as being unimportant because "It's just Henry" as I was formerly called. My mother especially uses this as an excuse for my sister's bullying and other situations which she would prefer not to confront, and my desire to be truthful has often got me into trouble as other family members have sought to conceal affairs, theft or other crimes both social and moral. I am made to feel like a non-person, a second-class individual, at home where my mother believes she needs to keep an eye on my bank account and can thereby take money out of it without asking. I enjoyed very little of my primary school experience. I did find refuge in the library because no other children went there.

What did you find most challenging about secondary school?

I found the whole experience challenging. Exercise was never tailored to individual needs and neither were classes. The available special assistance was often poor quality and subject to funding, which was itself too limited. Teachers were not fully aware of the needs and thought processes of children on the spectrum, and students used it as an excuse to ostracise and bully us.

What do you think the education system could do to improve support for individuals on the spectrum?

I think the educational system could institute mandatory training courses for teachers to help them understand and interact with pupils who are on the spectrum more effectively. There ought to be more adaptability in teaching methods to enable AS and autistic pupils to get more from lessons, and a firmer hand ought to be taken with bullying situations in which the victim is on the spectrum, which do not include the shaming and dismissal of the victim for enduring the effects of their condition.

Do you have a job? What are you doing with your life presently?

Currently, I am in Sweden at Lund University on an exchange year studying History and Archaeology, writing an alternative historical fiction novel, preparing for my upcoming dissertation and investigating possibilities for an MA in Canada. I am also heavily into historical re-enactment and am to my knowledge the only fully blind re-enactment archer and general combatant in the UK.

The important thing I want to highlight here is that Annie's experiences with bullying usually occurred due to other individuals' lack of understanding of her condition and behaviour. I experienced the same thing myself, and this led me to experience high anxiety because I saw cruelty in others easily and was anxious when being presented with new situations that I had not encountered before. This meant times were hard for me, and for my parents – both at home and in dealing with my school. But despite my socially weird behaviour, I was fortunate to have a strong group of friends.

FRIENDS

I met my friend who I have known the longest in primary school and I still speak to her now. She has two children and lives with her father. She can tell you more about how we met.

My longest-standing friend: I don't really remember the first time we ever met, but I know it was in nursery. I don't remember many things from when I was younger. I've got a memory like a sieve – it's terrible. The main memories I've got of Maddy is coming round hers and eating cheesy pasta and playing Beehive Bedlam on Sky. How funny! I was talking about her mum's cheesy pasta to my dad the other day. I remember when I went to Teen Cult with Maddy as well, the parties at my dad's for my birthdays and her party at the pub in King's Heath – her 16th I think – and my ice-skating party. That's all I can remember off the top of my head.

I never ate the cheesy pasta. My mum, bless her, cooked it just for my friend, because she knew I wouldn't eat it due to my diet issues. In adult life, pasta has become one of my favourite foods. Beehive Bedlam was a game in which you had to match three coloured bubbles together on the screen to make them disappear before the barrier came down.

I'd play it whenever my friends came over, and Super Mario on the Nintendo 64. I'd get cross if my friends didn't take the game seriously because it made me anxious as it wasn't the way I played games.

Recently, I was upset because we'd bought a new version of the game Risk and it wasn't the way I'd remembered it, so I decided I didn't like it before we even started playing, and I'm an adult now. The party at the pub was actually for my 13th birthday and was the first rite of passage, if you like, from childhood into teenage years. At the ice-skating party I skated on my arse as ice skating and dyspraxia are not compatible things!

My friend in primary school was the first friend who I ever felt safe enough to stop over with at her house. She was kind to me and so was her father, and her house began to fit into my routine way of doing things. Every Saturday I'd stop at her house etc. Other children made me nervous, and I kept myself to myself. I didn't like going to parties, even though the other parents tried inviting me at first. If I did engage in play with other children, I could be weird. I used to like eating rubbers, which I know now is a bit of an odd behaviour, but I'd still do it if I could, because I like the taste of them, and the texture in my mouth.

My other friend, whose party was spoken about previously, was a different kind of friend, and I don't think she meant anything by it or was trying to be cruel in any way, but she could often make me cry. She would make me believe stories that she told to scare me, or she would play hide and seek with me, make me be it and run away, leaving me to look for her. These are just harmless children's games and anyway, looking back, I think it was my fault for being a tad gullible.

ZQ: I didn't know Madeleine had autism.... I remember in reception she used to have a helper come in, but I can't remember what she did apart from helping her to get dressed with the orthopaedic shoes she had. I also remember Madeleine had trouble with handwriting and would use a special pencil. The more I think of it, I do remember she could be very sensitive; i.e. things would upset her, quite a bit, that wouldn't have upset most people so readily... like for instance, if she lost something like a scrunchie or pencil... and, of course, when she was being teased, but that is understandable.

So, I suppose I suspected something or other, but I never quite knew what. I mean, in all other ways I thought Madeleine excelled i.e. well-spoken and very bubbly and friendly. This is perhaps speculation, but I think she started (sometimes a little fiercely) standing up for herself by the time she was in Year 6. I want to say she was very loving as a child and would get easily attached to people i.e. friends and teachers, and I still remember once when I was late to her Take-a-Tumble – or was it

Harry Hedgehog? – birthday party; she was in tears when I got there, thinking I wasn't coming (bless her!)

So, my peers had noticed that I was different to them, but they didn't quite know how, and I didn't start going to the Youth Centre to socialise with them until later on in my school years because I was afraid of change, but I'm glad I did in the end because it was always fun.

SLEEPING HABITS AND A NEED FOR SAMENESS AND ROUTINE

Sometimes I cannot sleep and my mind is racing,
I often worry about the issues I'm facing.
I am wary of new places and situations too,
I often cannot sleep the whole night through.

If I go to a friend's house or the house of a lover,
The situation is alien to me and other.
I choose which side of the bed is mine to sleep on.
I cannot sleep with open windows or televisions on.
I really cannot sleep on the floor,
Because that is too much for my back to endure.
I cannot sleep if you are still talking downstairs,
Because I feel excluded or like I'll be caught unawares.

Some say I can't sleep because I drink too much caffeine,
But I had troubles before, so I don't get what you mean?
I'll end this verse now so we can carry on
I really don't care if you're bored of my song.

Another issue I had trouble with when growing up was sleep. Many people on the spectrum experience difficulties with sleeping. These difficulties can include "problems falling asleep, frequent waking during the night, early morning waking, short duration sleep, irregular or erratic sleep patterns, other arousals/disturbances, daytime sleepiness"[*]

I certainly had difficulties sleeping as a child, and I still have them in my adult life. One night I remember feeling particularly anxious and upset. Mum had already put me to bed, many times, but I could still hear her and Dad talking downstairs. I came down, tugging on Mum's clothes and she sighed as she put me back to bed again and again. Then, I sat on the landing and started to cry, "I want Mummy," and I think Dad got angry, but Mum was patient and just kept putting me back to bed. This had happened many times before, and so then Mum suggested that I looked at my picture books, which I remember well were Disney books, and from then on whenever I had problems sleeping I read. I lined up my books in some sort of order too, but I can't remember what the logic behind it was. (This reminds me of when my eldest sister and I used to play video shops, and I'd sort out all of our videos in some sort of order on the carpet, then we'd pretend to sell them to each other.)

It's really only in the last year or so that I think I have actually overcome my sleeping difficulties because I now have a bedtime routine that I stick to quite rigidly. Also, exhaustion from being on work placements helps – sometimes I fall asleep instantly because I'm so tired. I still cannot sleep in new places, though, due to anxiety, and the longest I've ever stayed awake is four days because I was excited and anxious at a music festival.

---

[*] from "Encouraging good sleep habits in children with learning disabilities" by Paul Montgomery Luci Wiggs, which can be found online here:
https://www.oxfordhealth.nhs.uk/wp-content/uploads/2014/05/Good-sleep-habits-for-children-with-Learning-Difficulties.pdf

Generally, I would advise anyone who is struggling to sleep, whether they are on the spectrum or not, to create a good sleeping routine. Try to go to bed at the same time every night and switch off all technology one hour before doing so. Scrolling on the internet for hours is known to damage the eyes and does not promote good sleep hygiene. If you cannot sleep, I suggest to try to read a book or get up and do a mundane activity, such as washing up and then try to go back to sleep. This has worked for me and is based on scientific research. If you want more advice about sleep hygiene, then I'd also recommend visiting the NHS website and its "10 tips to beat insomnia" page[*].

Parents, if your child is struggling to sleep, then I suggest you do not punish them for it. This may be easier said than done if all you want to do is relax with your partner and your child keeps coming downstairs to talk to you. Try rewarding the child if they exhibit good behaviour, such as staying in their room. Maybe keep a behaviour chart with them, and if they get so many gold stars at the end of the week, they can take part in their favourite activity or they can have a small gift. This is called positive conditioning and is also supported by scientific research.

HOLIDAYS

Many people on the spectrum struggle with going on holiday. This is due to the fact that it is a change in their day-to-day routine and is a cause of anxiety. They do not know what activities will be done or what to expect as it is a new situation. Older individuals on the spectrum may struggle to read the information boards at the airport, get anxious about timing or about finding where to board their plane.

---

[*] https://www.nhs.uk/live-well/sleep-and-tiredness/10-tips-to-beat-insomnia/

I know that when I was a child I must have been a nightmare to take on holiday, due to sleeping issues and my eating behaviours. My father loved to travel, and I have a number of memories of different childhood holidays.

One of my earliest memories is of a playground. I see it clearly in my mind sometimes when I think about my childhood. It's covered in sand and it has wooden play equipment. It has a wire mesh fence around it and some grass. Subsequently my mother has told me that this playground is in Spain in the Costa del Sol. It was sometime when I was six years old; it felt like my eldest sister hadn't been in the family very long, but she was four. The hotel that my family stayed in was lovely until my sister and I decided to draw all over it with red crayon, which I remember doing vividly, and we decided to jump on the beds.

On another trip to Spain later on in my childhood I was being a difficult child, and I got cross because Mum wanted to sit down on my imaginary friend whilst we were watching my sister go on the trampolines. I didn't want to go on them, because they scared me and I'd rather stay with my mother. On that same holiday I lost my Milo cat figure and threw a temper tantrum. Dad laughed, because I lost the cat in a lift called Otis, which was the name of Milo's dog companion in the film I loved. I watched Dad play on the pinball machines because they had cats on them. I drank milk with ice cubes in it, which had been given to me specially because I didn't want to drink anything other than milk or Ribena, but I didn't like the taste of the milk because it wasn't British milk, and I called the ice cubes ghosts rather than ice cubes.

During that holiday we went on a day trip to Gibraltar, to search for Ribena as it was the only drink I would consume. Mum had found some and packed it with us, but it leaked everywhere on the bus.

Another holiday we went on that same year was to Corfu. The hotel we stayed in was called the Hotel Sea Bird and there was a pool, which was lovely when lit at night. As we were checking out of the hotel our flight was not until the next day and so a man my parents befriended let us stay in his flat. He had two dogs, which I loved very much, and I was sad when we had to leave. I don't think my parents were, though, as Mum has subsequently told me that the hotel was awful. I got chicken pox and was really ill and Mum had to stay in the hotel and look after me.

When I was a little older we went to Jamaica for a week. There was a thunderstorm so I had to get out of the swimming pool. There were crab races on the beach, and Dad bought a strange mask. We went in the caves, but I made myself sick because I wouldn't eat any of the food there because I didn't like it. We then went to America for a week, and we met my uncle there. My sister was a brave child and wanted to go on the Tower of Terror. It is a ride the drops 30 feet to the ground. Nobody wanted to go but my uncle pulled the short straw and screamed like a girl whilst my sister wanted to go again. I was always too scared to go on rides when I was younger, but now I love them, well except for ones that spin because they make me ill, and I went on the Tower of Terror myself in Paris with my ex-boyfriend in 2008.

The main troubles with holidays were, of course, to do with the anxieties around change in routine, my dieting habits and fear of flying. Now that I am older, I have my own holiday routine that calms me down when I follow it. For example, I pack my suitcases about a week before and I write a list to make sure I have everything and I pre-pack food that I am sure they won't have. For example, I took Ribena and Red Bull to Venice with me when I went with my friend in 2014.

I can just about cope with flying if I have someone I trust sit with me on the plane. I do not like take-off and landing because of the sounds of the engines, and turbulence truly terrifies me.

I only used to trust my Dad because he was into his flight simulator, and I knew that if the plane crashed he could land it. Recently, I have been able to fly with my friend and my partner because I trust them and they help me feel safe on the plane.

HOW TO HELP A CHILD ON THE SPECTRUM PREPARE FOR HOLIDAYS

I think my parents tried their best to help me with routines on holiday, but it is always hard to combine the needs of a child on the spectrum with the needs of the rest of the family and actually enjoy the holiday. Personally, I think they were brave for attempting it and I thank them for it, because I did really enjoy holidays despite my anxiety; it was the only time we all spent together as a family and we did it once a year until 2007, which was two years after my Mum and Dad split up (which I'll talk about later).

If you experience anxiety during family holidays, try to communicate to your family what would help you be less stressed. Do you need an itinerary for each day? Do you need time outs? Are you scared of flying? Would you prefer to do certain activities over others? Always let your family know how to help you, because keeping it to yourself will stress you out and you will not have a good time or enjoy trying new activities. If you are non-verbal, try to draw for your family what you need or maybe you need someone who speaks sign language or Makaton to support you to communicate with your family?

Parents, if your child experiences anxiety during family holidays, ask what you can do to help them in a kind rather than intimidating way. It may be that they do not know what they need or are finding it difficult to express it to you. It may be that you have to leave them in the house with a neighbour, but if that is what they feel will help them to feel safe at the time, then you cannot force them to do anything they do not want to do.

ACNE, HORMONES, PUBERTY AND BODY AWARENESS

Another difficulty on holiday and growing up generally was body awareness. These issues can sometimes be difficult to talk about, particularly due to societal embarrassment and social taboo, but I would like to begin by saying there is no need to feel embarrassed. I certainly don't and it is my body I am discussing with you! For the most part, these issues need to be talked about and they are issues that any child comes across regardless of gender or disability.

Such issues might arise when it comes to swimming on holiday or P.E. or swimming lessons at school. Do you remember earlier when my sister pointed out that I have difficulties with boundaries? Well, my teachers were starting to notice that my boobs were developing. I was around ten years old when they started to appear, and the teachers seemed aware of them, but I was not. I would get changed for P.E. in our Year 5 classroom and I would just take my top off in a room full of boys and I was not wearing a bra because I did not need one until that point. My teachers had to ask my mother to buy me an appropriate bra and swimwear. It was around this time that we were shown a sexual education video which explained to the girls about periods.

I also started to get very spotty when I was 12 and I developed acne because I kept scratching my face as a form of self-harm, so I had to have two weeks off school and take antibiotics whilst my acne cleared up. (We later discovered that I have too much testosterone in my body, and that is one theory in the literature as to why autism develops in the first place.) I got through it, the time does pass, and

I believe that the biggest difficulty I had with puberty was, as I have mentioned, that boundaries were difficult for me to understand.

Youngsters on the spectrum, please don't be in a hurry to grow up because you will soon regret it if you go through your childhood without appreciating everything – even the hard times. Everyone experiences growing up and you are not alone with these issues; it's just some people may not be so willing to talk about them with you due to social embarrassment.

Parents, please don't despair; help your child through this time and remember that they are probably just as embarrassed as you are. Also, the time soon passes, but whilst you and they are going through it do not criticise your child or point out any bodily changes they may be going through. Comments like "Damn, you got spotty," or "Hey there big boobs," just aren't helpful whether your child has autism or not. I would like to finish this paragraph by emphasising that whatever gender your child is they will appreciate your support through puberty and a non-judgmental attitude.

Aaah we can breathe again now that section is over. I could feel you holding your breath as you were reading it. Yes, it's embarrassing and you can probably remember your own embarrassment as you are reading this, but I thought it needed to be written about as it is not often discussed. It is often an area of concern for people, but they cannot get help with it because it is not spoken about often in society. If you're affected by any such issues, there are many places you can go to for support, such as gender clinics, sexual health clinics, GPs and generally counselling and guidance support.

MY LAST DAYS AT PRIMARY SCHOOL

In Year 6 of primary school we were treated as being that bit more grown up. In Year 6 we were encouraged to think that we ran the school. We always played the recorder for most assemblies, and I was made a prefect. I wanted to be Head Girl, but only certain girls were ever chosen for that job. We had special duties in Year 6, which included making sure the younger children were behaving in the playground.

In Year 6 we had proper wooden desks with little slots for ink in. I loved to have all my stuff tidy and in order. I put all my books in order and lined pencils up in my desk. I hated when the other children went through my desk and messed up my order. We'd have our own coat racks for our bags and the classroom was at the top of the stairs so that the younger children couldn't disturb us when we were revising for our tests to get into secondary school. I always forgot where my coat and bag were until I learnt which peg was mine. I do a similar thing with cars as an adult because they all look the same to me, so I cannot tell which car is which unless I memorise the registration numbers or the car has something significant about it like a sticker.

Towards the end of Year 6, we performed our Year 6 play. It was three plays put together by a narrative, whereby an old woman read three children's stories. One of them was the Pied Piper of Hamelin, and that's the one that I worked on. I was devastated because a girl who couldn't play the recorder got to play the pied piper and I had to play the music for her instead of being on stage where I wanted to be.

For our final prize day, I won the prize for effort, which was a small poetry book, and a prize for music, which was a little trophy that still sits on my desk. The final book fair came around, and we got first choice of which books we wanted because we were leaving. On the last day of school, I wasn't sad. I wanted to move on and experience new things. I thought it was going to help me get rid of my "special" label, but I was wrong. We got to sit at the main table in the hall for Kiddush when we left, and the headmistress wished us luck for the future. Some of the girls cried, but my friend and I didn't. That day we took photos. Everyone wrote nice messages on our shirts. I still have mine. We wore medals that the boys had won in a football match against another school, and then we had one final food fight at lunch time before going back to one of the boy's houses.

SEXUALITY AND NOTICING BOYS

Here we are folks: the big one. I warned you that we would get to talking about issues like this. There is a horrendous assumption that people with learning differences or disabilities generally do not have sex or should not have sex. I have seen dreadful things written on social media, like if you have sex with someone on the spectrum then you must be a paedophile because spectrum people have childish special interests such as Pokémon or Dungeons and Dragons. This assumption is just ignorant. What if two spectrum individuals want to sleep together? What if a neurotypical person is supportive of the spectrum individual and loves them very much? Individuals on the spectrum are just as entitled to sex and love as anyone else. I have also read things such as what if people on the spectrum hurt themselves during sex because they don't understand or are vulnerable? Individuals on the spectrum may be vulnerable, and that is true, but that does not mean they are undeserving of love and affection.

I will now talk to you about my own experiences with these issues so that readers understand that it is normal for spectrum individuals to have sexually active relationships. So, I guess I noticed boys existed when I was around 10 or 11. Before that, I had a best male friend who I was platonically very fond of. Also when I was younger, there was a boy who I had been friends with since nursery school whose family lived in Turkey. This boy would kiss me on the lips and give me roses when I came to his grandmother's house, but our parents just thought it was sweet. Then my sister and I became good friends with two boys who were the sons of one of my mum's friends at the time, and we went round to their house and one day we played a game which we called "rudie nudies". I will not describe the details of the game to you, but as they were a religious family, that left some awkward embarrassment and some apologies going round from the two sets of parents.

On the day I left primary school, the boy whose house we went back to had a big swimming pool in the back garden. We had told our parents we were going swimming after school to practise and we went upstairs into one of the bedrooms and we all played truth or dare. I kissed a boy then, which I'd count as my first proper kiss.

My gender and sexuality are interesting. I believe I am bi-gender because I do not have much attachment to traditional concepts of gender. I believe that gender is defined by how you feel about your identity and not by whether or not you have male or female genitalia. What is between your legs is your sex, your gender is a social construct which is performative and defined by societal gender roles. For example, many people are still attached to the idea that pink is a girl's colour and blue is a boy's colour without any real evidence that it is the case other than the fact that many people seem to agree that it is so. I fluctuate between male and female genders, meaning that on some days I feel in touch with my masculinity and I wear suits and masculine clothes. On those days, especially when re-enacting, I strongly identify as male and people often call me sir and use male pronouns for me, which I am also fine with.

On other days I am more aligned with my femininity and have even been known to enjoy wearing dresses and having my nails done on occasion. I sometimes go out of my way to wear suits or dress in men's clothing as I do not feel that gender should be defined by the clothes you wear or the roles that society expects men and women to take on. I really hate being called gender-identifying pet names. Names such as love, lovely, sweetheart, sweetie, hun or darling are only ever used to describe women, and when women who are younger than me use those names I find it to be patronising and disrespectful. I know you probably mean it to be kind or you say it because you think I am a good or lovely person but it does not come across that way, especially if it is something you say all the time to everyone you think of as being nice or sweet. It just isn't genuine or authentic. I especially hate it when men who aren't my partner call me love or sweetheart. I am not your love or sweetheart – I hardly know you.

As a child, I did not relate strongly to other girls who played with Barbie dolls or enjoyed sleepovers and discussing clothes and make-up. Even though I did go to the odd sleepover myself, there were always boys there and I did not feel the need to surround myself with groups of girls.

I have always been accepted in many friendship groups as "one of the lads" and I am fine with this. However, growing up was difficult as I always felt isolated anyway and then when I could not relate to other girls and was called a tomboy it made things really hard.

When I wore my hair back in a ponytail at school the other girls would pull it and tell me it made me look like a boy, so I never wore my hair in a ponytail again until I had to for work in my adult life. I felt very lonely as a child. I have very broad shoulders and I am physically strong. I also have a deep voice and behave in ways that are often associated with men such as being boisterous and competitive. This means that I did not fit in with other girls my age and meant that I further stood out.

I do not believe I am transgender as I do not suffer with gender dysphoria, which is a condition where a person feels that their biological sex does not match their gender identity; although I am told you can be trans without experiencing dysphoria, I just do not feel that my gender is an important aspect of my identity. I am quite happy being female-bodied and it does not make a difference to the way I live my life. In fact, it's my view that gender should not matter at all and everyone should be able to live the way that they want to live without fear of prejudice, violence or harassment and be seen as a unique and valid human being. With regard to sexuality, I am bi-sexual because I am attracted to both men and women. I find *people* attractive, but it depends on their personality and how well I know them. I am not bothered if a person is male or female, although I did not find that out until I was in secondary school where I also dated girls.

I feel that my gender and sexuality were a part of the reason why I was ostracised and bullied at secondary school. Personally, I wish that gender and sexuality didn't matter and that we could all live and let live, but in light of the recent protests of parents due to teachers wanting to teach LGBTQ+ awareness lessons in schools, I think that these issues do matter and need to be spoken about. I also think that society needs reminding that disabled people can and do have sex and that it is a normal thing. People on the spectrum should be allowed to live their lives in the same way that any neurotypical people do.

I think the key thing to remember here is that everyone is an individual and everyone needs support in whatever decision they make. If you are gay, so what? If you are a lesbian, so what? If you are transgender or bisexual, so what?

Parents of children on the spectrum, it is your responsibility as a parent to ensure your child is safe and exploring sex in a consensual and responsible way. This may mean that you might have to have awkward conversations with them, but they should be supported to have a loving and caring relationship if they want one. Alternatively, they may not want a relationship in that way at all and that is also ok, but it is not up to parents to dictate whether their children have relationships or not.

And if your child is gay, lesbian or transgender, so what? Whatever they are, look after them and love them, no matter who they choose to be with. Be open and honest with them and allow them to feel safe talking with you about any given situation. It is ok not to know the answer to things. If you do not know, look it up on the internet or go to a local LGBTQ+ support centre to research. If your child does not feel safe talking to you, then they may hide things from you later on and you will not be able to keep them safe if they go clubbing etc. because you may not know where they are going or what they are doing if they feel unable to talk openly with you. Saying things to a bi-sexual person like, "Oh, you will grow out of it," is not particularly supportive or helpful. Gender and sexuality are permanent parts of identity and not something one grows out of.

When your child is young let them choose which toys they play with as they are growing up so that they can choose their own gender. I was scared of Baby Born dolls and Cabbage Patch Kids, but I loved Lego and X-Men figures.

I think it is important that boys play with toys like cooking sets and Baby Borns because it will teach them the skills they need to look after their families when they are older. My parents did not dictate to me which toys I played with and they allowed me to make my own choices, even if they did not always agree with them. They kept me as safe in all circumstances, without dictating how I should or should not be and for that I am forever grateful.

TO CONCLUDE CHAPTER 2

So, to summarise Chapter 2, I have discussed getting a diagnosis and the help I received at school. I also speculated over what might have helped me more. I talked with you about various sensory difficulties, anxiety around change and general anxiety. I discussed my relationships with my siblings and family holidays. I talked about difficult teachers, depression and my negative views of the world. I spoke with you about lessons I struggled with and lessons that I liked. I spoke with you about my primary school and my love of routine and order. I went on to discuss acne, hormones, boys, gender and sexuality. At this point in the book I am around 11 years old and will be going to secondary school. As we move onto the next chapter I want you to think about your time in secondary school. Did you enjoy it? Did you have many friends? Did you find it easy or difficult? Then think about someone on the autistic spectrum and all the sensory difficulties I just described to you in this chapter. What do you think the experience might be like for them?

CHAPTER 3
SECONDARY SCHOOL
AND SIXTH-FORM COLLEGE

(AGES 11-17)

CHAPTER 3
SECONDARY SCHOOL AND SIXTH-FORM COLLEGE (AGES 11–17)

A STATISTIC

"34% of young people [on the autism spectrum] say that people picking on them is the worst thing about school."

"Great expectations"
report published by the National Autistic Society 2011

MY SECONDARY SCHOOL

My parents didn't want me to go to grammar school, because they thought that I would struggle in a high-pressure setting. The secondary school I went to had the best special learning support, and I got into the school without taking an entrance exam. I hate it now when people undermine comprehensive schools. I just don't see what makes a private school better. My education was as good as anyone else's. Although children were bullied badly in my secondary school, it was still a good school academically. That school also played a part in helping me achieve, and helping me be who I am today. The school's motto was *carpe diem*, which in Latin means seize the day, and I have done ever since.

Of course, the move from primary school to secondary school wasn't easy. It was a big transition, and I always get ill during transitional periods because I don't like change. I get anxious when I do not have a plan and when I cannot control what will happen to me.

At this point in the book, I want to ask you to think about your time in secondary school. Did you enjoy it? Did you have many friends? Did you find it easy or difficult? Then think about someone on the autistic spectrum who's around 11 years old and of all the sensory difficulties I've just described to you in Chapter 2. What do you think the experience might be like for them?

I remember the night before my first day at secondary school as if it were yesterday. I was profoundly nervous, and I stayed up all night packing and repacking my school bag. I was so tired that I made myself sick. On the first day of school Mum dropped me off, and then we had an assembly to sort us into forms. The teachers did it in the style of Harry Potter, because the first film was coming out at Christmas.

I sat in the school hall with my legs crossed on the carpet for so long that they went numb. When my name was finally called to be in 7BC (which were my form tutor's initials) I tripped and fell on a boy who was also in my form, because I was so stiff.

FACING SEGREGATION AT SECONDARY SCHOOL

That same day I was taken out from the mainstream school into the special learning centre. The special learning centre was designed to help children with learning differences who needed extra support from the staff. The head of the centre was quite strict, and I'm sure she was only trying to help me, but I didn't like her very much because of how strict she was. (Looking back now, I feel differently and am grateful for everything she did.) When they asked me what my interests were, I took my recorder out of my bag and started to play it. I was trying to find something I could feel familiar with and make secondary school seem like primary, but it was really different. I was using the recorder as a way of trying to cope with the transition at a time when I had a few problems with social skills. As their parents will know, children on the autistic spectrum need familiar things around them.

WHAT MIGHT HAVE HELPED ME COPE BETTER WITH THE TRANSITION TO SECONDARY SCHOOL?

Maybe if I'd have had my helper from my first school come with me, things may have been easier. Who knows? What might work for me may not always work for other young people on the spectrum, either. You learn what works through trial and error. I suppose it might help if the young person has friends already in the school but that only marginally decreases the anxiety. Unfortunately, there is nothing that can be done to make transitional periods feel easy for someone on the spectrum. People on the spectrum feel anxiety around transitional periods because they are moving into something which is unknown and unfamiliar. They have learnt how to behave in one environment and are now being expected to learn a new set of rules and routines.

Parents, ways to help are that you can take the child to their new school for a visit and teach them what is to be expected of them in their new school.

If you are a young person on the spectrum who is moving on to big school, congratulations. Well done for getting this far and putting up with all the difficult and confusing people around you. I am not saying this in a patronising way; I am saying you should be proud of everything you have achieved so far. You might be scared of going into secondary school. You might not even want to go and that is completely normal. Remember life is an adventure and you are just moving on to the next chapter of your adventure.

Another thing that I remember really well about my first days at secondary school is a residential trip that we went on to the Bilberry Hills. I didn't know many people in my form, because I was a bit useless at making friends, but by the end of the trip I was really good friends with one of the girls.

Form tutor: *Maddy was always a pleasure to talk to. She was an individual, in viewpoints, opinion, appearance and some aspects of behaviour. She tended to speak first, without much consideration of other people's feelings. She is a voracious reader, staying up until the early hours of the morning to finish a book.*

She has a great imagination and can spin out a story with ease. Having said that, she always told the truth as she saw it; I could always rely on Maddy to tell me what had happened if any of her friends was upset by anything.

One thing I must mention is that she always appeared in advance of her years in her knowledge of the world around her; she has an opinion of world and local affairs. In addition, she has a strongly developed sense of right and wrong, and would speak up for her friends very loyally.

Maddy was quite ill, and likely to be off school for some time, so I decided to invite about four of her friends to accompany me to see her. I didn't know what to expect, but when we walked in the first thing we noticed was a huge parrot sitting in its cage in the corner of the room. We also noticed newspaper spread liberally around the floor under the cage. It was very hard to talk to her when the parrot was squawking, but Maddy seemed not to notice. As for her room! Her mum showed it to me, and it was a veritable tip; how she ever found anything I don't honestly know.

As part of the settling-in process, the school tutors took their classes to a one-night residential trip to a local youth centre, Bilberry. She was the main culprit for losing her belongings, but joined in with all the activities, although ball games seemed to cause her problems, e.g. catching the ball.

Head of the special learning centre: *My first impressions of Madeleine were that she was obviously very intelligent, and eloquent. She was confident, and ready to give things a go, even if they made her anxious – I'm thinking here of the drama production in particular. Madeleine was, and continues to be, very individual, which some of the* *less open-minded of the students didn't really understand or appreciate until later on.*

The thing Madeleine found hardest was taking advice about how she could improve her work. At times when she spoke, she was dismissive of others and frank/tactless in her comments – both to staff, and students. I think that in all respects Madeleine made exceptional progress, and as a result achieved highly, and made good friends. She also managed to stay true to herself.

I have just remembered – my very first memory of Madeleine is on the induction day when she pulled a recorder out from nowhere and started playing it! That really made me laugh.

As for whether young people should be made aware/diagnosed as being on the autistic spectrum, I think that it can be really positive if appropriate support can be put in place. Many autistic students find school (and life!) very hard to bear, and extra allowances/assistance can help. We get a lot of advice from Parkview Clinic, and the Communication and Autism Team, which helps us to decide what to do to make young people's lives easier. I think the whole process of diagnosis can help children to feel understood, and I think it makes things easier for parents who sometimes feel at a loss as to how to cope.

FIRSTS AND RITES OF PASSAGE

In secondary school any child experiences a lot of new things very quickly. They get their first friendship group, they have their first sleepovers, their first boyfriends and romantic attachments, they go to their first house parties and they host their first parties themselves. Teenage years are a rite of passage for any child whether they are on the spectrum or not, but because of all of the previous challenges discussed in the last chapter, children on the spectrum may find this time more overwhelming than others. I know I certainly did.

I started to experience a lot of firsts in Year 7, the first year of secondary school. I had my first ever laptop computer and I had my first big sleepover in March for my birthday. I took lots of photos of my friends, but the laptop was stolen at Christmas, so we never recovered the photographs.

I did my first big drama production, which was of *Fame*, in Year 7. I was in the chorus. This was important to me because it was the first real theatrical performance I did and I could explore my ideas about creating fantasies in a socially acceptable environment.

During the production of *Fame*, I got into my first ever social group. I met a girl who was in the year above me and I adored her. She never judged me and she would stand up for me a lot. We had sleepovers at her sister's house for years afterwards and she introduced me to two boys who were both gay and I loved them.

However, one of them always bullied me and played on my insecurities to make himself feel better; he made me feel very inadequate. That social group used to use me a lot. They liked to see what they could get out of me because my mother was very kind to them and gave them lifts home from school and let them borrow money. Now I wish I hadn't been as kind, but you're naive when you're 13, aren't you? That group of friends was important to me because they introduced me to the theatre at the school and they made it easier for me to socialise because I was routinely with that group. I fell in love with one of the gay boys in our friendship group and began a particularly difficult part of growing up, which was dealing with self-stimulation, obsessive traits and rejection.

GROWING UP

I believe that I forced myself to grow up too quickly. I wish that I had played with my action figures and Lego for longer and that I had continued to play Beanie Baby and Barbie musicals with my friends. When I was 14 a friend introduced me to MSN Messenger online. All of this technology stuff was very new back then, and at 14 it was a real risk to have the internet at all due to the vast amount of unregulated content that could be accessed. My friend's older cousin asked me to send him explicit photographs of myself and being young and vulnerable I did not see anything wrong with this and did so. Looking back, I think it was that day that I lost my childhood.

We went on a few dates together and he came to my house often to hang out with my group of friends because he was my friend's cousin, but later on he was verbally and physically abusive towards me. He was very racist and believed that Hitler had the right idea about what he did to the Jews. All of my other friends did not like him and warned me to stay away from him. I stayed friends with him for 13 years because I was too afraid of him to stop spending time with him. He married another woman and has not spoken with me since, thankfully, but I have included this paragraph to highlight how vulnerable people on the spectrum can be if they are left to their own devices. My parents did not even know this bit, but they will now that I am publishing this book.

Young people on the spectrum, please do not be in a hurry to grow up. Everything will happen when it is meant to happen. Do not put yourself at risk by meeting people online, and if you are being cyber-bullied then you can block the person or tell someone to make it go away. Talk to your parents; tell them if you have concerns. I know I have said all of this before, but I seriously cannot stress it enough.

Parents, please try to build a good relationship with your children. Encourage them to speak with you; ask them how their day went; ask them what they are looking at online – not in an interrogating sort of way but in an interested sort of way. Maybe play a game they like with them, because they will soon grow up and they won't be your children anymore; they will be adults with their own concerns and priorities.

MY FIRST SERIOUS BOYFRIEND

Some people on the spectrum struggle with social signals and sharing their space so much that they do not form meaningful attachments and prefer to stay on their own. Others enjoy social contact and yearn for a meaningful relationship. For some it takes them a while longer than others, and that is ok too. I would say this is the same for any individual whether they are on the spectrum or not.

My first serious boyfriend and I met outside a queue for a gig when I was 15. We dated for four years and we were very nearly married. He loved me for who I was and said that he found me to be beautiful despite the curvature of my spine which the other kids so gladly mocked me for. When I was 19, he asked my mum's permission to marry me and she said yes. My dad was not so keen on the idea and thought I could do better, but that is pretty much how most dads think about their daughter's first boyfriend. However, I think I did date him for all the wrong reasons. I was trying to get over the fact that the boy I first fell in love with and I could never be together because he was gay, and I was terrified of being alone. I could never accept that you don't need a partner to make you whole. I've only just learnt that recently.

I did love my boyfriend with all my heart, however, and we seemed to be a good match until I went to university. We went to the cinema together, and with him came a whole different friendship group and new sleepovers and new experiences. Once I was at university, however, I started to become embarrassed by him when we were out socially – but it wasn't him who was changing; it was me. My dad asked me to watch a film called *Educating Rita*. It was about a girl from a working-class background who wanted to better her life and go to university to gain an education. Her boyfriend wanted her to stay at home and get pregnant, and the film was all about her experiences of starting a new life at university. One scene in the film sees her boyfriend finding out that she has been taking the pill behind his back because she does not feel ready to get pregnant yet. He reacts by burning her university books, and I showed the film to my boyfriend and he cheered when the character burnt the books. I knew we were different then. My boyfriend and I had a good relationship and we only ever argued twice in four years, if I recall correctly. I'll only relate the one argument to you, though, because it is the only one that is related to being on the autistic spectrum.

My boyfriend was a creature of habit and I don't think he ever meant to hurt me, but one day whilst play fighting he told me to "shush, you Mongol". He didn't know why the word had such a profound effect on me, but it felt to me like he was singling me out and commenting on my learning needs. That's not what he was doing at all; he was only saying it because that was how he and his brothers spoke at home, but it upset me, and he cried because I wasn't speaking to him. He thought I was going to break up with him. I wouldn't have broken up with him over something so petty, but I was hurt for a very long time afterwards. I still care for him now and I wish him all the happiness in the world with his partner and his children.

Sometimes others say cruel things that to them are just words because to them they have no special meaning. The use of language is very powerful and words like "retard", "spacca", "Mongol", "spastic" or "special needs" are all highly negative and drenched in negative stigma. For a lot of people those words just mean slow or a little bit dim, but those are people who have usually never been oppressed due to how they look or a label that they have. To someone who is bullied for being on the spectrum those words are highly offensive and hurtful because they have been used to deprive us of our rights and to demoralise and put us down for the last one hundred years, if not more.

One of the most influential writers on social stigma, the sociologist Erving Goffman, saw stigma as a phenomenon where individuals are rejected by society as a result of attributes they possess which might be: body differences such as physical defects, blemishes of character which are perceived as weak will, or passions which society believe are unnatural. If you possess any of these stigmas, then you are likely to be mistreated by the rest of society whom Goffman describes as "normal". Goffman, writing in the 1960s[*], also states that specific stigma terms in society such as "bastard" or "moron" are used in daily conversation without much thought as a source of metaphor and imagery and that society makes a variety of discriminatory assumptions which may reduce an individual with a difference's life chances because society views that person as unhuman due to their flaws or perceived negative characteristics.

The reason that I mention this is because I feel that it is very important in this particular example. My boyfriend used the terms he did because society taught him that they are acceptable. He used them without thought to my feelings or even that they were harmful, and because of this he oppressed me without even meaning to and made me feel like a second-class person, "unhuman" to use Goffman's words. Everyone should consider how they use language a little more carefully to avoid oppressing or hurting others in any social setting.

---

[*] In his book *Stigma: Notes on the Management of Spoiled Identity* (1963)

SOCIAL RELATIONSHIPS

Self-stimulation, often called "stimming" by individuals in the autistic community, is a behaviour commonly connected with autism which means a repetitive movement or behaviour. It has been reported that youngsters with autism gain pleasure from self-stimulatory behaviours because they find it hard to gain reward from normal social interaction – behaviours which are repetitive such as body rocking, head banging, arm flapping and biting, which seem odd to adults but for a child create a sense of pleasure and stability. The behaviour can also be related to sensory issues and used to block out other input of information. Sometimes I complain about too much external input if I cannot process everything that is going on around me. I engaged in banging my head on the wall and I clap my hands repeatedly if I am overexcited. Both of these behaviours seem odd to others who do not understand the spectrum and other children bullied me because of those behaviours. I also body rock and head bang when I feel anxious and until recently I suffered with quite severe panic attacks because I simply found the world too overbearing.

When it came to forming social relationships, my friendship group often told me that they were being further bullied in school because they were associated with me. I found this very difficult to deal with. I also had difficulties in forming appropriate relationships because I became attached to individuals very quickly.

I repeatedly form the same sort of attachments which spring from what has been called "separation anxiety"*. I cling to the person who I am attached to whether or not they reciprocate my affections, due to being a child who experienced insecure attachment patterns, such as extreme distress when mother left me alone at any point. It is almost like whether they want to or not,

---

* a term coined by Mary D. Salter Ainsworth and Silvia M. Bell in their 1970 journal article "Attachment, exploration, and separation"

whether I want them to or not, they become my primary care giver and the centre of my focus, attention and obsessive behaviour.

I exhibit obsessive thought patterns and behaviours. The boy I first fell in love with once said that he felt like he couldn't have a relationship with someone else, because he felt that I wouldn't let him. This is a behaviour that did not stop until well into my adult life and caused me to get hurt romantically. I still exhibit obsessive thought patterns and behaviours as an adult, often after a row or if I feel my partner has left me. I used to get intense attacks of anxiety at the thought of being left alone. I could not bear confrontation as I was growing up, particularly being shouted at. This would result in me crying, hiding or leaving the room. This has got better for me as an adult because you cannot cry every time someone shouts at you if you work in healthcare, but I always still prefer to avoid confrontation if I can.

The boy that I loved who was gay and I argued a lot, because when I was younger I thought he was my ultimate best friend. I didn't realise that best friend is a myth and that when you're an adult you have four or five close friends. This boy used to use the fact that I loved him against me. He'd bribe me into doing things for him by saying he'd kiss me, and because I was blinded by love I believed him. Looking back now, I'd say that I confused loving with liking and I did things that you're only supposed to do in a relationship like buying Valentine's Day presents. I was vulnerable and let myself get hurt emotionally, because I was constantly looking for a relationship and only now that I'm in my early 30s have I stopped doing that.

The boy took an overdose one year, but it didn't kill him. The feeling of loss nearly killed me, though, because the idea of losing my friend was worse than losing a scrunchie or pencil. At that point I realised that human beings were more valuable than inanimate objects. I loved him with all my heart, and the idea of him not being in the world was a very painful one. I couldn't understand what would make him do such a thing back then, but I understand completely now. Sometimes I thank a metaphorical god that I am too scared of what is on the other side to commit suicide properly. I feel squeamish when I have to have an injection or see anyone taking an injection, because I am reminded of the past when I visited the boy in hospital and the doctor took his needles out in front of me.

I experienced my first physical fight in Year 9, because I slapped him round the face. Looking back now, I handled the whole situation really badly, but I think I probably did it because I felt lonely and I felt that he was supposed to be there for me forever but he just wasn't. I couldn't communicate my needs correctly to him and because of this I became frustrated. He retaliated and we ended up fighting for quite a while until our friends split us up. If I could go back, I don't think that I'd apologise, because he hurt me. We had loads of arguments because he was supposed to wear a best friend's necklace that I bought him. I did not understand that he had the choice whether to wear it or not. He wanted to run away at one point and because I was unhappy at school I promised I'd go with him, but nothing came of it. He and I weren't all bad, though. When we got on we really got on and I was in love with him, which was what caused the problems. He was funny and handsome and my first love. He was also gayer than anyone I had ever known and was great to dance with on nights out.

When I got to be alone with him just laughing and talking it was special. He encouraged me to drink one hell of a lot of alcohol, though, so I began to develop difficulties with alcohol. I thank him, though, because he was a big part of the person who I am today.

JN: I hadn't realised at school that Maddy was autistic. I was aware that she was different, but I couldn't quite put my finger on what it was.

At times her behaviour could be uncomfortable. For example, if there was a big group of us, I felt that she would try harder than everyone else, almost like she was trying to prove a point.

For example, when we all went out, Maddy always felt uncomfortable and sometimes she put up a wall because she felt threatened.

If I'm totally honest, I wasn't very keen on Maddy at first because she was "different", but it just goes to show that you should never judge a book by its cover, because she is a kind, sensitive, warm friend. When we were younger I don't think Maddy knew how to contain herself, and sometimes would do certain things to try to fit in or try and be "normal". It's only in recent years that her behaviour starts to make sense.

One of my fondest memories, from younger years, being close to Maddy was when we would just chill out, eat loads of crap food and watch TV! We did this a lot; she would sometimes go a step too far, though, and do crazy things like pouring beer onto her ice cream to see if it tastes nice.

Now this boy is a high-achieving hairdresser for a popular company and his wedding reception was the first gay wedding reception I ever went to. I am glad of those experiences because they taught important lessons and are a very important part of who I am.

WHAT CAUSES MY MELTDOWNS?

If I feel like I have been treated unjustly, that my rights are being threatened or taken away or if I feel that I am losing a person I am close to I can have meltdowns, or extreme anxiety attacks, because I find strong emotional responses challenging. I also get this if I have lost something and I feel that the object is important. There are other reasons why I might have meltdowns and it's hard to explain exactly what they are. Meltdowns can be related to overbearing sensory stimulus or anything from the bus being late and my plans changing to feeling under pressure, people playing loud music on the bus and anti-social behaviour on public transport. It is fair to say that I have most of my meltdowns on public transport these days, but I guess that is because I spend most of my time commuting. Alarm sounds can make me meltdown, especially car alarms or repetitive piercing sounds.

I can usually sense that a meltdown is coming, and I can usually calm it down or at least try to prevent it enough so that it does not become problematic in social situations. For example, if I get an anxiety attack on the bus, my heart usually starts beating faster and my chest gets tighter, then I sweat and then I cannot breathe. If you don't know what this sensation is, it can often feel like a sense of dread and like you could perhaps be dying. To calm this down, I slow my breathing by taking deep breaths and I ground myself. This means that I remind myself that whatever is making me anxious is only temporary and will not last forever; then I focus on each specific part of my body individually and imagine it calming. I imagine my chest becoming freer and my heart rate slowing down. I do this until I feel calm and can carry on with whatever I am doing.

This is not a strategy that I learnt straight away, and I remember many afternoons in student support because I could not calm myself down. Having meltdowns is one of the curses of being on the spectrum that when I was younger used to make me wish I was a neurotypical person.

Trying to deal with it whilst growing up, experiencing romantic attachments and managing social relationships can take a lot of energy, so my advice would be for any person with Asperger's to look after themselves through this process and not to beat themselves up about being on the spectrum or to feel guilty for their behaviour. You cannot help being on the spectrum and it is a lovely part of you; you just need support to deal with the side effects.

I had to stand up for a particular friend a lot because she was profoundly autistic and other children used to bully her, because she had nervous panic attacks. She was the one whose parents didn't let her go into town by herself that I mentioned earlier in the book. I helped her because I was able to vocalise to the teachers what was wrong for her. I also related to her because people had been unkind to me in primary school, and so we helped each other. She wrote me a sad poem one day about how I was one of her best friends and it made me angry about how cruel society can be. The other children used to say things like, "Oh you are special … special needs," and laugh, and it made me incredibly angry and I learnt to stand up for myself and my friends.

I remember realising how cruel the wider world was on the morning of September 11th, 2001 when the first bomb hit the Twin Towers in the United States. I was coming into school and I had swiped my ID card into the turnstile to get into the building. I was walking to my form room and one of the girls shouted to me, "Come into the assembly room." I followed her and on the big screen everyone was watching the attacks. That day we could all start lessons a little later due to the shock and upset of the attacks, and lots of time was spent discussing them in class. It struck me how cruel the wider world was then and I have had a keen awareness of political issues ever since.

MATHS AGAIN

I hated Maths lessons so much I stopped going to them in secondary school, hence the reason why I only have a Functional Skills Maths qualification. I will go back and do my Mathematics GCSE one day; I just need to find the time to do so. I know I need one, but I just don't like it.

One day, we were being asked to solve a particular problem and I perceived my teacher to be bullying me; she moved me away from my friend, because I was talking in class. I grew angry and responded by throwing a chair out of the classroom. I threw the chair because I knew that it was the only way I'd get the lesson to stop. I didn't get a detention, however, because I cried to get out of it. I did that a lot in those days.

My eldest sister: All I remember is seeing a flying chair come out of the classroom as I walked past.

I feel that if I had been better supported in Maths, I would have been able to gain a GCSE like everyone else did. I did have a private tutor and she was good for a while, but the bullying that I experienced made me hate the subject so much and now I just switch off from it.

I think teachers could support children by using real-life examples that actually apply to the individuals they are teaching. Nobody can cook at a young age, or at least not many people can, but what they do is share out their lunches and swap things they want, so why not teach percentages that way? For example, if Dave gives his friend half of his chocolate, what percentage will he have left? If a situation did not apply to me in Maths, I found it really difficult to understand the task that was being asked of me due to thinking literally, and even many of my neurotypical friends feel the same way about it. Although I particularly hated Maths, I had special interests that were just as strong as my hatred for mathematics.

THEATRE AND SPECIAL INTERESTS

As the charity Ambitious about Autism explain on their website, "Many people with autism have a highly focused level of interest in particular topics. Some special interests begin in childhood, but some are picked up later in life." This is often harmless and can, in fact, be beneficial; however sometimes a special interest can become an obsession, and this is more problematic, if an obsession interferes with an individual's quality of life.

It is certainly true that I developed a special interest in theatre during my time at school. My first productions were the school plays in primary school I mentioned in the previous chapter. I carried this interest on to secondary school where they mainly focused on musicals. I went on to be in every musical that my secondary school ever did until I left sixth form. There was the production of *Fame* where I was in the chorus, *The Sound of Music* where I played mother superior, *Oliver Twist* where I was Widow Twankey, *Return to the Forbidden Planet* where I was in the chorus, and more. I won various music awards and public-speaking awards. In sixth form I went on to study Drama as an A- level and we got to do several productions throughout the year. We did a play called *Find Me* by Olwen Wymark and we got to create our own collaborative piece, and also go on lots of trips to the theatre. After school, I continued my special interest by joining clubs such as the Midlands Arts Centre (M.A.C.) youth theatre and Spotlight at the Birmingham Hippodrome. I met one of my best friends there and she had this to say about being friends with someone on the spectrum.

NB: I first met Maddy when we were 16 years old at a drama group in 2005/2006 when we were working on a production called City Child. *She was one of the actors and I was singing soprano in the chorus.*

I did not know that Maddy was autistic and she did not tell me until much later on in our friendship. I must have known subconsciously that she was on the spectrum because I have a lot of experience with my own family members. I always listen to Maddy and ask if she needs help; I allow her time and space to process things and I try to let her do things for herself.

I have way too many favourite memories with Maddy. I have loved all the shows that we have created, written and performed together. She is so talented and I like to see her shine. I think that schools could do more to support young people on the spectrum. I think that they need to teach kids that thinking differently is not a sign of weakness and that everyone is great, not just the people who think like you. Also, that getting the best grades is not the most important thing. Exams are not always the best way to demonstrate ability; sometimes the ability to understand is key.

I have been friends with this lovely woman for 15 years and would not have met her if it was not for my special interest. Theatre has allowed me to make friends and interact in groups. I also used it as another valuable coping strategy. The theatre allowed me to become a character which was not myself. What I also love about the theatre is that it can be used to teach others about issues in society. I use it to express my emotions and it always makes me feel calmer. If I have had a meltdown, sometimes the best thing to do can be to put theatre show music on. Theatre can be used to show others feelings and experiences that they might not have themselves and it encourages people to experience empathy. It also teaches reflection and allows people space to explore the feelings that they have. I love political theatre that forces audiences to discuss world affairs and I have a keen interest in using theatre to raise awareness of mental illnesses to educate the public about such conditions.

So, on the one hand my special interest in theatre has not been a problem and has been a very good thing for me. It has been a problem, however, at the times when I was so busy with its extracurricular activities that I did not sleep because I was learning my lines and when I did not speak about anything other than the theatre and had no interest in other people's hobbies, lives or feelings if they did not care about the theatre. My special interest could have become a further problem when I was doing my exams. I was very angry when they did not cast me as the Drama teacher Mrs Darbus in *High School Musical* because I was in my last year at school and they wanted me to focus on my exams. I was taking on too much and the teachers could see this, but I could not and I felt like they did not want me to have the lead role.

Because I loved theatre so much, I thought I might like to apply to go to drama school. I applied to go to the Royal Academy of Dramatic Arts (R.A.D.A.) but it is a difficult process with eight audition stages to it. I got halfway through and had to travel to London on my own each time, which was very anxiety-provoking. I am glad I did not go to R.A.D.A. because it would have been a high-pressure setting and I would not have received the help that I needed. It was better for me at the time to receive the support I did in a university setting. (However, now I am older I would love to go to Drama school and it is a dream of mine to make it happen somehow.) In the end I chose to study Drama and English Literature at university, which was a much better idea even though it was still extremely anxiety-provoking.

I have had a few other special interests in my time too, such as historical re-enactment, which is only a problem when I spend money that I don't have on kit and shows. The biggest special interest of mine which is problematic is that sometimes specific individuals become special interests and that can lead to obsession if it is not dealt with correctly at the time.

I am still friends with many of these individuals, but it did lead to problems with my relationships and social groups as I was growing up. You have already heard from one of these individuals (JN above) and will hear from others, and I'll talk about this more, as the book continues. It takes a special kind of person to realise that they are an autistic special interest and not run away, continuing to support the individual instead. I am attracted to personalities and people who are kind and genuine. It is very scary when you first experience an obsession, especially if you do not understand what it is or why it is happening. You cannot explain to the person involved or ask for help because you don't know what to say or what is happening to you in the first place. You just know that you feel scared, confused, frustrated, infatuated and sometimes angry that it is happening at all. You know that you want help but you don't know how to ask or what to ask for.

INTERVIEW 4: A YOUNG MAN DIAGNOSED WITH ASPERGER'S

I will now interview a young man on the spectrum who wished to remain anonymous for the purposes of this book. He spoke of his special interests in theatre and of how school was difficult due to not receiving the correct support.

Tell me about your diagnosis?

I'm diagnosed with Asperger's and I am 27 years old.

What age were you when you got your diagnosis?

I was diagnosed around six years old.

What are you studying at the moment?

I am not currently studying anything.

Do you have any special interests?

I enjoy playing video games, watching movies – my favourite genre is horror – and I also enjoy drama.

Do you have any sensory difficulties?

My sensory issues are loud noises, bright lights and touch, to an extent. How I have learnt to deal with them is to try and calm my mind and focus rather than thinking about it too much.

What did you enjoy most about school?

I enjoyed Science at school and Drama because I felt understood and could express myself with those subjects. I also enjoyed History.

What did you find challenging about school?

I was more or less kicked out of mainstream school. The headteacher there also didn't believe I have Asperger's. I then went to a special school, which was difficult because they still didn't understand special needs, which was strange. One thing I found difficult was dealing with emotional overload and the teachers not really taking the time to actually understand me.

What do you think schools could do to better support individuals on the spectrum?

I think more time to understand each person and patience – so, understanding what each person needs and how to respond correctly and not to just tell people off because what they might do could be considered naughty.

What are you doing with your life presently?

I'm about to work on a show for a group called Spectra, but I've also been working as an assistant Drama practitioner in schools with Open Theatre Company.

The interviewee's answers demonstrate that having special interests on their own are not necessarily a problem and that teachers need to take time to understand each individual's needs.

HEALTH PROBLEMS

Not only was growing up itself an anxiety-provoking time for me, along with things like studying for my exams to worry about, I had difficulties regarding my health to deal with as well. My family and I discovered that I had scoliosis of the spine when I was 15 years old and in Year 9. My spine grew with a curvature and so I was developing a hump on my back. Some of the children were very cruel to me and called me "Hunchback of Notre Dame". I applied to the NHS for surgery and I was on a waiting list for over six months. I went into hospital for the surgery as I was doing my final year exams. I had over two weeks off school and had to go to catch up classes when I returned to school so that I would not fail to get into sixth-form college. Dad bought me a portable DVD player so that I could watch films whilst I was in hospital and I brought my laptop so that I could continue to do my coursework.

The doctors took my spine out of my back and replaced the offending curve with a titanium rod which equated to about £15,000 worth of metal. I relearnt to walk again with the help of a glorious nurse from the Royal Orthopaedic Hospital. I complained that I did not want to eat my apple or brush my teeth, but she managed to get me to do both, even though I spat the toothpaste at her afterwards.

Mum stayed with me all the way through the experience, even when I complained I could not sleep and did not let her sleep either by holding her eyelids open every time she tried to. My boyfriend at the time was very supportive of me and he came to visit me quite often. Mum would buy me McDonald's because I did not like the hospital food, and he would eat my chicken nuggets if I had fallen asleep and let them get cold. I got so cross with having to stay in hospital that I tried to discharge myself. I was bored and I felt like I was missing out on all the cool parties at school. I had brought my coursework and my films, but just doing that every day was really boring. I felt like I was getting nothing done by lying in a hospital bed. I simply got up and walked to the reception desk. Mum tried to talk me out of discharging myself and helped the nurses to put me back into bed.

I told her then that I hated her and I've regretted it ever since. I was just frustrated because I believed that she was on the nurses' side instead of mine. Eventually, I managed to go back to school, and I did well in my GCSEs regardless.

I think what might have really helped me in hospital would have been if there had been some groups at the hospital that I could have gone to. I also think that if my friends had visited me more that would have been great, but there were limitations on visiting hours and my friends had to go to school themselves.

My parents did all that they could under the circumstances, but the one thing that they did wrong was that they tried to use humour to alleviate their anxieties and Dad joked that I could be in a band called "Camel". Mum laughed and because of the bullying that I experienced at school I felt like this was the worst thing I had ever heard. My parents were devastated that they had upset me as they thought I would find it funny. Parents, please, I know that life is stressful but do not make jokes at your child's expense. They might be sensitive and find your jokes hurtful.

I also think that filling out the autism passport might have helped, but this scheme designed to help people with autism to communicate their needs to doctors, nurses and other healthcare professionals was only developed in 2014, so nine years after my operation. Although it is sad in a way that society needs such paperwork in order for people to get their needs met, the autism passport, also known as "My Health Passport", is a very helpful resource and can ensure that your needs are properly catered for whilst in hospital. Ask the nurses or doctors at the pre-operative assessment for support to fill one in if you are unsure.

If you have health concerns such as I had, the most important thing is to research the hospitals first and make sure you have chosen a decent one. If you cannot do this on your own, then get support from family or friends to research. The Royal Orthopaedic was marvellous and was one of two hospitals near enough to where we lived that performed the surgery I needed, but you really need to know the hospital and trust the surgeons who you will be working with.

My advice to any person going through this is to have realistic expectations. I expected to go back to school immediately and to walk immediately, and this was just not the case. Realistic expectations are the key to recovery in this type of process. Be realistic about what you can achieve and take each day as it comes. If you set yourself goals each day that are achievable, you will find that the time passes quicker and you will be able to do more each day, rather than focusing on things you cannot do.

Get to know the nursing staff taking care of you, and ask questions about the science behind your illness. Science is your friend and helps you to understand what is happening to your body. It gives you a sense of control, and you have to do as much for yourself as you physically can even though it hurts. Roll yourself in the bed if you are able and it is safe to do so; don't wait for the nurses unless you are unsure. Certainly, brush your own teeth and eat your breakfast without help if you can still do it yourself. Do not assume a position of helplessness by making the nurses do it for you. You will be out of hospital quicker this way.

Depression is a natural thing to occur after an operation, especially if you are experiencing high levels of pain. I wish I had been told this at the time as it was a very frightening feeling for me. Always talk to someone, your family, friends or a counselling service; if you keep the feelings inside, then the pain will last longer and you will be less able to find a solution to the problems you have. Sometimes just talking makes the pain feel better. Similarly, do not isolate yourself. I spent all of my time in my bedroom upstairs and became very lonely.

Spending time with family and friends is key, and if you do not have good family relationships, then call somebody or connect with your friends online. If you feel you have no friends, then try to make some during this time as it will feel a lot less unbearable if you are not going through it alone.

I would also advise altering your meaningful occupations – these are activities that have meaning to you. If you are someone like me who loves sports and competitive activity, being told you are unable to participate in sport for six months can be devastating. So, when I was in hospital the second time I took time to learn more about the theory behind my favourite activity and I spent a lot of time making the clothing so that my costumes would be perfect when I could train again, and that took my mind away from the fact that training was something I couldn't do.

Maintaining your occupational identity is also important. Theorists believe that identity is represented by the things that you choose to do and a loss of identity results in depression or feelings of hopelessness or confusion. For me, I am a historical re-enactor, partner, daughter, sister and was at the time a student. I continued to do work whilst I was off school so that I could keep my identity as a student. If I had been a re-enactor when I was younger, I would have continued to learn history so that I did not feel I had to stop being a re-enactor, even though I would have been unable to participate in exercise. Whatever your hobbies or interests are, you can find ways to adapt them so that you can still engage with them on some level.

As an adult, whenever times are hard for me I take solace in my religion. I practise mindfulness and meditation. If there's anything that helps you focus and makes you feel calm, I would advise you use it, especially if you are afraid of MRI scans like l am.

SEXUALITY DEVELOPS

I discovered I was bi-sexual in Year 8; when I was 13 years old, I developed romantic feelings for the girl in our friendship group who I had first met. We kissed a few times and I think perhaps we stated that we dated for two days, but kids are funny things so I will not count that as a real romantic relationship. I also confused loving and liking again and thought I would get married to another of the boys, but he too was experimenting with his sexuality and so we would, naturally, not wed. Basically, we were a group of very close friends who were exploring our sexual and spiritual journey together, and we were bullied at school for being the gay group and the goths and whatever else got shouted at us as we walked home from school, but we did not care because we were strong individuals.

Young people on the spectrum, please protect yourselves during this time. It is fine to experiment with your needs and desires but do so in a safe way. Use protection and do not feel pressured into having sex. If it does not feel right for you, then simply do not do it. In my experience when I was younger, sex was a major focus of your time at school. You would talk about who was dating who and you'd be viewed as boring or uncool if you were not sexually active. Most of this is down to the way sex is portrayed in films, television shows and popular culture. Have sex when you are ready to and not before then.

It doesn't matter if your friendship group are all having sex and think you are not cool because your life experience is different to theirs, and they may regret some of the dumb stuff they did when they are older. I have a friend who was still a virgin at the age of 28 and it did not matter. We did not love him any less because of that. Sure, people might make jokes and comments but that is just British humour. It does not mean you are a weirdo or are unloved. Please do not take the gossip and banter seriously.

Parents, please do not despair, help your child through the stages of discovery, and if you can do nothing else be there to listen with a non-judgmental ear. These issues will occur whether or not your child or relative is on the autistic spectrum, so if this section offers no comfort at all apart from the fact that you are not alone in these experiences, then I will have achieved what I have set out to do.

RELIGION

I mentioned earlier taking solace in my religion. I am a Pagan. I discovered this through my group of friends when I was 14 years old, although I had sensed my spirituality from around the age of 12.

One of the boys in our group suggested we be in a coven together. A coven is a group of witches who practise their craft together. Paganism began in about 10,000 BC during the Palaeolithic Age. It was a time where primitive people were nomadic and had to hunt for their food, following the herds of animals to survive. This was where the belief of the god of the hunt first appeared. The men worshipped the sun, the stag-horned god and the language of the animals, as hunting was crucial to their survival. The women, who were the child bearers and the healers, were those who took care of the tribe and were looked upon as having more power, as they were the givers of life.

It was during this time that the women discovered that their bodies were in tune with the lunar phases, and therefore they worshipped the moon and the goddess deity, and they were the ones who led the rituals. There were some men, however, who stayed behind from the hunt with the women, as they were too old, sick or injured, and this is how there became priests in the lunar cult.

In around 8000–7500 BC, agriculture was discovered quite by accident as the food the women stored in the ground began to grow. With the realisation that people could plant and grow their own food came the realisation of the mystery of fertility. Up until this time the deity had been the goddess of the lunar cult as men did not understand their role in the cycle of life until this point. The discovery of agriculture proved that men also had a part in creation. Prior to this, there had been a division between the men and the women for the most part, and after this discovery they had to work together and they no longer needed to follow the herds for food to survive. This was when they became "paganised", the word Pagan meaning "country dweller". Now people were able to settle in more than one place and began exploring and discovering mysteries of life, death and rebirth.*

Pagans worship the natural world around them and believe that the world is made up of energies and an equal balance between the goddess deity and the god. Without the two the world cannot exist, as we need both to create new life. Pagans also believe that the elements and the environment play an important part in the development of the world. The world cannot exist without the earth, air, fire, water and spirit, so people began to worship those gods and gods for the weather, as if there is plenty of sun there can be fruitful harvests etc.

There are many different types of Pagans, Witches and Wiccans, and all believe different variations of the above. I am an eclectic Pagan, which means I take various teachings from all doctrines that I find beneficial to me and have created a set of values and moral principles based on those teachings.

Pagans can practise the craft solitarily or in a coven of others. I joined a coven with my friends when I was 14 and I began to practise the craft. I remember terrifying my eldest sister and some of the pupils in the school by saying I was going to cast spells on them whilst they slept.

As I mentioned earlier, my father's family are Jewish. My mother's family, on the other hand, are mainly atheists from a French background. But both sides made comments such as saying that I would grow out of it. It was worse at school where my religion

---

* See "The true meaning of Paganism" article on the Ancient Origins website here: https://www.ancient-origins.net/myths-legends/true-meaning-paganism-002306

slowly became another thing for which I was being bullied and ostracised, along with my sexuality and my Asperger's syndrome. I am pleased to say that I am still a Pagan, though, and would like to be hand-fasted (that is to have a Pagan marriage) one day. Now, I am certain that my family will support me in this however I choose to marry and whomever I choose to marry, even though they may not understand my decisions. I cannot stress enough how important it is to have support from your family when being faced with difficult situations, and it certainly helps if you find yourself being bullied for who you are. However, I know that some of you may not have sympathetic or even supportive families, and I cannot imagine what you have to go through. Keep fighting, friend, and know that if the world seems like you do not belong it is only so that you can change it for the better and create a new path for others who are like yourself to follow.

BULLYING

So, now I was a 14-year-old, bi-sexual, Pagan with Asperger's and instead of being bullied for being overweight (which I still was) I was being bullied for being a weird, gay, goth kid – bullied for being different to the other children. I used to like doing assemblies for my form tutor, and I got bullied for dressing as a goth for one assembly. I got bullied for showing off my jujitsu skills in another, and finally I got bullied for saying I wanted to be an actress in the third, so I stopped doing them. I used to get my head hit off my locker in the morning by some of the popular kids, and I got tripped up in the corridors on the way to my lessons.

My group of friends liked the gothic style and we listened to different types of music. The clothes we wore got us bullied, and one day we were attacked in the park by a gang and were hit with a metal pole. The police were involved. It was then that my head of year and my form tutor got involved to try and stop the bullying. I'd never told them, because I thought it was weak, and I thought that I could take it. I wrote poems about it, and one day in class my teacher thought I was suicidal because of a poem I wrote. I was also bullied by a girl in our friendship group who was a foster child and she disliked me because of how close I was to the boy I was in love with. Some girls printed off my ID card pictures and put them in the locker rooms with mean comments underneath them. I was elected onto the student council, and I think I was only elected because the class were taking the piss, but it looks good on my CV and I really enjoyed it, so it can't have been a bad thing.

I used to get taxis to school in the mornings because I was in the special learning centre and because Mum worked nights and wanted to stop the bullying, but one day I didn't go into the centre as I was supposed to in the morning. I went to the park with my friends because taxis made me feel different from the other children.

Eventually, the bullying at secondary school gradually stopped and I could begin to feel happier there. My parents supported me through the difficult times and had many meetings with my form tutors and the head of the school about how to make things better.

Young people on the spectrum, if you are being bullied, please speak with someone about it. Keeping things locked inside of you won't make the bullying go away. If you are being threatened by the bullies, still tell people because there is nothing that they can do to you that the police or a teacher or parents cannot deal with.

Parents, if your child does experience bullying, please speak with their teachers as soon as possible to get it stopped. Your child may not want to speak about it because they might be scared or embarrassed; however, you will know the signs. Are they becoming withdrawn or overeating? Are they afraid to go out after school? If you notice any of these things, then speak with your child straight away to see if they are ok. Tell them that you will talk with a teacher they trust and you should get help quite quickly. Again, though, please do not go behind your child's back and always communicate what you are doing at each step of the process.

MY PARENTS' DIVORCE

My early teenage years weren't all doom and gloom, though – I was much happier once the bullying had stopped – and nor did I spend all my time at home in my bedroom. I had my first part-time job at a shop called Spar because the boy I loved worked there, and I went to my first house party, which he went to too. (Unfortunately, that party didn't end well. The boy got so drunk that he was throwing up, and Mum had to come and collect him from the house we were at, because it got shut down by the police. That scared me off house parties for a while, but I liked them again later when they were in my own student house, because there I had control over who came and I could fall into bed at the end of the night.)

However, there was another issue for me to deal with. Mum and Dad had started to argue. I don't know if they'd been unhappy before, but there was one particular occasion that was the first time I can recall them definitely arguing. It was over something stupid. My eldest sister wanted to sit in the front of the car, and I didn't want to sit by the youngest, but she didn't want to sit on her own in the middle. That was what started it. Then Dad let me sit in the front, and my eldest sister had to sit by the youngest; then they made silly noises all the way home. Dad warned, "If I hear that noise one more time, you'll all be walking home," and then my eldest sister did it again and he said, "I'm going to belt you."

However, I yelled, "If you hit my sister, then I'll hit you back," and then everyone was quiet for a while, but my eldest sister made the noise again.

Then Dad yelled at me, "Maddy, shut up you stupid child." I was upset because I was the only one not to make the noise and I hated to be called stupid. If I hadn't been through all the bullying in school, then I'd not have reacted so badly, but I knew that Dad didn't mean it.

He meant that my behaviour was stupid, but it made me feel inadequate and so to be deliberately irritating I made the noise myself.

Dad slammed on the car brakes, but after he'd calmed down we drove home, and he and Mum argued for a good hour or so afterwards. I went upstairs to my room to block it out.

The film *The Notebook* came out in July 2004. It is about an old man reading a story to an old woman, who is losing her memory, in a nursing home. The story is the story of their love for each other which he has written to try and help her remember things. He reads the story to her every day in the hope that she will never forget that he loves her. Mum and I cried because no man had ever loved us the way the protagonist loved his lady in the movie. Mum cried for a long time and I was sad because she was so upset. I didn't realise that she and Dad were still arguing then.

In October 2005, Dad, my youngest sister and I went to the Walsall Illuminations with Dad's new partner. I knew Dad was friends with her because she'd been to my 13th birthday party back in Year 8. He'd not yet told us that he and Mum were not together anymore. I knew Dad wasn't happy in our house, but I didn't know why, and all I wanted was for both him and Mum to be happy.

It's horrible when parents split up, and Christmas 2005 was when Mum and Dad had finally had enough. Our family always has a big dinner on Christmas Eve, and that year my little sister got stuck under the table. Mum and Dad had a row of some sort. I can't remember what was said, but I wrote the following entry in my diary:

Saturday, 24th Dec 2005

We were going to have a nice Christmas dinner; the only time of the year where we sit as a family at the table and we couldn't even get to pudding before we started fighting. This is probably our last Christmas with Dad and I hate it. I hate the thought of him not being here. I hate Mum being unhappy. I hate my sisters fighting. Happy fucking Christmas everyone. Happy fucking families. All I wanted was one proper family meal. Can't even manage that. I feel so un-Christmassy. I don't wanna wake up tomorrow. Why is there always changes and why do they always hurt me?

PS: Went downstairs to say goodnight to Dad. He can't even hold me for a hug. I wanna hold him, hug him but no. I wish he would say he loved me to my face not on text or email. All he could say to me was that I needed a Christmas bath.

When they split up, I felt like Dad had abandoned me, because we didn't spend very much time with him then, but I spoke to him about it recently and he wants to try to spend more time with us. I also felt, however irrational this is, that it was my fault Dad left, because I was not good enough, and that I didn't try hard enough to make the family happy. I knew some time before they did that my Mum and Dad would split up because I could sense they were so unhappy. In a way, I was glad when they did split up because I knew that they would be happier this way.

Everything was ok in the end. Mum and Dad eventually divorced, and Mum is happier than she has ever been. Dad is happier and he has a nice house and a really cute dog called Oscar. The only bad thing was that the divorce had a profound effect on my youngest sister.

WHAT WOULD HAVE HELPED?

I do think it would have helped if Dad would have been honest right from the beginning and told me directly at my 13th birthday party that he had a new partner instead of introducing her as his friend. This was also the truth, but when I was young I only saw friends as being platonic and it confused me when the two of them began to live together.

I guess divorce is hard for any family, and my parents only did what they thought was right at the time. I also hope that now my father is retired we will spend more time together. I continued to live with my mum in the house that I was used to living in, and I think that helped massively. Having to change houses as well as getting used to Mum and Dad splitting up might well have been too much for me. I think I personally should have spoken more with my dad about my irrational ideas that it was my fault he was leaving. I know this is not true now, but the idea plagued me for a long time when I was younger and I found it difficult adjusting to visiting Dad in his new house. Something my Dad did do very well, however, was when we went to spend the night in his new house a few months after he left home and he prepared a breakfast menu with scrambled eggs and all the things I liked to eat on it. That time was challenging for me because I find loss and change incredibly difficult. With any change one normally experiences a loss of something, even if it is a loss of a routine or a way of being. And as I mentioned before, even losing an object can upset me – let alone a change in relationship or a death of a pet or family member. Each person deals with grief and change in their own individual way. It is a journey and a process for anyone, whether they are on the spectrum or not.

LOSS AND PETS

Each person on the spectrum can react differently to loss. This does not mean that they are doing it wrong, rather that they each need time to process it differently. Some people will need time alone; others may become non-verbal for a while; some may cry, have trouble sleeping or may choose not to acknowledge the situation entirely.*

We lost our family cat Wooly, and I found that extremely hard to deal with. We had already lost our other cat, Tabby, and I just did not want to experience it again. Death just terrifies me. I cannot deal with it easily. We replaced Wooly with two little kittens called Roxie and Rogue, who later became known as Black Nose and

---

* See "Autism and bereavement: a guide for parents and carers" on the Autism West Midlands website here:
https://autismwestmidlands.org.uk/wp-content/uploads/2020/03/Autism_and_Bereavement_March_2020.pdf

White Nose because they had different markings on their noses. We still have Black Nose now 16 years later. I couldn't believe that the family wanted to replace our cat so quickly, but I think that was their way of dealing with the loss. I didn't like the new cats at first, because I don't like change and they were not the same as our previous cats, but I quickly grew to love them to pieces. As I have mentioned earlier, I cannot stand the feeling of loss. I started cutting myself as a way of dealing with my emotions. I did not learn emotional regulation techniques until very recently. I believed that if I hurt myself I could not hurt or upset anyone else. Now, though, I wish to show myself kindness and self-compassion and don't want to do my body any damage, but it took me a long time to reach that conclusion.

In July 2007 our dog Scruffy got very ill and she was not the same after that. Eventually she collapsed on the roadside when we took her for a walk and she never recovered. She finally died on Boxing Day 2008 and I cried for hours. I didn't think I could handle ever feeling like that again.

We got a new dog in April 2009. Mum didn't want to get one because we didn't want to feel the hurt of losing one again, but my youngest sister wanted a new Bull Terrier. We got a dog called Jock, but we didn't have him very long because he'd been mistreated and he became aggressive. We had him for five months in total and Mum had become very attached to him. In August 2009 when I was home from university, we had to have the dog put down because he attacked another dog in the park, and it had a bad effect on my youngest sister. Mum blamed herself; she thought she should have done more for the dog. I think now sometimes she regrets the decision. I just buried my head in the sand and pretended it had not happened.

The hardest experience of loss that I had ever dealt with until recently was when I found out that my grandpa had died. I was really sad and I cried for quite a number of hours. I struggled to get up to go to my class at university, but we had an exam that week and so I felt that I had to go. A good friend really helped me because he told our group leader for me so that I didn't have to say it again and he was really supportive and hugged me. I found out that Grandpa's funeral was on the day of my exam and Grandma told me not to come if it would disrupt my studies. So, I went to my exam, and to other classes, but it was hell and I just wanted to be with my family. I really regret not going to Grandpa's funeral and I often feel very guilty about it.

Young people on the spectrum, I know dealing with loss hurts and I know it feels like you will never be happy again. Your routine has changed; the person or thing you loved is no longer there. They are still there; they are with you in your memories, the stories you tell about them and in your dreams and often in your values and beliefs. Grieve in your own time; do whatever you need to do to help yourself move forward again. Perhaps you could write your loved one or pet a letter, song or poem? Perhaps you could look at photographs of them before you go to bed, but please understand this: they do love you, they have always loved you, and they would want you to continue with your life and be happy until you meet them again in heaven, Valhalla or wherever you believe you go to when you die. Please look after yourself and help yourself to keep going, even if it is just for your family or one special friend.

Parents and other family and friends, how should you help support someone on the spectrum to deal with loss? It is important to allow them to grieve and express their feelings in their own way. Support them to understand you are there for them, and validate their thoughts and feelings, even if their response seems strange or odd to you. Do not compare their grieving to that of others who are not on the spectrum as it may take someone on the spectrum longer to recover than others. If you yourself are grieving too, try to talk with them about your feelings as well and let them know that they are not alone. You can also seek family counselling if the grief becomes too hard to bear.

For further support with helping youngsters on the spectrum to deal with loss, I'd recommend Marci Wheeler's article "Supporting individuals on the autism spectrum coping with grief and loss through death or divorce", which can be found online.*

EXAM STRESS AND A-LEVEL CHOICES

At the same time as my parents were splitting up and I was about to go through the health problems I described above, I had other pressures about me. I needed to prepare for the Year 9 SATs (standard attainment tests) exams. (Up until 2008 these assessments were required in secondary schools at the end of Key Stage 3. So, every child my age experienced them. Schools were under more and more pressure to get the best results so that they could look good during Ofsted reports, and in turn this stressed out the children who are supposed to be achieving the results.) After the SATs exams came GCSEs and then once we had finished our GCSEs we were supposed to pick A-level subjects and do work experience. At this point, I still did not know what I wanted to do with my life. The scoliosis of the spine was becoming noticeable at this time too and it would need to be operated on before I finished my exams. I saw a photograph of myself with my curvature and I became really upset and sobbed to my dog Scruffy and my mum. The whole thing seemed like too much for me and I did not know how I was ever going to cope with all this.

I think if the school had done some things differently, it really would have helped. There is a lot of pressure at school to decide your future then and there. I think this attitude is one that needs changing as nobody knows exactly what they want to do when they are 16 years old. In this current political climate, the best advice you

---

*https://www.iidc.indiana.edu/irca/articles/supporting-individuals-on-the-autism-spectrum-coping-with-grief-and-loss.html

can give a young person is to show them all the different career paths that are out there. You can show them which careers go with individual subjects that they enjoy the most and what they need to do to get to those careers. I found that the careers advice services never helped if you said you had an interest in the arts or in film because most people who work in those industries are freelance or own their own businesses, but there was never any advice given about what freelance was or about how to start out on your own. Those choices are tough, but they are worth doing if you feel, like I did, that there is no job role that exists that fits your skill set or interests.

It is best not to bombard individuals with information and many leaflets, and it is best not to force them to attend talks and workshops about careers and CV-writing skills. Yes, those things are important, but everyone realises this in their own time and their own pace. Some people never realise this but are no less valid in society than anyone else. It is also best not to criticise people for achieving at their own rate and to individualise learning plans for people.

Young people on the spectrum, if you are experiencing exam stress the best thing you can do is prepare. Know when your exams are. Have a timetable of exams in order of when they are occurring so you know what you can study for. Make sure you are getting enough sleep. Stop revising at 10pm and make sure you do socialise with your friends and do other things during this time; exercising helps because it releases adrenalin and helps you to focus and think more. I find that the treadmill or the bike at the gym are my thinking places or swimming.

In terms of picking A-level subjects, you should pick them according to what career you want, or if you do not know what career you want pick the subjects you enjoy most – this was what I ended up doing.

Some A-level subjects like Law, Business Studies or Health and Social Care are obviously related to possible careers; others like Maths, English or Physical Education are more generic but nevertheless valuable and could lead to careers like teaching or, in the case of Maths, accountancy and finance.

If you want to go to university, then always check what the entry requirements are for the universities and courses you are interested in are because they are different for each one, and this may determine what subjects you choose to take at A-level.

For work experience you just have to use the internet and research which companies offer work experience. I would advise you look at companies which declare that they are disability positive because this means that they have had some training in how to support individuals who are disabled and are likely to discriminate less. Some companies do apprenticeships and summer experiences, but I would always try and get work experience related to whatever field you are thinking of for your career. Ironically, I did not do this myself because there were no work experience opportunities available in theatre at the time in Birmingham; however, the Birmingham Hippodrome now has work experience opportunities for young people to apply for. I worked in Cadbury World for two weeks instead because I love chocolate, but it was one of the best jobs I have ever had and it allowed me to develop transferable skills such as communication and speaking with the public. It also gave me experience of what the working world was like, so it was a worthwhile and valuable learning opportunity.

Nothing will be handed to you and it might take hard work in the current economic climate to get work experience, but it is worth doing. If things don't work out immediately, young people on the spectrum, please don't get frustrated and never see yourself as worthless. You are not and you can achieve anything you set your mind to. There may be limits to what you can do due to your disability, but adults should always help you to understand what your strengths are and support you to engage in activities and jobs that you enjoy.

Parents with children on the spectrum, please help your child find work experience which is suitable to their needs. Don't ever write them off and think that they won't be able to work. Even if they have a seemingly mundane job as work experience, it can still be a positive thing and give them a feeling of maturity and responsibility.

MOVING ON FROM SECONDARY SCHOOL TO SIXTH FORM

In 2006 I was 16 years old and moved from secondary school up to the sixth form. In June there was the secondary school's leaver's prom and it was an amazing night. I looked really good for the first time ever. Before that I'd never really put much effort into my appearance, and all of the people who had ever bullied me at school told me how sorry they were. They danced with me, so that night meant a lot. It was because everyone had expected me to go as a goth to the prom, but I had decided to be different and wear a big pink princess dress, which was beautiful.

That summer, Italy won the World Cup in Germany, Dad moved out of our house and the night before I got my GCSE results I stayed up all night worrying – playing Guitar Hero and completing all the easy levels. When the results came, I got two Bs, five Cs, a D and an E. Everyone was proud of me, because I was always told I wouldn't get that far. Later, I resented it at university when everyone bragged about how many As they'd got and laughed at anyone who failed their Maths GCSE. I felt that it undermined how well I'd done, and I just didn't say anything when they started those conversations.

I burnt all my old school exercise books to say goodbye to secondary school, and I was happy to be moving on to sixth form, but because it was my school's sixth form nothing would change very much. Looking back now, I wish I'd have gone to Solihull Sixth Form College instead, because the teachers there were supposed to be better, but I was being my Asperger's self and didn't want to change.

I started sixth-form college in September 2006. I studied Drama, English Literature and Psychology at A-level. I had wanted to study Law, because at one point I thought I was going to be a lawyer when I was older, but Law wasn't available as an A-level at my college, so I moved on from that dream. However, I enjoyed sixth-form college. For our Drama exam we changed the play *A Doll's House* by Ibsen into a modern-day scenario. We also did our own piece about mental illness, and since then I've always been interested in merging psychology and theatre together.

In 2007 I was 17 years old and everything was stable most of the time. I had got a job as a cleaner and I worked there for three years on and off. I eventually left in 2009, because it became challenging to coordinate with university, but I regretted leaving that job when the recession hit because it took me ages to find another one. I got my ex-boyfriend a job there too and he worked there for at least three years. My best friend at sixth-form college worked there too. We had to do some horrid jobs like scraping chewing gum off desks and cleaning the swimming pool. The ladies who worked there were unpleasant toward each other. They tried to pull me and my friend into arguments, but we would not entertain their behaviour. I got closer to my friend due to working with her at the cleaning job, and this is what she wrote about being friends with me:

EC: I've known this amazing girl for a very long time now, and from day one I knew about the problems she faced. I've never considered her as any different to myself and in fact... I don't think I've ever met anybody as intelligent. Of course, there are things Maddy does that other people will find a little strange, like not eating certain foods because of their colour or seeing things in a different light; but this is what makes her unique and interesting. We sit and laugh at all the little things, because they only begin to scratch the surface to the deeply fascinating person that she is. Her sense of humour is one of the things I love the most... Most people don't find funny the things we roll on the floor laughing about, like our "cheese people" stories or our cow humour [or] "Bob" the rubber mask. I wouldn't change the way she is for the world and, as the saying goes, never judge a book by its cover.

DRIVING

A lot of the issues I'm discussing with you fall into the category of growing up, and with growing up comes a whole load of societal expectations. For example, you're supposed to start thinking about your career and about learning to drive. For my 16th birthday, I got given learn-to-drive theory books, so I knew that my family wanted me to learn to drive a car. I started trying to learn to drive later, in 2007, but it was distressingly challenging for me. The dyspraxia renders me very uncoordinated. I struggle with spatial-orientation difficulties, so knowing how much of a gap to leave between the car and the pavement is difficult for me. I also find right-left discrimination challenging, and I have a slow processing speed, meaning that I find it difficult to interpret information which is being given to me quickly. This makes driving tough as you need to be able to make split-second decisions and understand the signs on the roundabouts before you get to them.

Driving is incredibly problematic for me because it is an intense sensory experience and I have to process a lot of information very quickly, which I find challenging. I know that many people with dyspraxia can and do drive but for me driving was a struggle.

The first time that I drove Mum's car I drove it into a bush because I couldn't work the steering wheel and we had to call the AA. I do not find it particularly helpful when people make negative comments such as, "I'll make sure I'm off the road when you're out, then," or "Look out, she's out again." I know that this is British humour and they say that sort of thing to everyone, but I felt like those comments undermined my confidence. I had over forty lessons and three instructors. I tried to switch to an automatic car to see if that'd make it easier, but my instructor undermined my confidence saying that I had reached my full driving potential and that I probably would never be able to drive, so I was upset.

Until very recently, whenever I tried to drive a car I was very nervous and scared of buses on the road. I got a new driving instructor and my sister told him I was on the spectrum. He helped me to learn with diagrams and was very calm when taking me out on the road because he knew that I got anxious. I am afraid of the immense responsibility that if I were to crash it wouldn't just be me I killed. I want to say that all young people on the spectrum should have the same opportunity as everybody else to drive, but if it is unsafe then, whether one is on the spectrum or not, I would advise against it. I would also say that the more you practise the easier it becomes and, although learning to drive is a battle that I am still yet to conquer I am a lot better driver now than I was at 17.

Driving pretty much emphasises every part of my condition that I struggle with, but I keep going with driving lessons because being able to drive offers such freedom and mobility. All of that stuff I've mentioned about public transport would disappear if I could drive and I am sure my determined nature will enable me to do so eventually, even if I have been trying to learn on and off for the last decade.

MUSIC FESTIVALS

Do you love rock music as much as I do? Rock music festivals are amazing social events, which allow you to have so much fun. The Download Festival held annually at Donington Park is the one I know well, but there are many different festivals in many different countries. They are very anxiety-provoking events but well worth the experience if you have a good group of friends to go with, and I would say this to anyone whether they were on the spectrum or not.

Parents, this is another big one. Let your child take risks and take risks with them. Allow me to explain. Download Donington is a large rock-music festival and only allows certain types of bands to play there. It opens on the Wednesday afternoon and closes the following Monday afternoon. The first year I went in 2007, I had to go on the Friday and could only stay until the Sunday because I had exams. I'd wanted to go previously, but Mum hadn't thought I was old enough to go alone until I was 17. My mum took a risk allowing me to go to that festival. What if I'd have been crushed in a mosh pit? What if the security was not good enough? What if I felt alone, anxious and afraid and wanted to come home? All these what ifs would be enough to drive any mother batty, but mine took a risk and decided to follow me into the unknown. If you have already tried to go camping and your children with autism do not like it, please do not sue me. I am not saying that every child on the spectrum will enjoy rock music. What I am saying is that there will probably be an activity that they like which you consider a risk. If they like ice skating and want to compete, they may injure themselves. Same if they like football or contact sports. Allow them to experience those things for themselves and decide for themselves rather than protecting them from all possible harm and danger. They will need to fend for themselves once you are no longer able to care for them.

I was very nervous that first year that I went because I feel awkward in social situations often, and I don't like change, so this was a very big deal for me. I'd never been camping in a tent before, let alone with people I didn't know very well, so my mum was worried about how I would take it. I stayed up all night worrying the night before we left. On the way there, we picked up my friend and listened to music. The festival itself was great. The only hint of trouble was because the nu metal band Korn and the emo band My Chemical Romance were playing at around the same timeslot on different stages and some people were upset about it. I got scared at the time because I hadn't been to a festival before, but I'm ok with that sort of thing now because I know that it's just banter between the crowds. Other scary things were trying to find the other people that I was camping with and trying to remember where our tent was.

But I must have loved it because I went to Download Donington every year for the next ten years. The festival is really well organised and there's always loads of security there, so Mum didn't mind me going back again. I only had to take a break from going in 2017 due to studying my course, which made me terribly sad because I had been going religiously for ten years.

I used to take my youngest sister with me, because she likes the music too and I enjoyed spending time with her. When she was old enough, she went with her own friends for a while. When I first went to Download I didn't even know how to pitch a tent, but now we think of what we need and we always buy pop-up tents. All you have to do is pitch it to the ground rather than try for hours putting it up. I hate carrying the bags, though, because you always have so much stuff to take – beer and tents and so on, so by the time you get to your spot on the campsite your arms are aching, you've already been sweating, so all you want to do is sit down and have a drink and a chat for a bit.

I've only ever been seriously hurt there twice and both times were my own fault, because I wasn't careful in the mosh pits. In 2010 I dislocated my shoulder and it hurt like hell carrying the crates back to the car on the Sunday night. My little sister had to help me carry my stuff.

But I love Download because it's such a community of people and I feel that I can really be myself there for a few days. Nobody cares what your career is or how intelligent you are or what grades you got at school; they are just there for a good time and hardcore rock and roll music. Unfortunately, each time all good things have to come to an end and after the weekend you go back to reality — searching for a career and doing work towards that career.

HOW TO PREPARE FOR FESTIVALS IF YOU ARE ON THE SPECTRUM

If you are considering going to a festival, I would advise you to write a list of all the stuff you'll need for the five days. Most important things are your medication, your ticket, your money, your clothes and any stimulation toys you might have. I always take my noise-cancelling headphones as well. With anything else, if you forget to take it, you can buy it when you're there, but it makes the trip more expensive. I would also advise you to write down the stage times and stages of where your favourite bands are playing so you don't miss anything. Go with a good friend who understands you and you know will look after you. Drink and party responsibly and never feel pushed to do anything. If you don't want to do it, then don't. Go back to your tent. Your tent is your safe space. I used to try not to share my tent with people because I preferred to be alone if things got too much for me, but I have shared with people I was close to in the past, and now when I camp I go with my partner.

Of course, there's the crowds to deal with. Crowds can get too much, especially when there are over one hundred thousand people there, but if you feel overwhelmed by any stimulus then remove yourself from it. You can always find a quieter patch of grass to take yourself away, and most festivals offer quiet camps or disabled camping. You do get a different atmosphere if you stay there, but it is still a lot of fun and quite safe.

Other than that, all I have to say is have fun, enjoy yourself and experience life.

Parents, if it is the first time your child has been to a festival, then do always be on hand to pick them up and take them home again if they do not like it or become overwhelmed. Ask them how they are by text and remind them to take their medication if they are taking any. Most importantly, though, try not to worry. Your child will be fine, and you are taking a huge step by allowing them to experience this amazing opportunity. Thank you!

APPLYING FOR UNIVERSITY AND LEAVING SIXTH FORM

When I was in sixth form, they took us on a residential trip to Nottingham University and during that trip I decided I wanted to go to university. I also decided that I wanted to go to Nottingham or a university in London because I loved London so much.

When the time came to apply, I looked around Worcester University, a university in London and Coventry University. I was interviewed for Coventry University and accepted into Worcester University, which would be where I would have gone had I not got into my chosen university in London. I think I did well at the interview for my London university because I went on my own. I went there on the train by myself without my parents because they wanted to see if I could manage. This was the first time I had ever travelled on a train by myself and trains always made me anxious. Even as an adult I am nervous on trains because I don't like the thought of being late or not being able to find the correct platform. I also do not like how loud they are. I can go on trains a lot more now because I have accepted that it is just something that I have to do if I need to get around. Mum had come with me on the train to Worcester, but I went to London on my own and that gave me enough confidence to go on my own on trains again afterwards.

For three years running (2006-2008) I went to Wales with the special learning centre for three days in the summer. When I went for the final time in 2008, the teachers were all really proud that I was going to university. They also said that it wasn't usual that somebody from the centre could help them to organise the other children. I knew that I'd grown up a lot then. It meant a lot to me that although I was on the spectrum, I could still help others who had more severe learning difficulties than me. It was then that I realised that I could use my experiences to help other people, but I didn't discover what I wanted to do until I went to university.

When the time came, I was ready to leave by the end of sixth form. The school was changing and when the new headmistress joined there was barely anyone left who we knew in the school. The teachers didn't put much effort into our leaving. They just did a small do in the sixth-form centre, which was just six boxes of pizza and a stereo. It didn't make me feel like I was wanted in the school anymore, so I was glad to be moving on to university. I got three Bs for my A-levels, and I believe I could have got three As, but I didn't do as well as I could on my final exams because I went to Download 2008 the weekend before my exams.

That summer I went on holiday to Bulgaria with Dad and his, then, partner. Dad did not always agree with some of the decisions that I made. For example, when I was 15 I'd got a tattoo and I know I got it for all the wrong reasons; I got it because I knew that Dad wouldn't approve. (But now that I'm older I have learnt to like it. It makes me unique, like being on the spectrum.) I felt bad because Dad said that we never told him anything about our lives. I tell him most things now (and soon he will know everything when this book gets published).

Bulgaria was the second holiday that we went on with Dad and his partner, and we were slowly adjusting to the idea that he and Mum were not together anymore. As I've said previously, there is nothing that can remove anxiety during periods of transition for a child who is constantly anxious. All you can do is be there for them and let them know that everything will be ok.

I've talked in this chapter about a lot of firsts and a lot of growing up. Many of the issues I've talked about are things that can happen to any person or child at any stage of life. They are not unique to individuals on the spectrum, but what does make them unique to such individuals is the way that we deal with them due to our different world outlook and the sensory challenges that I discussed earlier. This unique way of dealing with things does not change once you are grown up; you just learn new coping strategies and more suitable ways of dealing with situations. The unique way of dealing with things also applied as I was about to face university – which provided many challenges, many experiences, much anxiety, but also some amazing fun.

But before I talk about university in the next chapter, now is a good time to hear more from two other individuals on the spectrum.

INTERVIEW 5: SARAH

I have chosen to place this interview here because the interviewee discusses issues such as socialisation and bullying which I have discussed during this chapter.

Introduce yourself

I'm Sarah Kaye, 25 years old. I like lists, Netflix, dark humour and purple stuff.

Tell me about your diagnosis

I was diagnosed very early, at the age of four, with Asperger syndrome and dyspraxia. I have had some issues with mental health and am currently on the waiting list to test for borderline personality disorder.

Do you feel that your diagnosis helped you in anyway?

I am glad that I have an explanation for some of my more frustrating features, such as misunderstanding of social gestures and the physical stimming to release inner tension, which to a stranger can make me seem a lot younger and/or presumed to be less intellectually capable than average. While I hate the difficulties that come with having Asperger's at times, I wouldn't get rid of it permanently because the little quirks like the tics, fascination with pop culture and unique processing of information are features that do define me in a good way and are what my family and closest friends have grown to accept and love …I hope.

What difficulties did you face in secondary school?

I had a lot of problems with bullying and finding a friendship group that I fitted in with throughout secondary school. In my younger years I think other pupils found me annoying or rude, even when I wasn't intending to be, so combined with various personalities, some more aggressive than others, that caused a lot of unpleasant incidents to occur. Even with a uniform code and an all-girls environment, there was a large focus on physical appearances and I often felt humiliated for not being able to pick up on the habits needed to make myself look "pretty" with flattering hair and make-up (hormones kicked in [and] some pretty bad skin breakouts). I grew more self-aware and improved my social skills as I got older, but by the time I got to Year 10 and 11, I'd grown sick of being forced to take subjects I had no interest in and arguing with less understanding members of staff. I developed a slightly more rebellious attitude and started prioritising my time with older mixed crowds I met outside of school, simply because that's what made me happy. I came out with fairly good GCSEs, but I think I'd have been more motivated to give classes my best shot if I hadn't felt so isolated from everyone else. Sixth-form college was a much nicer experience as I had the choice to do subjects of genuine interest and wear whatever I like, therefore giving easier opportunity to engage with like-minded people.

Describe any sensory difficulties you might have

Sensory difficulties were definitely present as a child. I vaguely remember screaming in a shop with my mother at a very young age, which must have been challenging for her, to say the least. Yet at the time I could not verbally explain that it was simply because I didn't like the colour of the floor and literally just wanted her to take me out of the place.

I also hated the sensation of stickers on the skin and even over worn clothes, so wasn't very appreciative of them being frequently distributed as "rewards" in primary school. However, one that caused bigger problems was being shouted at, especially in an aggressive manner. Both at home and school, I could never handle someone telling me off in raised tones because it made me feel scared and sick. I remember shaking a lot as well as ringing in my ears. To this day, it always feels like I'm losing grasp of my surroundings, which results in a meltdown.

How do you deal with sensory difficulties as an adult?

As a young adult, I no longer scream at colours. I'm still not keen on any sticky fastenings, purely because the texture makes me cringe, and the sound of other people brushing their teeth is another annoyance that became more noticeable as I got older. However, if I cannot avoid a scenario featuring these sensations, I'm capable of the "grin and bear it" technique (maybe with not so much grinning) for as long as I absolutely have to. I can cope with going to noisy venues like clubs in the present day, but again, my own preferences will frequently lead me to state that I'm "more a bar kind of girl", in terms of going out with friends. Aggressive shouting still remains more problematic. No matter whether it's my family, an authority figure, a friend, stranger or some douchebag boyfriend doing the yelling, I still go into a state of mind where I break down, cry, and am vulnerable towards hurting myself out of resentment towards the way I am. Drawing others' attention to the shouting always makes it even worse as it contributes embarrassment as an additional unpleasant feeling. I don't like to be left alone in these states as loneliness is another additional horrible feeling to what already feels like an overwhelming amount. I'm aware a lot of people on the autistic spectrum don't like to be touched, but unusually, gentle holding and getting a hug if we've got a close enough relationship actually works well in calming me down. Otherwise, the next best thing someone can do is to take me somewhere as quiet as possible and sit with me, talking and listening in a calm and sympathetic way, giving as much assurance as possible until I feel better enough to regain self-control. Luckily enough, I have quite a few brilliant friends who know exactly how to do this should tough days occur.

What are you doing with your time presently?

I'm currently in my second year of a Drama degree at university, which I enjoy immensely. I've always loved to act, as it allows me to imagine how various characters in different scenarios would feel and behave, which I credit to improving my understanding of others socially and emotionally, hence making my personal interactions with others often more meaningful experiences. I'm very glad I recently had the opportunity to move out of my parents' house and give living with friends a go. It took a lot of determination to convince myself that I was eventually ready, but I'm loving the independence and fun it brings. I get sad sometimes but know there's trustworthy people I can talk to about, if need be. At this point, I'm worried about what I'm going to do for financial means once I can no longer stay a student, especially as I crave a lot of independence. This may be low self-esteem speaking but I don't think I'm good at much else aside from acting, which is obviously an insanely competitive industry. I'm a bit of a mess who occasionally feels broken. But at least it's a gradually improving, socially fulfilled, purple-haired mess who can feel mended by laughing. A lot.

The interviewee's positive attitude provides valuable insight into how keeping positive enables any individual to face extremely difficult situations.

INTERVIEW 6: ALEX

I will now interview someone who has had great success in writing his book which is also on the topic of coping with the education system whilst being on the spectrum. I would like to thank him for encouraging me to finish writing my own book, which has been a work in progress for the last ten years – and also for reminding me that we are all individual and we all have our own individual stories. He is 22 years old, and despite not going to university, he has been very successful so far in his chosen fields of television and radio presenting.

Introduce yourself

My name is Alex Manners and I am 22 from Solihull. I present talks on "My Life Living with Asperger's" to many different schools, universities and businesses and have just written and published a book called *That's Not Right! My Life Living with Asperger's*. I also host my own children's radio show every Sunday morning and have started my own "Autism & Football" campaign.

Tell me about your diagnosis

I have Asperger's syndrome, a form of autism.

What age were you when you got your diagnosis?

I was diagnosed with Asperger's when I was ten years old.

What are you studying at the moment?

I'm not currently studying or in any form of education.

Do you have any special interests?

My specialist interest is football. I go to bed thinking about football and I wake up thinking about football. During the 2018/19 season I completed a quest to watch a match at all 92 English Football League grounds. I can name all of these 92 grounds along with their capacities. My bedroom is full of all the shirts, programmes, badges and memorabilia that I have collected over the years. Football has also given me another focus in life and has been a great way for me to relieve my stresses.

Do you have any sensory difficulties?

Certain noises really affect me, such as the sound of a ticking radiator or a ticking clock. A ticking radiator sounds like someone is right next to my ear banging on a drum as loudly as they can. I also can't stand the feel of thick, itchy cotton labels in the back of shirts, or the seams at the end of socks. My grandma often has to unstitch the seams and sew them on back to front. At school I hated the feeling of clay when it became all dry on your hands. This is why ceramics was always one of my worst subjects when I was in secondary school.

What did you enjoy most about school?

To me, school felt like prison, so there were not many parts of the day I actually enjoyed. However, one thing I used to enjoy about school was a lunch club that we had called "The Den". Lots of my friends used to go there and we always had fun playing dodgeball and table tennis. In fact, for some of my friends this was the only part of the day that they enjoyed. During my time at secondary school, I used to take a taxi to and from school with about five other people. The taxi rides used to be great fun as I got on really well with everyone. The taxi journeys used to relax me before I arrived at school and many of the people in my taxi went to "The Den" at lunch times with me.

What did you find challenging about school?

Two of the things that I found most challenging about school were the homework and the uniform. If I am wearing dark-coloured clothes such as blacks and greys like the colours of my school uniform, then I feel like I am hiding my personality and can become depressed. This is why I never felt myself whilst at school. I used to think that school was for work and home was for play. To have to do more work once I got home used to get me really stressed. I would spend lessons worrying about whether or not we would get any homework at the end. Subsequently I was not able to concentrate on the work. Many other aspects of school used to also make my anxiety and stress go through the roof. These included having tales told on me, teachers who I felt did not treat me in a nice way or who did not acknowledge my Asperger's, and timetable changes.

What are you doing with your life presently?

At the moment, I present talks on "My Life Living with Asperger's" and "My Time at School". I present these talks to many large businesses, insurance companies, councils, universities and to teachers and pupils. I also take along copies of my book called *That's Not Right! My Life Living with Asperger's*. My book is also available on Amazon. As well as presenting talks, I also present my very own children's radio show on Solihull Radio every Sunday morning.

I have started on a number of projects to ensure that rail travel is made more accessible to people with less visible impairments. Like the work I do with football clubs, I have done the same with companies looking to re-develop train stations. My ambition is to be a TV presenter and I have had numerous interviews on the TV and radio about my Asperger's as well as having written many articles for magazines and websites. I also appeared on series ten of *The Undateables* on Channel 4. As you can tell, I am always very busy and will never give up until my ambitions have been achieved.

Why did you decide not to go to university?

I chose not to go to university because I did not think it would benefit my career. My ambition is to be a TV presenter, and I believe it is my personality, hard work, determination and real-life experience that will enable me to achieve my dreams and not a qualification.

What do you think schools can do to support people on the spectrum?

I think that in schools it is the teachers that make the biggest difference to a child with learning difficulties. I think teachers should have training on what autism/Asperger's is and the impacts it can have on different people. I also think that, above all, they need to have empathy for the children they are teaching and allow the rules to be changed or amended to give those children the support that they need. These will most often be small changes that won't affect anyone else such as allowing them to listen to music for five minutes or not having to do their top button up. These changes will often be beneficial for everyone.

Alex decided not to go to university and is doing well, which is perfectly fine. There is often a belief that you have to go to university to succeed or to be viewed as intelligent for having a qualification. Neither of those things are true, and there are many successful intelligent people who did not go to university. (There are also many people with qualifications who went to university and are absolute idiots in high-powered jobs, but to name some I would have to get into politics, so I shall not go there.) Each person is different. Not everybody needs a university qualification in order to be successful and if you are hardworking and ambitious you can create your own success.

CHAPTER 4
UNIVERSITY
(AGES 18–21)

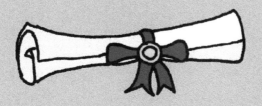

CHAPTER 4
UNIVERSITY (AGES 18-21)

A STATISTIC AND AN INTRODUCTION

"In 2008 2.4% of the student population were said to be on the autism spectrum."

Journal of Autism and Developmental Disorders 2019

In this chapter I am going to discuss university life and how challenging that is for any young person but especially for someone with some of the difficulties that I've been describing throughout the book. Again, I would like to remind the reader that what worked for me may not work for every young person on the spectrum; I am merely providing insight into a complicated social system with its own set of rules and processes.

This chapter has been my favourite one to write and also my favourite one to live, in many respects. I hope this will guide you through the process a little and show you some of the anxieties that you might face if you are on the spectrum and also some of the things that your parents may worry about too. I'd also like to point out that these anxieties are faced by many students and parents who have no experience with autism at all. So without further ado, here we go folks: the big chapter! Let's sit back and have a bit of fun. Mind the anxiety, though – there's always a little of that lurking somewhere about.

A POEM ABOUT UNIVERSITY

On the first day I was nervous, I knew nobody there
I'd moved to London and I was scared.
I had moved to escape from my troubles and fears
But they had travelled with me and so had the tears.
The sensory challenges, and difficulties making friends,
The apologising for existing and feeling the need to make amends.
I studied Drama and English Lit
In many lectures I had to sit.
I read many books and learnt new things
I learnt to let go of mother's apron strings.
I learnt about life like cooking and paying bills,
I learnt about positive thinking and new social skills.
The things that I learnt there I use every day
And despite the depression I wouldn't have done it any other way.

IS UNIVERSITY THE RIGHT THING FOR YOU?

Is university the right thing to do or can you go out and make money without gaining that qualification? Will you succeed or won't you? Since the fees have gone up, is it advisable to do a subject that you'll be guaranteed a job in, or do you follow your passions and take subjects like Drama or Film?

Young people on the spectrum, I would advise you to go with what you feel would work for you. Do a subject that you enjoy if you want to go to university, but do not feel pressured into going either. University brings out the good and the bad in all of us, but it isn't for everyone. A degree doesn't mean everything, and you're not a failure if you don't go. You have to do what you feel will make you happiest. Your mental health and wellbeing are more important than any career or job you may have. But if your reason for not going to university is that it is scary and makes you anxious, I would suggest that you try it and see what it's like for a while. You shouldn't avoid things that make you anxious; you learn far more when you go out and experience new things.

The great thing about having Asperger's is that we are a determined bunch, and even when it feels like the world is crashing down around us, we still push on until the end. You can do anything (and everything if you put your mind to it). As I said in previous chapters, there may be limits to what you can achieve due to your disability, but that should not stop you from experiencing everything you can. Do not feel pressured by my words if the world feels too much for you. By all means rest; your mental wellbeing is most important – but I always say that my Asperger's doesn't define me; it's part of me. It does not stop me from doing anything that I want to do. I fully embrace the quirky weirdness of it all, and I know, if it wasn't for my Asperger's and my determination I wouldn't be where I am today.

Parents, I think if your child is academically able and wants to go to university, then the answer is always yes. If you cannot afford it, do not worry. The student loan only has to be paid back once your child has a job paying them over £27,295 a year, and in the current economic climate that is unlikely, so the money is neither here nor there. Yes, your child will succeed if they are determined. You cannot give them success; you can only help them to prepare as much as you can. Let your child study what they want and certainly do not force them to go to university. If it is not right for them, then they shouldn't go, but equally do not stop them from going if they want to either.

FINDING ACCOMMODATION: HALLS OF RESIDENCE AND HOW TO APPLY

Before coming to London, I had to go through a process to apply for accommodation at the university. Universities often have a range of accommodation and when you receive the application form or find it on the university's website (however your institution wishes to do it) you can pick which accommodation you want in order of preference. I got to live in a house called Pooley House because it was the best halls to fit my needs, although it was one of the university's most expensive living arrangements. Each room had an en-suite shower and its own fridge and internet cable. Pooley was big so that I didn't get anxious when living alone, and the en-suite shower meant that I didn't have to worry about sharing it with anyone. It made me feel anxious that you could not go and view your accommodation beforehand, though. You viewed it online through a virtual tour, paid your money and moved in on the move-in date.

I was very nervous about the idea of living in halls of residence, and I found it very hard to deal with at first, being constantly anxious about who was coming into my space. I think universities could make this better by having at least two students with learning differences living in one house, because then they'd know that they were not alone and would have someone else that they could relate to.

MOVING IN AND ANXIETY AROUND CHANGE

I had got accepted on a joint honours course studying Drama and English Literature. I'd have liked to have studied just Drama, but I thought that Dad would disapprove and I also didn't know what kind of job I could get from studying Drama alone; so I combined both of my interests. Mum ordered all of my household appliances and Dad agreed to pay for all of my books in the first year, as well as giving me spending money and buying me a brand-new printer.

I was very nervous a few nights before the move to London. I went to my Dad's to say goodbye and I had nightmares on his sofa all night. I also acquired tonsillitis and was exhausted from coughing. When the time came to move I was very tearful. Mum and I moved my stuff in over the course of a few trips back and forth – for one thing, I wanted to go to a friend's party to say goodbye on one of the evenings. To start with, Mum, my boyfriend and I moved half of my stuff in, collected my student card and keys, and then went for a drink in the student union.

I got upset and angry whilst we were moving stuff in because my boyfriend and my friend knocked on the doors of my housemates and made friends with them but I sat in my room sorting my stuff because I didn't know what to say to them. I knew nobody and was very distressed when my family finally left me on my own. This is a very normal thing and later I found that a lot of my colleagues who weren't on the spectrum had been anxious, homesick and upset too. I cried for a while and then decided to go to one of the freshers' week parties.

FRESHERS' WEEK

I loved freshers' week. Freshers' week is basically induction week at university, but there are a load of parties in the evenings and you meet a whole lot of new people. That first freshers' week party I went to was a traffic light party at the union bar. A traffic light party is where you wear a shirt in accordance with your relationship status: green if you're single, red if you're taken and orange if you're being mysterious. I decided to wear orange because nobody knew anything about me at university. By the end of the traffic light party,

I felt like I'd already known my housemates for my whole life; we got on so well.

Let me explain a little about freshers' week. I think it is very important that everybody gets involved in freshers' week, whether they are on the spectrum or not, because it is the first taste of university life you will get. You'll make all sorts of new friends and you'll have a lot of fun, but you also need to be very careful whilst you're going about it. There is the potential that you may end up being unsafe if you behave in a silly fashion, but if you are careful then it is fun and rewarding. I want to give you a flavour of what student life is like but also place an emphasis on safety. Freshers' week is only fun if you are careful and keep your wits about you.

The second party of the week was pound-a-pint night in the union bar (which they called Manic Mondays or Happy Mondays back then). I went there alone – not recommended if you'd like to get home safely – and got drunkenly lost on the way home because I couldn't find my way back to my halls of residence. I really missed my Mum again that night and I nearly went back home due to being lonely, but I'm glad I did not.

On the Tuesday of freshers' week we had a bonding session in the flat because all of my course mates had gone to a club but none of my flat had got tickets; so we stayed in and the two of our housemates who were American exchange students taught us a new drinking game called "the ring of fire". Basically, the last person to pick out a king from the pack of cards has to drink everything that's in the middle cup – and oh my goodness, do you get drunk! I never used to drink that much until I went to university. I used to use it to deal with my social anxiety. Drink made me confident, loud and crazy; so I used it to help me most often in a club or pub setting, anywhere where I was expected to dance. Drink helped to combat my anxiety and phobia of meeting new people. Now that I am older I do not need drink to help me make friends, and so my drinking has decreased as my age has increased.

During freshers' week I enrolled on my course, I got to look around the Drama department, and I met my new professors. I met my advisor from my English course and went to a talk given by the headmaster. His talk was about graduation mainly. He told us that we should be aiming to achieve that goal and showed us pictures of the ceremony. At the time I thought I'd never reach that goal. We were given exam numbers. Mine was HC613. This made me feel very sad and lonely; I still didn't have a firm group of friends and I thought all anybody would ever know me as was a university exam number.

I joined loads of societies during the week: the music society, film society, the theatre company and the student magazine to name but a few. I made a Facebook profile because it was the only way that people communicated with each other about events and now I am slowly trying to limit the amount I use Facebook.

On the final day of freshers' week I auditioned for the University Players' production of *Twelfth Night*, but because I had never really acted Shakespeare much before I didn't get the role. (Now, I'm better versed in it after completing my dissertation on Shakespeare.)

I went home to Birmingham after freshers' week still not feeling like I knew many people, but I was enjoying myself immensely. I'd never been able to plan my own things before and not have to worry about what my family wanted me to do. I felt like an adult for the first time in my life.

And later, in my second and third years I went on to volunteer to help run freshers' week as a member of Freshers' Crew, doing things like helping the first years move into halls, and that was really fun too.

LIVING ON CAMPUS

I found living in halls of residence strange. There were seven of us living in a flat, three boys and four girls. Two of the boys were American exchange students in the first semester, and in the second semester we had students from different countries and cultures living with us. I found it difficult to start with, because there were always people that you didn't know coming in and out of the flat. The cleaners came in every Monday and the electricians were always in. As there were seven people, they each had a set of friends and so there were always loads of people in the flat. Also, there were house parties constantly and you found yourself complaining about other people's music. After a while I did get used to living in halls, but when I first moved in it was very hard to deal with.

Nevertheless, my university campus was lovely. I had especially wanted to go to a campus university rather than a university where the departments were spread all over the city because I struggle with direction and locating the buildings would have added a new layer of stress. The campus was pretty much in a great circle, so you were never very far from help and support. You had the counselling services and the disabilities service on campus and also the sports hall and the great hall where a lot of the activities and society meetings took place. There was a small student shop where you could buy your food and toiletries from, and there were coffee shops and a WHSmiths so that you could buy your books. There was also a small laundry room and a great big library so that you could study.

Also, living on campus meant that your friends were always in close proximity, and it was nice to just have to walk to their flats to watch films or have dinner together. I enjoyed going to my friends' flats for various parties and socials, but I soon realised how much my mother did for me at home and I started to miss her terribly. I first discovered that you had to separate your black clothes from your whites and your colours when doing my laundry at university. I also learnt not to leave my things unattended as somebody took all of my laundry out of the machine when it was finished and it fell on the floor as I was not there to pick it up. I also started to learn to cook at university, and that gave me great difficulties.

LEARNING TO COOK

I did not take to cooking very easily and I remember having to phone my mother to ask her how to boil a potato so that I could make myself some mash. I also bought myself a whole chicken and I had not read the label stating that it was halal meat and I tried to fry the whole thing in a pan. There was also one particular occasion I remember when a colleague, who was in my class at university and who I liked a lot, decided after one class that he was going to come to my flat for breakfast and he particularly wanted a bacon and egg sandwich. Well, I never used to eat bacon until I came to university, and I didn't have any so I had to borrow some from my housemate, and then I sheepishly just stood staring at the eggs in the pot. My colleague realised that I didn't know what to do, so he laughed at me and stood teaching me how to cook eggs on a hob. Looking back now, I think that every day of my life I use the knowledge I gained from my time at university, even if it's about practical things like cooking – so I think it was a really good experience for me.

A lot of the food that I ate in my first year was frozen food that I had bought from the student shop (and later in my final year I got so desperate for money that I remember eating chocolate spread out of a jar for three days because I had too much pride to ask Mum or Dad for money before the student loan came in).

I struggled to follow recipes when I was younger and I did not really learn to cook until I was in my late 20s and I began to experiment with recipes for shortbread or cheesecake. A word of advice for current students: cooking when you are drunk is a very bad idea! I once tried to cook spaghetti Bolognaise after drinking and I woke up the next morning to find I had not turned any of the appliances on and there was minced meat all over my kitchen floor. It was not a good look, I tell you.

Students, if you are struggling to learn how to cook, then YouTube is a fabulous resource. When I was growing up YouTube was not as widely accessed as it is now, and I bet if I had YouTube during my first degree I would not have had so many cooking disasters. It is advisable to start to learn when you are young, though, as cooking is a skill you will need throughout your life. I guess what I'm trying to say is that cooking is a skill which improves with practice and moving away from home is a good time to learn how to cook or improve your existing skills.

Parents, trying to teach your children to cook from a young age is a good idea as it empowers them, gives them the life skills they will need and helps you too because you can get them to do little jobs to prepare the dinner, such as cutting carrots or peeling potatoes.

I also think that schools should teach a full Life Skills class. Whilst they did do Cooking and Design Technology in my school, these were individual subjects which you could pick and were not mandatory. I believe that all children should learn how to cook, sew, clean, manage taxes, pay bills and be equipped with the general life skills that they will need for survival as an adult.

LIVING IN LONDON

Looking back, I think that living in London was a challenge for me all by itself. I remember when I got fined on the bus because I did not know how to load money onto my Oyster card. If you don't know, an Oyster card is London's equivalent of a bus pass but you can use it on the tubes (the London Underground) as well. I soon realised what an incredibly big city London is. In the first few weeks of living in London I went back home to see Mum and my boyfriend, and I didn't know that you had to be on time for your coach otherwise National Express would charge you for another ticket. So, I used my autism as an excuse and cried to get a refund. Now, folks, I do not condone using being on the spectrum as an excuse for bad behaviour, but if you can use it to your advantage and beat the system full of ignorant people then by all means do so – especially if it means you get refunds or reduced train tickets.

All of the new sights and sounds affected me in a sensory way, and in my halls of residence I began to punch the walls when the fire alarms sounded. They happened so often, especially in the first week, due to students starting to learn how to cook and failing miserably. I hated the alarm sounds because they hurt my ears, and when it first happened I was afraid and rocked in my room. I did not know I was hypersensitive to sound then. I only found that out through going to research at the National Autistic Society when I started to write this book. Eventually I got used to the alarms and even had time to grab my video camera and film one so that my group of friends could relive the memory once we moved out of halls. When we moved into a shared house the fire alarms didn't happen at all – one of the many advantages of living in a shared house as opposed to halls of residence.

Living in East London was difficult as the levels of crime were high. There were always police sirens sounding down my road during the first year of university, and during the second year there was a stabbing round the corner from our student accommodation and we were robbed one evening.

London was a fast-paced environment, which meant that I was always on the move all the time. I started to lose a lot of weight in London as I was walking everywhere, which was one of the positives about it, but I remember feeling tired all the time and I began to drink Red Bull a lot.

Sometimes I wonder whether going to Worcester University might have been better as it is quieter than London, but I learnt a lot of things about myself and my coping strategies during my time in London, so overall I would not rate it as a bad experience.

NIGHTS OUT AND CLUBBING

Of course, there are loads of places in London for nights out and to go clubbing. I personally have learnt that, as a rule, I do not like clubbing because of the loud music and being anxious when getting separated from groups of friends. However, I think it is something everyone should experience because it is something that you can say you have done. Also, I have had some good experiences. The first time I went clubbing in London was to Fabric in Farringdon in 2008. I went with some people in my Drama class and we had a really good night. I also enjoyed going to a club called Ruby Blue in Leicester Square, which we went to quite a bit. I familiarised myself with the layout and I grew to like it because it was routine that we went there to celebrate occasions. There are all sorts of clubs for all sorts of musical tastes, and the only bad thing is going home at three in the morning and having to take the 25 bus in the freezing cold back to your student accommodation. Again, it's advisable to go with a group of people because getting home on your own is a nightmare. I feel nervous and anxious in clubs if I ever get separated from the people that I'm with. I felt anxious in a lot of social situations and I used alcohol to combat the nerves and social phobia during my degree.

There were also many other events I went to, such as a fancy-dress party for my Law housemate's birthday and Boat Balls where you had to dress up in your smartest dresses or suits and dance the night away on a boat that takes you along the River Thames. There was also the university sports night which was called "Hail Mary". Hail Mary happened once a month, and if you were in a sports team you showed off about how awesome your team was. I was always proud of my fencing team and so Hail Mary was always a regular occurrence.

But on one of the nights out at the start of my second year I went to Zoo Bar for my friend's birthday party and I ended up going to A&E that night with a friend because he'd decided to try to fight a gang on the way home and they got the better of him. He was ok in the end, but we stayed there all night and I went to my lecture next day with blood stains on the front of my shirt from where I had held him. (Don't worry, I wore a jacket over it.)

So, there are things you need to watch out for. I would advise students to be careful and go out in groups. Never go alone, especially if you've only just met the person that's invited you to a party. Do not get involved in gangs, and if you stay together you will have fun in a safe, controlled environment.

DRINK AND DRUGS

Drinking can be a major problem at university, because it's an activity that is highly encouraged by everyone. During the first half of my time at university, my drinking got worse and worse – I'll talk more about my personal problem with alcohol a bit later. We found ourselves using it as a form of entertainment. I liked the feeling of being out of control when I was drunk. I liked getting silly and emotional, and liked it because everyone tells the truth more when they are drunk. I still like to drink now, but as an adult I do not think I have an alcohol addiction – because when it's not available I don't need it. I do not like most types of alcohol, and as an adult I've made it a rule to only drink something if I like the taste of it rather than drinking for the sake of it. I've taught myself to like beer and ale. I like vodka when it's mixed with orange juice or Ribena. I also like alcopops, but my favourite drink of all time is Jägermeister. It is a herbal, medicinal spirit. I especially like it when it's mixed with Red Bull because it tastes very sweet. Originally, I drank because I didn't have to be myself, but now I am reasonably ok with being me and I would like to give up drinking altogether because I've reached an age where hangovers hurt so much that they are not worth the few hours' fun the night before.

Students, please do not feel as if you have to drink at university. I know it is hard because it is encouraged a lot, but never feel like you have to do anything you do not want to. If you're going out, always think about how you are going to get home at the end of the night. Always go with a group of friends, and remember that eating is not cheating. Always eat before you go out and remember to drink water as it helps keep you hydrated. You will be less sick this way, I promise.

Parents, don't worry if your child is getting drunk at university. They will have a lot of pressures that they are dealing with and this is something, unlike their sexuality and gender, which they will grow out of. Seriously, ask my dad if you are concerned. It's just another thing to experience and as long as they are careful then they will be fine. It is much wiser letting them do it safely in your knowledge than having them do it behind your back and getting ill. The same can be said of drugs. Both are passing stages and people usually grow out of it. If you find that you do develop an addiction to either, there are helplines that you can call and professionals that you can see. Please do so sooner rather than later as the quicker you access help the quicker you can solve the problem.

Drugs are easy to access in London and so you do have to be careful. Students, if you are trying drugs, always do so in a safe environment such as your room. If you can't do that, make sure you have a friend that you trust who you know will support you to get back home. Do not get into money difficulties through trying drugs; it is never worth the stress. If you do find that you are becoming addicted, then talk to your university counsellor or doctor immediately. Finishing your degree will be worth more than the evening of fun that drugs may bring you.

Parents, please don't worry about this. Not many people become addicted to drugs through trying them at university. In fact, if you think back, I am sure that you may have tried something at some point; so don't despair, just talk with your child and be there for them when they need you. They are growing up and becoming educated adults. Just be there for them, enjoy the ride and take pride in their success. You may be thinking, gosh this all sounds a little too much. I don't want my child getting involved in any of this stuff, so I won't be letting them go to university. Stop those thoughts right there and carry on reading. University is not just about getting drunk; there are serious aspects as well. The course work is really hard and there is a lot of reading to go with it. Students feel immense pressure when there are deadlines looming. You may have experienced all of these yourselves and have just forgotten what it's like. I'll be talking a lot more about those serious aspects as we go on.

FIRST LECTURES AND CLASSES

So, if you're wondering about how much work I actually did at university, the answer is lots of it. By the time freshers' week ended there was already a general atmosphere of nervousness as students knew they would have to buckle down and study. I quickly began to feel the pressure of deadlines and exam stress. But let me tell you a bit here about my first classes. It's the very first lectures that I will never forget, because I remember thinking that I was too stupid to be at university. Lots of people think this, but I remember feeling quite alone with the thought. I'll never forget not knowing a soul in Drama class and then coming out feeling like I'd known my course mates my whole life. For our module "Making Theatre Work" we had a wonderful teacher called Jim. We had to research a theatre practitioner called Robert Lepage on the first day. In the first class, Jim asked us about our skills and he made me bring in my clarinet to play it in front of the entire class; I felt exhilarated. University teaching was nothing like anything I'd ever experienced before.

That feeling also frightened me, because everyone was so disorganised when we worked together for Drama and I was not used to working in a large group of 30. So, there were many times when I ended up crying, because my Asperger self didn't like change and conflict. I always find getting back into studying after long breaks very tough and challenging and so I struggled in my English lectures for a few weeks before I found the right speed to work at. I loved the Reading, Theory and Interpretation module, because even though it was hard I had a really good lecturer to help me out.

Reading, Theory and Interpretation–seminar leader*: I taught Maddy in her first year of university, as her seminar leader for the Reading, Theory and Interpretation course. This is a challenging course, in which students are introduced to a lot of new texts and ideas very quickly, and it can knock the confidence of some students at first. My main recollection of Maddy is that this was never the case for her – she was always one of the most engaged students in the seminar group, and always seemed prepared to tackle new ideas. We read Robinson Crusoe near the beginning of the course, and she sent me a piece she'd written on why she hated the text – it's always nice when students have that kind of original and lively interests in the texts we discuss. She certainly participated in discussion – I remember she sometimes tended to address her thoughts directly to me rather than to other students, but this is by no means uncommon. I thought Kieran and Charlie were some of her closest friends in the group.*

I did not know Maddy was autistic, and in fact I was quite surprised to hear that she was. I suspect this is due to my probably stereotypical preconceptions about autism – that an autistic person would lack social skills and find it difficult to empathise with people – and I don't see those qualities in Maddy. I also suspect people are generally more likely to see autistic characteristics in boys, as the condition is most often discussed as being experienced by men.

As to the question of whether autism should be diagnosed – I don't really feel qualified to answer that question. I suppose that as autism is a scale, I do wonder about the point when a personality type becomes a condition, and whether there is the danger of trying to categorise people rather than accepting difference. However, if a diagnosis can help people to achieve their full potential, then it must be worthwhile.

SOCIETIES, FRIENDSHIP AND FITTING IN

I mentioned some of the societies that I joined when I talked about freshers' week earlier; it was soon time for me to attend some of the sessions of those societies and I was worried about fitting in. Well, the term "university" stands for everything that's universal and I began to learn about things that I'd never taken an interest in before. I didn't know that much about politics then and I certainly didn't know about capitalism, Karl Marx or the proletariat. I started to learn about ideologies and cultural capital. I joined a merry band of socialist students to try and figure it all out, but I didn't get very far. My first hug at university was from one of the boys who had joined the socialist party. It was special to me, because that was the first time that I felt like I really belonged at university and that I was not alone.

I wasn't bullied at university; it was one of the only places where I felt accepted, but there were still a lot of prejudice and people who judged and criticised. I went to a party at the union called "Heroes and Villains". It was a fancy-dress party, and I wore a black cloak with a top that said "I am my own hero" on it. I was sad because in the morning one of the lads phoned me telling me that my classmates in Drama didn't take me seriously because I was on the spectrum. He was trying to warn me about their prejudice, and it was then that I realised that I wasn't at university to be liked; I was there to get a degree. Students must stay true to themselves and passionately stand up for what they believe in. They shouldn't try to change for other people or they'll wind up very miserable and feel like they have no identity anymore, except for the group of people they hang out with.

Although I wasn't bullied, I did have some troubles with people not understanding my behaviours and not being able to help me through. There were a few of my friendships that broke down because of this, one of which I am still very sad about, to this day. Despite the setbacks, I made some very good friends in first year of university – one of whom was a Law student who I met in halls, and she later became one of my housemates in my final year because we got on that well. I also met a Drama and French student – she played the lead female role in *Knocking Over the Chair*, which was the first play that I wrote and had performed at university. I also made friends with a Biomed student and a single honours Drama student who went on to become my housemates in the second year.

Law housemate: Although Maddy is not the first person that I have met with autism, she is definitely the closest I have ever felt to such an individual. Living with her during our first year of university meant that we got to know each other very well. She is a great friend to have: caring, always tells you what she thinks, and above all always makes you laugh, especially the cow obsession and drunken nights. We have our ups and downs – but which friendship doesn't?

I think it is safe to say that finding friendship groups and worries about fitting in are natural worries that any young person going to university might face. Students on the spectrum, don't worry if it takes you a while to find a group of friends; you want the right ones that will support you, not friends who will judge you and talk about you behind your back. You want friends who will help rather than hinder you, and it does not mean you are a loner or an outcast if it takes you a while to find them. I would say that it means that you respect yourself and you know what type of people you want in your life. Never stay friends with someone who mocks you for being on the spectrum. They are not your friend in the long run.

INDEPENDENCE (AND PAYING THE BILLS)

I bet this all seems like a lot to take in: moving to London, living in halls, joining societies, studying, making friends, going to parties, learning life skills... Well, it was, but it strengthened my character and made me a better person. Looking back, I think that first year of university was moulding me into the adult that I am today. I started watching the news and reading newspapers. I was becoming more independent – I had to start paying my rent; I had to check the post box for letters, bills and documents from the uni; I had to learn to go to the doctors by myself and book appointments; I had to learn to do things like call the electricians when our freezer broke; and I had to learn how to do my own laundry. I didn't even know how to use the washing machine when I first came to university. Now I do it like it's second nature. I didn't have my mother to drive me everywhere, like she usually did at home, so I had to walk everywhere. I had to get supports for my feet because they didn't like the daily abuse that I was giving them. I began to take an interest in festivals that we didn't celebrate at home, such as Pancake Day and Thanksgiving, and, pretty much, I lived how I wanted to.

True, university is a scary, terrifying experience – yes, don't get me wrong – but that's because it's all about changes. I had all of these experiences because of change, and even though I still don't like change I feel that I wouldn't have experienced what I had without it. Even though university is scary, it's also a wonderful experience, and, like my Dad says, I grew up more there in a few years then I ever did when I was at home.

I remember when I began to realise that I had to start to pay bills, and it really frightened me the day I got my first letter from a water bill company right after a really complicated lecture.

What can I say about paying the bills? Well, it is a frightening concept for us adults that children don't realise exists until they start to live on their own. I really think colleges should offer Life Skills classes which include bills, money management and paying taxes. How can you live an adult life if you don't know how to pay a bill? Well, I did not and the idea that I had to pay to watch my television, have a glass of water or have gas and electric was terrifying to me. I got some good advice from the student support centre, though, and as in my first year I was responsible for my own money, all I had to do once I received the letters was call up the companies and arrange a monthly payment. Simple really, isn't it? I went back to my lectures in confidence knowing that my water, gas and electric were set up on a direct debit until the end of the year, which I would change once I got into shared accommodation.

It was my second year where things got a bit complicated and as I was living in a shared house all five of us needed to pay the bills. Some house members were telling me they could not pay on time etc. and as it was my name on the accounts, I ended up paying a lot more than I should have done. The only advice I can suggest for students is never agree to put your name on an account in a shared house. By all means, put the correct money in the group pot – in fact, I'd encourage this – but never take full responsibility as it will ultimately end in arguments. If you are as bad at mathematics as I am, definitely do not take responsibility for the house accounts. If you need more advice on how to pay bills, you should be able to find help at your university. I found there was always somebody in the student support centre to speak with who would offer me good advice.

FINDING PART-TIME WORK

Finding part-time work whilst studying at university can be a really positive thing to do, both for the sake of the experience and your CV and for the extra money. But it can also be a difficulty. We had a careers advice service, but they were not particularly helpful if you did not have your five-year life plan set out ahead of you. Art students were given various sheets with jobs that you could do with an arts degree on them which we were encouraged to look at, but most of them required you to do another degree or did not sound very appealing. Nobody showed me how to write a CV or how to fill out a covering letter and I taught myself everything that I needed to know. After a lot of searching, I eventually found a part-time job as a ticket seller in a club, but we were never given the money we made. I then sought help from the disability department and they found me a job as a student mentor, helping other students with Asperger's on campus to make friends, settle in and organise their workloads. I did this for a year.

As I've already mentioned, in my second and third years I also volunteered to be part of the Freshers' Crew for freshers' week and that was really fun. I hadn't even known that they existed in my first year. You applied via the student union and if you were accepted you received training to learn about all the buildings on campus and about all of the social events going on during freshers' week. The union staff were lovely people. We got loads of benefits out of being on Freshers' Crew, such as a T-shirt and hoodie and a couple of free entries into the union for the week. I made loads of new friends and felt like I was helping the university community. It was a really good experience and beneficial to everyone involved.

I also worked as a volunteer for an online site called BeatBullying where I offered a supportive ear to youngsters who were being bullied either at home or at school. It was there that I first learnt how to make safeguarding referrals and that I felt immense value when being able to support others through times of stress and difficulty.

I think finding part-time work is difficult whilst you are studying, but like anything you just need to persevere. I would advise students to use this time to gain experience: do apprenticeships, work as weekend events assistants, do free courses in your spare time. Anything you can do to build up your CV and gain the experience that you need is excellent. It does not matter if you don't know what you want to do in five years' time, but you do need to have experience and work on building yourself a decent profile. Once you work full time Monday to Friday, you will have a lot less time to work on this stuff than you do whilst you are a student; and don't you complain to me about your 9am lectures that finish at ten so you can go home and get some shut eye, because believe me you are living a fine life.

INTERVIEW 7: CATHERINE

I will now interview another colleague who is on the spectrum. She moved to Reykjavik, Iceland to study her PhD and has experienced similar challenges to me – but even further away from home as she is originally from Warwickshire.

Introduce yourself

Hi, my name is Catherine Langford. I was born in Warwickshire, England in the early 90s. I went to a private school in Coventry (yes, it's private but I wouldn't be here now if it wasn't for the amazing support I gained from that school). I went to sixth form at the same school, took a gap year (not a conventional one, I might add), and then studied for four years for a MSc Palaeontology degree. And if that wasn't enough, I'm now a 20-something year old, presently hopping between Iceland and England whilst I study my PhD! I have a range of diagnoses, but presently Asperger's is the easiest one to explain. I enjoy the occupation of dressing up as historical people, grabbing weapons (all safety checked, I assure you), and then bashing the living daylights out of each other (within the standard health and safety event rules, of course). I enjoy baking, writing, listening to books and watching the *Game Grumps* Let's Play series (and cartoons), listening [to] (sometimes playing) music, and walking my dog.

What is your diagnosis?

Oooh I have a range. To be honest, I always feel that it's a checklist of weirdness that makes me who I am! The earliest diagnosis I can remember was my dyspraxia, and I remember getting really good therapy for that at one of the local places in Coventry. Then, it was around primary school, I think, I was diagnosed with dyslexia – I remember going into a special room and having private lessons with a couple of other students. We were totally the cool kids! However, I wasn't diagnosed with my Asperger's syndrome until the middle of secondary school. To be honest, I am glad that I was finally diagnosed. I have no idea who figured it out, but it has made life a lot easier. I'm not going to lie, my mum is a GP, and my dad worked in schools with kids with learning disabilities, so it has meant that I am lucky enough to have family, from the start, who know more and are super-understanding. However, it wasn't until just before I started university that I was diagnosed with DiGeorge's syndrome. It finally made sense of everything, my myriad of learning difficulties, and my selection of underlying health issues. It's rarer than Asperger's (1 in 1000) but it doesn't mean that I'm any different – well not that different!

What age were you when you were diagnosed?

I think I was diagnosed around the middle of secondary school – which really helped as I do believe it was just before my GCSEs. This meant I was able to develop different types of strategies to help. But it also helped me understand what I was going through at the time. During that period my hands felt like they were falling apart, as (until then) I had been undiagnosed for my obsessive-compulsive disorder (OCD) as well. I was so glad I was diagnosed around that time because I was able to start preparing myself for the future ahead, with knowing why I struggle with things more than others.

What are you studying at the moment?

I'm actually studying for my PhD for some reason (I'm kidding I love it). I wanted to go back to university. Presently I am studying the early human occupation of an area of North China – using tiny little microfossils to try and unravel what on earth (pun intended) is going on with the ancient environment at a particular period in time.

What do you enjoy about university?

I enjoy that I can work on my own, in my own free time, and I only have to work for my own gain – and if I don't work hard enough, my loss. I feel that even though university is a steep learning curve, it really helps with your confidence.

During my undergraduate and my master's course, even though it was hard graft at the start, there [were] lights at the end of the tunnel when I got to the finishing line. I found that once I got settled (and got out of my dire student housing) I really found my pace. I can owe a lot of my success to the people I met at university and the people who increased my confidence. I think if it wasn't for the Druam re-enactors I would not have had the confidence that I have today.

I also loved my department and the people in my department. I feel that the Geology department at the University of Leicester was key for my enjoyment at university. In itself, it was a medium-sized department, and it was an easy department to work around. It was easy to get to know the building and then I felt I could get to know the lecturers. Most people would probably think that it was nerdy getting to know the staff, but I feel that makes me feel far more confident within my surroundings. The head of first/fourth year has become one of my good friends, and I got to know the technical staff too.

The fact that the University of Leicester department had such great people (I really can't stress that enough) meant that I didn't feel alone. It also helped that there was an accessibility area, with dedicated staff members to help every step of the way; this made me feel even more comfortable.

I mainly enjoyed the friends that I made at university. I have a firm, small and close-knit group of friends from school and before university but I had never been very social within the rest of the school year. For the first time in my life, I felt comfortable enough to make friends with the entire year – it was probably because I was a lot more kinda confident than I had been at school. I made my best friend at university. We try and meet every time I am home in Iceland, and make time for each other. She's helped me through so much. For example, when my grandma passed away in my second year of uni she was late to our lecture the next day because she had gotten up early to bake me a cake.

I also met my long-term boyfriend at university. People say that Asperger's people can't deal with relationships. However, I think that they are incorrect. It's hard to get it started, and I was so panicky with everything! – although now we're settled I know that I love him to pieces and he's a wonderful person. He puts up with so much from me and I just think that he's perfect.

Have you found it difficult to make friends at university?

I think, during my undergraduate degree I did probably have issues with making friends. I was probably a bit too loud and overbearing in the first few weeks when I started. I can't remember really because presently, due to the societies, department and friends that I made at the University of Leicester, I have become very outgoing. I try to forget about the bad times and focus on the better times. I had a solid group of friends and was settled and happy in Leicester University. It was a tough year to actually get through, but when I was on the roll it was good to get into the flow of things.

However, I have found it much harder to make friends whilst I have been doing my PhD. I think when you are in a different country it is a slightly different environment. I had to get used to a lot of new things very quickly but I have had help from some really good people. I still found it difficult to settle in. I think it has been a far greater learning curve than when I moved to Leicester. I've been in Iceland for a year and a half now and am finally feeling somewhat settled.

What were the biggest challenges you faced at university?

I will warn you in advance, bullies follow you everywhere. I don't want sympathy but I have had my fair share throughout the years. However, I had an absolute arsehole in university – to the point where I didn't want to go back – but then I realised that most of the year was on my side and that gave me the confidence to overcome his pettiness. The fact that the rest of the year (and professors) were supportive enough to raise my self-esteem, dispel my paranoia and realise that I wasn't part of the problem. Someone who my mum calls the "hag" and I call a "sycophantic vindictive little woman child" nearly got me fired from my PhD. It is all sorted now, but due to the trials that I had learnt to overcome in my earlier years, these helped me to overcome my personal struggles with this woman. However, when you have people on your side, and you make sure that they know that you are an exceptional person, then they can help you throughout.

One thing that I have had to learn to overcome (at university) is stress and becoming too overwhelmed. When this happens I tend to shut down. This means I tend to lock myself away and become incredibly unresponsive and lonely. I have managed to overcome this by forcing myself to do things to get myself out of my loneliness bubble. I find that whilst dealing with stress that it is easier to compartmentalise. I tend to try and work rounded hours from 9-5 pm and sometimes at the weekend. I do try to manage my work, and I tend to micromanage to extremes! When I get stressed I tend to hyper-focus on one task and forget about other tasks in my workload. I have started to understand where this is a problem and have found ways of coping (including lots of tea and breaks from work, with shorter days) to try and manage my time better. My stress amalgamates with health problems, so I have to really deal with it quickly before it gets out of control.

I found when I was at the University of Leicester going home over the weekend (as I lived in Coventry) helped with my stress. However, whilst I'm in Iceland I find it harder to cope with. I try and keep busy at the weekends and have tried to elevate my other interests, such as gaming, drawing and writing. Whilst in Iceland I have to be very careful with what I do and when I do it. I can get very tired and shut down when I'm stressed, so trying to keep up with my sleep is important for me. Even if it means that I have a little bit less of a social life! This is why I found life in halls (in Leicester) really hard, because (as it was a university halls) it was rather loud and everyone was out partying all the time in freshers'. I felt a bit left out and uncomfortable about it all because I preferred having money and sleeping to getting completely sloshed (I learnt that after the first week or so), but when I moved into my own house it was a lot better as I was able to have a much easier routine and I knew where everything was. Also, my room wasn't freezing and actually had heating, which was a bonus! – although it was still hard to try and fit into everyone else's routine.

When my boyfriend moved out at the end of fourth year (he moved to Reading for a new job and I was working at a job in the Leicester department) I found it really hard to live in my house. All my friends from my year in uni had left and I felt a bit more alone. It was difficult and stressful living in the house (even though I had lived there since halls). All of the change was far too much and I began to feel overwhelmed. I couldn't deal with the issues within the house. I was lucky as I was able to go home over the weekends (and because Dad was retired, he'd sometimes drive me back on the Monday morning). My boyfriend helped a lot too during that time. I would have struggled even more in that time without my boyfriend and my family.

I find that the hardest thing to do is not having as much support in Iceland as I had at Leicester. For example, when my original support worker left they managed to set me up with another one straight away. Even though it was really hard when my original support worker (Tess) left – I cried a *lot* – I was able to adapt and move with the change. It was difficult but my new support worker (Donna) really helped me move on with the change. I couldn't thank both of these wonderful ladies enough for helping me through every challenge I faced at university. Nonetheless at University of Iceland I have managed to get help (from an amazing woman called Johanna – she lets me look after her dog sometimes at the weekends!), but as it is a much smaller community here, I find it is harder to find people to gel with. It is also hard to work with a supervisor who doesn't really *get* you, but it does help when I have Johanna on my side. My supervisor seems to be far more relaxed about everything now that he has Johanna to help him understand.

What do you think you will do once you finish university?

Hopefully, I will be in a job that I will be able to enjoy. I know I can't deal with a high-pressure job (I suppose I could, but I would have to deal with a LOT of changes and make changes to deal with; I would be constantly tired and probably not very happy). I would prefer something to do with public relations in the museum industry. My personal dream job would be to work within a small group of people that get along with each other and accept me for who I am! To be honest, I really would love to be able to work part time, front of house in a museum alongside kids and to do research and running it behind.

Do you have any sensory issues? How do you cope with them on a daily basis?

I have several sensory issues, but I never really thought about them until now. I have just dealt with them in ways where they are not much of a problem anymore. If we were to compartmentalise them, I have some issues with touch and sound.

Personally, I hate sounds that are out of the norm. For example, I hate high grating sounds (like polystyrene on polystyrene, or when you have to clean the rosin from your viola strings, or the sound when someone rubs their fingers across recycled paper of a book). For example, I also hate low repetitive sounds, because they just grate on my nerves and I just can't shake them. For example, where I live on University of Iceland campus I can hear the bass from the parties they have in the park, and I cannot concentrate, nor sleep! I hate repetitive songs that get stuck in my head too, as it makes me anxious and upset because I cannot concentrate!

I also hate large, crowded, noisy environments. I have learnt to steadily cope with the environment. I think it's because I become overwhelmed with everything that goes on and I cannot calm down. The worst environment for me is the tube in London, or any airport. My worst experiences generally included times where my anxiety was raised because I was in a heavily populated area that I didn't know, or I was with a group of people and I didn't know what was going on.

I have managed to alleviate these problems by focusing on other things. When I travel in London with my mum, and my sister (my dad can't walk very well so he doesn't go to London with us) or my boyfriend we have developed ways of coping. My mum normally just allows my mind to wander, and she is very good at telling when I am getting upset and consequently helps me calm down. I tend to just play Pokemon, go on my phone to focus away from my anxiety. My boyfriend is very good too; he's learnt that if I'm in a busy area and I'm getting panicky he can just give me a cuddle when we are on the train, and he doesn't mind holding my hand and distracting me with talking about anything to help. I also really want an assistance dog, to help with my anxiety in regard to moving around on public transport or going to new places. I also think it would give me a bit more room. I *hate* being pushed around and shoved, especially when moving. Because Asperger's doesn't necessarily have any visible cues, people just don't think and jostle you like anybody else. This doesn't help and I try not to get angry when this happens. It's hard but I have found ways to cope. The way I cope with the travelling is to know what I'm doing, and when I'm doing it, inside and out. That normally helps, but not as much as an assistance dog!

I tend not to go to gigs or concerts etc. as the large crowds and multiple people really increase my anxiety. But if I do go to large events, I like going with a group of people and I like knowing where things are, like the toilets, the exits etc. I also have my little patterns to help me cope with the situation. This is why I prefer to go to the theatre rather than massive gigs as I have a more enjoyable time.

In regard to touch, I hate rough things, like sandpaper – because it feels weird on my skin and makes me actually shudder. I also don't like eating particular things because of their texture. I *hate* cooking my own pasta, because I find I can never get it right, and it's always slimy – although my younger sister loves the squishy sound that pasta and that type of food makes, so always has to make that sound. I used to get SO ANNOYED with that – and she knew that too! I think I stopped eating pasta for *years* when I was a kid because of the texture. I also don't like eating certain ice lollies when they have wooden sticks, as I have to be really careful to avoid the wooden stick so it doesn't cause me to shudder and feel sick. However, I really like smooth, cool things, such as stones. If I know that I'm going to be in a stressful environment, I sometimes take my favourite stone along for the ride to help me calm down. Currently my favourite is a smooth, sub-angular, vesicular piece of black basalt that I found at the black beach in Vik. It's a wonderful thing just to hold when I get stressed. I also really love my "fidget cube"; if I know that I'm going on a long or difficult journey (like flying or travelling to a new place by train) I tend to keep one in my pocket, just to make sure that I have something to play with if things get stressful.

To deal with these sensory things I have learnt to ignore or accept them – in regard to sounds, and people. I try to be organised when I'm going anywhere, carry as little possible (normally my phone, wallet and headphones) and have my music on when I know where I'm going.

However, I'm not sure how many people have to deal with this, but I find it really hard to recognise facial expressions. So, for the longest time I didn't like watching what I would call "human or real life" movies as I didn't understand them. I loved cartoons and things with animals because they were so much easier to read and understand. *The Blue Planet* and *Walking with Dinosaurs* was my favourite documentary series for the longest time. But I have gotten a lot better with recognising facial features of friends I have known for years, but not with friends or people I have not known for very long. I find that I am desperately trying not to ask what they are feeling or what they are doing – as I know this annoys them! Consequently, this is why I find cartoons so much fun. I really enjoy them (even though some of them might be for kids, I find watching them as an adult means you get ALL the jokes so they're twice as funny) as I do not have to concentrate on the facial expressions because they are so easy to read. However, I have found that I am a bit slow on picking up things in live-action programs that I haven't seen before. For example, I have to pay close attention to new programmes and I get annoyed when people talk over them as I have to concentrate. Now I am older, I enjoy comedy, documentaries, sci-fi and the odd drama. But for comfort I tend to watch the same things repeatedly as I now find them relaxing.

How do you think universities can help individuals on the spectrum to have a better time in higher education?

I had really good support from the University of Leicester; even though there were changes that I struggled with within the Accessibility Department, I managed to cope because I was so well looked after. It was only thanks to Tess and Donna that I got the care I needed in regard to helping me with my master's thesis, third-year dissertation and my mapping project. They also helped me with exams, when we realised that the best place for me was in a quiet room on my own with the least distractions possible. I was even able to bring in a comforter for some of my exams (which was a little Pegasus figurine from the *My Little Pony* cartoon called Derpy). Because the plastic was smooth, cool to the touch and not easily breakable, it helped me realign my thoughts when I got stressed. Because I was in a room on my own (with Tess or Donna) I could play with Derpy in my hands to relieve my stress. Leicester was good for me because the support was tailored towards my requirements.

Personally, I think every university in England should have some sort of "Accessibility Department" to help students with disabilities – not a "safe space" but somewhere where the people who run the department have specific training in counselling and providing help to those who need it. If the university cannot provide this, there does need to be some sort of specialised counselling for people with disabilities. I also think that if they cannot provide a department (Leicester's was a small computer room with a couple of offices and a check-in desk) they should at least provide a constantly monitored quiet and calm environment that students can feel comfortable and safe in. I also think that the professors should have some basic counselling training – especially if they are going to be heading a tutorial group, or are going to be a master's or dissertation tutor.

I wouldn't be where I am today if it wasn't for the kindness and understanding of the folks at Leicester. I find that even though there are still issues with consistency in regard to mental healthcare in the UK, it is steps above the help provided in other countries. Although I have found my own help within the University of Iceland (and I couldn't be more grateful for the support) I find that I had to be far less subtle overseas.

I also think, if they can, that universities should definitely try to employ a comfort living space – some place where people who need strict routines and feel uncomfortable in new places can live, like halls for other people but one that has particular sets of rules that people can follow. I think it would be awesome if a place like this was near the university and students with disabilities could stay there. I think my first year would have been far more enjoyable. I know that this is hard to do, but I think some universities should definitely consider this option for people on the autistic spectrum, or with mental health difficulties, as it would seriously help with their comfort and routines. Also, I think these places should ... have [someone] like [an] on-call person ... that can help with difficulties in particular hours.

There are changes that the universities in the UK can make, and I don't think that having consistent guidelines would actually help. This is because the situations can become normalised and things will fall to the wayside. I do believe that help and support for people with disabilities really needs more understanding within the general system. I truly believe that there should be as much effort as possible to make a tailored experience for each student that makes the leap to university. For me this was helped – not because they had a department (well that helped a lot) – but because of the people that they had at Leicester. I feel if they have the right people who are willing to help, then that sets everything else in motion.

THEATRE COMPANY

I began to really cultivate my theatrical interests at university. I'd joined the university's theatre company during freshers' week. I attended the group religiously every Wednesday evening after lectures for the whole of my first and second years at university. In the first year the theatre company wasn't very developed. The only major thing that I did with them was the variety show in October where we put together a bit of a thing from the Flat Pack. Flat Pack was an improv group which had been set up by the third-year Drama students. We performed the piece in front of other students. I auditioned for a play called *Back Bone Slap*, but I didn't get in and I felt betrayed by the theatre company because I'd helped them do the variety show, but then I realised that in university it's a tough competition and I was lucky to have done any of the things that I did.

In the second year, however, we had a Pinter festival and we dedicated a weekend to his plays because of his death in December 2008. I was in a production called *One for the Road*, which was brilliantly staged and quite difficult to perform. I played a guard and our responsibility was to lead the audience around the performance space, but in character. I dedicated that performance to my friend in that show because we had to be authoritative and at that time I was not very confident or assertive and did not believe myself to be authoritative, but he helped me to get into role and supported me throughout the entire performance.

I applied for the position of Social Secretary in the theatre company in the second year, but I didn't get chosen. I felt betrayed by them after all the hard work I'd done. However, I realised that it was not about how much work you do but about how the vote was cast, so I stopped being self-centred and moved on.

RELATIONSHIP PROBLEMS AND SPLITTING UP WITH MY BOYFRIEND

Whilst all these new things were going on I was becoming a new person. I was becoming interested in the world around me and in culture and in the theory behind theatre. My boyfriend had stayed the same and I missed him terribly during the first few months of university. When I went back home to see him, however, I realised that our relationship had changed. I was not the person he fell in love with anymore and our relationship was not going to work.

So, my boyfriend and I began to experience problems during my first year of university. I was becoming a different person, but he called me posh because I liked to read books. Apart from this, I was falling in love with one of my colleagues on my English course. I met him in a Shakespeare seminar; I found it ironic that when we met we were studying *Romeo and Juliet* because it was a play about love. I can still remember him commenting on how strict our teacher was in the first seminar. I didn't love him then. I didn't even really know his name, but as time went on I fell in love with him and I loved the way he read out the texts. I just loved the sound of his voice, which was, of course, another sensory thing, although I had not realised this at the time. He helped me carry my shopping bags back to my flat one day and I invited him in for a cup of tea. We got on really well and it was then that I began to feel something for him. I went back to his flat during the second week of classes and I enjoyed spending time with him when we were out of the intellectual setting. I liked having classes with him, too, because I realised that he was one of the most intelligent men that I knew. I always had a laugh in lectures because he pretended to do a radio voice over for Nottinghamshire radio station on my Dictaphone. I was in love with the sound of his voice and I hung onto everything that he ever said to me. When I found out that he had a girlfriend I was devastated, but I still wanted his friendship, so I said nothing to him about my feelings for him. I obsessed over the idea that I liked him. He played squash and football on the lawn outside our flat, and I used to watch him from my kitchen window. I met his girlfriend later in the year and she was a lovely girl. He made risotto for us and he sang to us in his room. I was envious of his girlfriend, but I was glad that he was happy.

I didn't want to hurt my boyfriend, but I knew that something was wrong in our relationship. I spent many nights lying awake crying because I didn't want to hurt anybody. I knew then that I needed to sort out my relationships with my boyfriend and my colleague, but I didn't know how.

In the first few weeks of university, I had, though, realised that marriage to my boyfriend was not what I wanted that early in my life. We were socialising in my flat and everyone went around the table saying where they'd travelled and what they hoped to achieve in life. One of the Americans was a 21-year-old virgin and as an 18-year-old in a sexually active relationship I had so much respect and admiration for him that I decided I wanted to travel and that I didn't want to get married right on the spot.

As for my colleague, I could not cope with the intense feelings of attraction that I had for him. The trouble, of course, was that we both had partners and he was obviously not interested in me in a romantic way. He was a very good friend of mine in first year and we would go to each other's flats to hang out and listen to music. He could play the guitar very well, so I often asked him to play for me. He was very supportive when my grandfather died and he came to my 19th birthday party. We played in the snow together when there was a snow day in first year and we went sledging with his girlfriend. I introduced him to my boyfriend and they got on well, but I was starting to compare the two of them. I took my boyfriend to a Shakespeare lecture the once and I sat with him and my colleague. I was in the middle of the two and my boyfriend played his Gameboy under the desk and completely lacked interest in what the lecturer was saying. My colleague took notes as he wanted to better his life and I was beginning to see where the flaws in my own relationship were. Trouble was that my behaviour became obsessive, and I used to look into my colleague's flat window to see if he was home (he lived on the ground floor of my building so you could see into his flat). I wanted to make sure he was ok. I would invite myself into his flat without reading the social signals he was giving me that he was busy. I would constantly speak about him with my flatmates, and all of this became too much for him and he began to think I was weird and creepy.

I have stated that I believe that my romantic attachments stemmed from separation anxiety and a fear of being alone. I liked the feeling of being in love and so I did it again and again, whether or not the response was appropriate for that situation. I believe that feeling like I was in love was a self-stimulation behaviour I engaged in at the time because I liked the feeling of getting a hug. Hugging was a new sensation for me and the situation was always unfamiliar. So, a new person and a new hug would provide new sensory feedback for me. I feel also that my romantic attachments stemmed from having people as special interests, and I would continually talk about the person and try to find out everything about them. The behaviour got quite dangerous at times – not in a sinister way, but I always wanted to know what my special interest was doing, so I would find a way to be where they were. At this stage I was around 19 years old with no vocabulary to describe these feelings, sensations and behaviours. I just knew that I had no control over them. Other people thought they were weird and didn't like them so much. I did not know what they were and I was frightened by my own behaviour and intensity of feeling.

Finally, I split up with my boyfriend in the summer when I had finished first year. I felt guilt about this for many years afterwards, but there were serious difficulties with our relationship. The main ones were that he seemed to really want a child and I knew I was not ready at the time, and that he really liked to have sex and expected it from me when he wanted it. I only enjoy sex if I am not expected to do it. I do if it is with the right person and I feel stimulated and happy, but I was having sex with my boyfriend just because I thought I was pleasing him, and it did not feel right. He wanted to marry me, and I wanted to marry him at one point, but I was frightened and I knew our relationship was not working. University was moulding me into a mature adult and I could not play Pokemon games for hours anymore or sit designing new creatures on Spore. I loved him with all my heart, but I knew I could not give him what he wanted most in life. It turns out now that he has children, so he got what he needed, just not from me. I was very sad when I saw pictures of his children on the internet because I realised that it would be very difficult for me to give anyone children at all, not just him. I could not find the words to tell him what I needed to, so I wrote him a letter. I felt guilty for a long time about that. He deserved to hear me say those things, he deserved to hear me confess that I needed different things to him, but I could not do it and I was a coward.

According to the American author of books on Asperger's Rudy Simone, "There is always going to be some internalization of blame. Most of us whether we care to admit it or not, have a considerable amount of embarrassment and shame to contend with – for not being able to handle the little day-to-day, ordinary experiences that other women seem to manage just fine."[*] I think this is part of the guilt that I felt – not only did I feel I had treated him badly, but I felt I could not hold down a relationship like society believes "normal" women should do. I was not society's idea of a normal woman. I did not realise then that I am not a woman at all. I am bi-gender. I am an Asperger person and that means that I construct relationships in a different way to how others might. I don't do small talk and I don't do trying to interpret metaphors or silent treatment. You either tell me what you mean directly or nothing will come out of the situation. Neurotypical men often find it difficult that I have traits which society often attributes to being manly, for

---

[*] Rudy Simone *Aspergirls: Empowering Females with Asperger Syndrome* (2010) p.56

example too much testosterone in my body and presenting with a lot of male traits – such as over competitiveness, exhibiting strength and muscle, a strong dislike of small talk, and being confident.

After I split up with my boyfriend, I continued to cause problems for my colleague. He invited me to his house for dinner and by the time we had finished drinking wine and watching *The West Wing* it was too late for me to get back to campus. I slept on his sofa whilst he and his girlfriend slept together upstairs. When he came downstairs in the morning he came down without a top on, and I could not bear how much I fancied him, so I told him so. Of course, he did not reciprocate the feelings and told me to draw a line. When I was becoming unwell psychologically in second year, I liked to tell people what I wanted to be true instead of what was the actual truth, so I told my housemates that he had kissed me. He found this out and was incredibly scared of me from there on, with good reason. He started to tell people that he only hung out with me in first year because I was autistic and he felt sorry for me. I was told by my housemates that he said he hated me and he would not come to events if I was invited. One of the girls I lived with in final year had a Halloween party at our house and invited him. I was away for the weekend so he came, and I heard he slagged me off all night, so I was incredibly upset but my obsessive behaviour was still in the way so I tried several times to apologise to him. In the end, I believe I shouldn't have bothered, but I was young then and I thought that if I could apologise for the lie I had told that he would somehow forgive me, but he never did and I did not really speak with him again until my graduation day.

I wrote my first play *Knocking Over the Chair*, which I mentioned earlier, as a tribute to my colleague and my boyfriend. I did not know I could write plays until my colleague jokingly said to me in a lecture, "Why don't you write a play with me as the main character?" As I did not realise he was joking, I did write the play and I hope one day that he will get to read it, even if he never tells me so. It was first performed at the university in 2009.

WOULD YOU GO ON AN EXCHANGE YEAR AS AN ASPERGER STUDENT?

In the first year of university I found out that you could study for a year abroad. Being an exchange student at an American university really appealed to me, but it was one thing to want to live independently in London to study and it was another thing to want to do this abroad in America.

Nevertheless, I wanted to do this because I felt it would make me even more independent and I wanted to see America. My family were petrified but they were very supportive, so I went about the process of applying to go there.

Unfortunately, even though I'd got as far as choosing my modules and everything, I realised I didn't have enough money to go and I didn't know how to sort out funding. I later applied for Camp America instead, but I didn't get a place because I needed to have experience with groups of children; so I didn't get to live out my dream of being a student studying in America. I've been on holiday there a few times before and I love it, so one day I will go again, but probably not as a student. In a way I'm glad I didn't go because I wouldn't have had the experiences that I did in London in second year if I'd have gone away.

When I was applying for Camp America, my personal adviser wrote this about me and I was very happy.

I didn't think that this description matched my view of myself, so I was taken aback. For example, I'd never have thought of myself as having good spoken communication skills and so that's why it made me happy. Sadly, I missed out on the Camp America opportunity, but I would still love to go and volunteer abroad somewhere and I may still do this but later on in life.

16th December 2009

Dear sir

I am happy to provide a reference for the above-named student whom I have known for the past two academic years in my capacity as personal adviser at the School of English and Drama. Maddy's written work across all courses at university demonstrates her enthusiasm for her subject matter and sound understanding of English and Drama as academic disciplines. In Year 1, she consistently achieved "B" grades across all her courses, and it is likely she will obtain a BA (upper 2nd class honours) degree when she completes her studies in 2011.

She has shown herself to be a motivated and capable student who has fully participated in seminar discussions with thoughtful contributions. She has the ability to communicate effectively in both written and spoken English, and is adept at guiding debate amongst her peers and asking challenging questions. At the same time, she has shown herself to be an able team-player, and clearly enjoys working with other students on a variety of curricular and extracurricular projects.

I believe Maddy to be an understanding and tolerant student who has committed wholeheartedly to her studies here at the University. I am sure she will prove similarly dedicated and responsible as a Camp America Counsellor. I have always found Maddy to be a co-operative and trustworthy student and have no hesitation in supporting her application to the Camp America Summer Work placement scheme. I recommend her as a worthy candidate.

MOVING INTO SHARED ACCOMMODATION

After the first year ended it was time for me to leave halls of residence and make arrangements to move into shared accommodation for my second year at uni. Due to being on the spectrum, I found leaving halls was very hard for me because it was a change. I spent a lot of that week crying. I found it hard to say goodbye to people. Going to the last of the student evenings for the year at the New Globe Pub really upset me and I used alcohol to combat the strong emotion. I cried when I took my photos off my walls and when it was time for us to clean the kitchen so that we'd get our deposits back.

I was going to share a house in the second year with my Biomed student friend and others, and she and I started to arrange house viewings as our university had a website with recommended landlords and you phoned them up to arrange viewings. There were a lot of problems with who was going to live with whom. Originally a friend from my English group was going to live with us, but then he decided that he didn't want to, so we were then stuck looking for another person. Finally, after a lot of messing about a graduate friend of mine decided to live with us in September, but I had to pay extra to cover his room as our house was on a group contract. I didn't get the money back until he moved into the house, so I was financially stuck for a few months.

The day after the final party of first year my mum, my boyfriend and I loaded my stuff into the car and dropped my keys off at the university. It took forever to leave because everyone was queuing and so we didn't leave until 1pm. I went back to London to collect my results during the summer, but it was a lot of hassle getting there for the day. I had to sleep over with a friend of mine, who already had a house in London, for the night. I was happy because I passed into second year and I knew I could have a good summer break. Unfortunately, there is not much you can do to make moving house easier. It is stressful whether you are on the spectrum or not,

236

but now I have done it so many times I have a moving-house routine and I am used to it. It was just harder back then because it was only the second time I had ever moved anywhere.

Living in shared accommodation brought its own challenges. I moved into my student house in the summer of 2009 and I found it incredibly difficult to live so closely with four other people. However, we had some great times there, including some amazing parties, and I lived there for a total of two years. There were some different housemates over that period. Originally, I shared the house with three female students, respectively studying English, Drama and Biomedical Science, and my male graduate friend who was studying Politics. He later moved out and a female English Literature student moved in, also my Law student friend who I'd lived with previously in halls.

I was very nervous about moving into a new house and I didn't talk much when I was sat in the removal van, moving my stuff down to London. My Drama housemate had got there before me. She had collected our keys from the landlord and was there waiting for me when I arrived. It took us ages to set up the internet. Because I went for an internet stick rather than a router first, it took me until the December to have working internet in the house. We had to use internet cafés and the university library until I'd got it set up. A friend of mine stopped at our house for the weekend, because he still didn't have anywhere to live at that point, and he scared me about living in the house. He pointed out all of its flaws, but I thought it was wonderful and he was wrong. We decorated the place to make it more homely and it took my Biomed housemate and me most of the first semester to do it. My graduate friend gave me the money that he owed me for the deposit that I paid for him, so at least I had money for freshers' week.

There were five of us living in the same house together, in a four-bedroom house. We converted the living room into a bedroom. Our landlord was into dodgy dealing and we never saw an inventory for the house and I ended up passing on contracts to new people who moved in. We got on fine as housemates most of the time, but as you'd expect in any shared living arrangement we got under each other's feet and we argued sometimes.

As a house, our main problems were as follows: the walls being so thin that we could hear when people were talking about each other; general hygiene and the lack of washing up and housework getting done; dependency on each other and alcohol; loud music; sharing of stuff or not sharing of stuff; paying for items that were communally used by the house, such as loo roll and washing-up liquid; and whether or not it was appropriate to bring men back to the house.

The Politics graduate had a habit of breaking things and I know that it was him who broke a laptop and hair straighteners, even though he denied it. He had a cutting sense of humour and used biting remarks as a sign of affection. I'd have been worried if he didn't insult me, because that would have meant that he just couldn't be bothered talking with me. He sometimes emails to ask how I am after graduating. He wrote this about his time living with me.

Politics housemate: You know what the gist of it is, though, in truth we get on perfectly amicably and should do so again when our paths cross. You gave me carte blanche to say what I want, so it should be ok. So, if I say hi when I see you, I'm not a hypocrite. [I] would qualify by saying it was my own fault for being too lazy to find anywhere else to live, and in truth as soon as I moved out I let it all slip from my mind.

The great problem was that my bedroom was next to yours and your voice is scandalously baritone. Gravelly, penetrating, whatever it was, it cut through the walls and stopped any other activity. There also seemed to be a musty smell coming out of there that I couldn't explain. I could sometimes hear phone conversations as I sat. The repetition and self-delusion was soul destroying at times.

The cow pyjamas were a bit much and I remember you once scared my sister whilst wearing them. This was hilarious.

In the living room we co-existed ok, notwithstanding The Exorcist–*style laugh you sometimes unleashed when a character from* Family Guy *did something very mildly amusing. But it wasn't you who chose the crap stuff to watch. And I seem to recall it was your TV. I will stop clarifying things for time's sake, but yes I was shit at cooking and washing up etc.*

In the kitchen your cooking just made me feel sorry for you. There's something about an ostensibly grown woman cooking smiley faces in cow pyjamas that's just a bit tragic, particularly when your hair was straggled around your face like that girl from The Ring *films. And sometimes you didn't really cook the food and you would put cutlery away which was still covered in food. I wondered at times how you survived.*

We had some decent conversations that weren't an issue, and you listened to me warble about a woman I liked. The day she texted me, only because she wanted to arrange to meet with YOU, was an all-time low point. Honestly. I realised after that the world in my head bears no relation to the outside world at all. I should be grateful in a way.

Oh yeah, and when you were drunk you were intolerable, rude, bitter and lashed out. Or fell asleep on the carpet. It was too much. I love a quiet life and so often in that house it wasn't possible. But genuine best wishes all the same.

Biomed housemate: *When I decided to make the move from the quiet, peaceful countryside called home to the hustle and bustle of London to embark on what I knew would be a massive chapter in my life, I was fully aware that I would be exposed to numerous challenges academically and socially. However, nothing could have properly prepared me for the arguments, tests, drama and wicked fun I would have after meeting Madeleine Levy.*

I met Maddie in first year, and to be honest my first encounter consisted more of a panic and concern for that fact that she was

239

cooking chicken not only in a microwave but then continued to eat it even though the centre was still pink and raw. However, over time this then developed into a motherly affection, for an eccentric, strong-willed character. Yet my real relationship with Maddie only truly blossomed in second year when we ended up living together.

I don't even know how I can condense the events at 9 Parnell Road into a paragraph. We very quickly developed a very close relationship which she found difficult to deal with, and I think anyone who knows Maddie would relate to the fact that she can become very attached to certain people and I happened to be one of them. She is a very loyal and protective friend, especially to those that she attaches herself to. However, this can cause a lot of strain in her relationships as she sometimes forgets that her friends are capable of looking after themselves and that they managed to survive 18 years before they met her. I remember one night we had all drank a fair amount and she ended up shouting, "I'm not your keeper," which just amplifies my point that no one expects her to be. The irony of this, however, is that I feel like I have spent most of my time being Maddie's keeper. For someone who is such a clean control freak as me, to live with someone who could not grasp the difference between a tea towel and a dish cloth was at little a challenge, not to mention her amazing ability to attempt to wash up without soap and water!!!! STRANGE! Yet one thing I will say is she was always willing to learn and do better, which to me was one of her most endearing qualities.

Me and Mads had a lot of wild times together, and everyone knows that Maddie is a horrendous flirt, but even though we all joke that she fancies everyone, it's probably to do with the fact that she always sees the best in people. I had a pre-conceived idea that someone with autism would be shy and struggle in certain social circumstances, but I haven't met anyone as social and popular as Maddie is, and if I have learnt one thing from Maddie it is to never judge a book by its cover.

One of the times when I found it difficult to live with Maddie is when she got angry and expressed this with violence – like the time when she decided to hit me with my own flip-flop. I grew up in an environment where violence was never seen and instead our opinions were expressed vocally, whereas Maddie's social circle at home was quite the opposite. I know she found it difficult to deal with my volatile temper and strong will, and sometimes this fear turned her into a bit of a coward in terms of saying how she felt. However, no one could say Maddie was a coward when it came to standing up for herself physically, like the time she fought off a group of chavs with a duvet, and when she ran to our friend's rescue as he was being beaten with a pole. In this respect I am very grateful to Maddie as she has toughened me up and drummed street sense into me, and I can say definitively that I never feel safer than when I am with Maddie.

Logic!!! Let's say doesn't come naturally, like the time when she locked herself out of her room and decided that the most rational response would be to throw a brick at the door, then go at it with a knife and then finally beckon chavs into the house to break it open. It took her a few hours to realise if she rang Bob the electrician then she could have got a spare key. However, this is where I feel I have been able to pass my experience onto her, and in this way you could say we kind of live in symbiosis and that our differences kind of work for us.

Maddie is one of my closest and best friends and probably the biggest challenges that tested our relationship involved that of a BOY!! Liking the same boy as your friend can always test you. Even though initially she hated me and couldn't see why things never worked out for her, I am a strong believer that everything happens for a reason. Since then, I have never seen Maddie so determined and driven. She has motivated herself to take on so much more – I even saw her eating vegetables the other day. As a result, she is now a smarter, well-rounded and a more independent woman ready to conquer anything.

I found it very difficult living with my housemates. My Biomed housemate liked to play loud music in the house, and I later found out I was hypersensitive to sound and it hurt my ears. I found it incredibly difficult to express when I disagreed with their actions or I wished to confront them about something, so I took to writing passive-aggressive notes, and when I was drunk I lashed out at them with too much strength because I spent most of the time repressing what I actually needed to say to them.

WHAT WOULD HAVE HELPED?

I believe that if I would have been true to myself and actually said what I needed to say rather than hiding behind fear of hurting or disappointing anyone, I would have had much more genuine friendships in my second year of university. I also believe that if I would have lived for myself and not tried to please others all the time, then they would have met the real me faster. I believe that if I would have learnt self-compassion then, I would have stopped drinking alcohol and that would have helped me faster. I should have learnt to say no and to respect myself rather than drinking. If I had not agreed to take responsibility for the house accounts and money, I would have had a better time of it as well. My advice to students would be to always stay true to yourself and do not try to please anybody. You are all there with the purpose to finish your degrees and you do not have to like each other or behave in ways to make your housemates like you. Just behave in a respectful, tolerant way and then everything should be fine.

OTHER CHANGES IN THE SECOND YEAR

During my first degree I had to fill out module forms every year. However, when it came to choosing modules for the second year, I still thought at the time that I would be going to America, so I chose no modules for semester one. This meant that during the second year I was allocated classes that had spaces left, which was incredibly difficult for me, and I didn't enjoy learning about Chaucer. There was an unequal balance between practical- and seminar-based classes and I ended up with a whole semester of seminar-based classes in second year. I found it hard to concentrate in class, so going from one three-hour seminar to the next was difficult. It would have helped if the module forms were easier to read and if I had support to fill in the forms, but everything is being done online these days, so I imagine it is much easier to choose modules if it is done via an internet system.

Exam term was also a really difficult one for me in second year. During exam term nobody had any classes and you'd just revise for exams all month. Whereas in the first year I had a written exam to focus on and friends around me, in the second year I had no written exams at all, but I lost my friends for a month because they were revising. I'd have given anything to be revising like my friends, but I had to entertain myself because they were all working. I felt really isolated and bored.

ALCOHOL DEPENDENCY

I think it's true to say that in 2009 I became dependent on alcohol. I believed that I needed it to be able to introduce myself to people. Why would anyone want to speak with me? I was a useless autistic weirdo. I needed to have my stomach pumped after one particular party and there are many embarrassing photographs that have occurred as a result of drunken antics. I used to take a hip flask of Jägermeister to my lectures and I was told that if I did not stop drinking I would be thrown off my course. My Biomed housemate and I became particularly fond of the two-bottles-of-cheap-vodka-for-a-tenner deal in Iceland supermarket. This vodka was so cheap it tasted akin to paint stripper – not that I have ever tasted paint stripper, but I can imagine it would taste like that. We paid five pounds each and usually drank the two bottles during the student evening called "How's your father?" that happened every Thursday night at the New Globe pub. As alcohol is a depressant, I used to wonder why I felt so low all the time. Funny that!

Students on the spectrum, if you are drinking because you feel low about yourself or because of your social anxiety, then please stop and get some counselling and support. Drinking does not make you cool or popular; it just damages your liver. It is also a depressant, and if you stay up late at night drinking and sleep all day, then you will wonder why your body clock is messed up and you are struggling to wake up for classes. It is fine to have a drink every now and then. I still like to have a pint with dinner, but I am not doing this because I feel bad about myself or because I am afraid of socialising; I am doing it because I like the taste of it. As I said before, alcohol is a very sociable thing at university, but do not be peer-pressured into going out drinking every night. It is very expensive and not all that fun. The hangovers hurt like hell. If you don't get them, then good for you, you are lucky. Please drink responsibly and stay safe at university.

Parents, as I've said before, if your child is drinking a lot of alcohol, then please do not worry. This is a phase that they definitely will grow out of – unlike their sexuality or gender. Be there for them, talk with them, but do not pester them or try to tell them how to cope with it because they will probably rebel against you and drink more just to worry you purposely. Alcohol is a very expensive habit and students soon realise that they don't have enough money to continue to do it constantly. I sought help from the university counsellor and soon realised that my drinking was connected to my incredibly low self-esteem. I have had a lot of support to build this up over the years, and, parents, I recommend that as soon as you spot your child has low self-esteem, do everything you can to help them build it up again. There are counsellors who can help with this, but sometimes just sitting and listening can help too. You would be surprised how powerful just sitting and listening non-judgementally actually is.

IT HAPPENS AGAIN

Just as I'd obsessed over the colleague I mentioned earlier, I soon came to obsess over someone else. This man was a friend of my Politics housemate and had been invited to a house party we were holding. He eventually became my Biomed housemate's husband, and in a way he changed my life. He is one of the few people who I've obsessed over who did not run away instantly but tried to maintain a platonic relationship with me.

My Biomed housemate's husband: When I met Maddie at her house party she forced a cake with a gummy ring into my hand. Then Maddie tried to kiss me in her living room. Although the details of this night are hazy, the ending I just described occurred around four in the morning after a few drinks, but this more or less sums up what I feel was Maddie's behaviour towards me. Oscillating between boisterous friendship and worrying obsession, she could often create uncomfortable evenings between us.

I think the main issue in our friendship has been her difficulty in distinguishing between platonic and romantic love. On nights out she would drape herself over me but then claim there was no meaning in it when questioned. Her affections towards me while trying to build a friendship meant there were many tense nights where I had to feel guilty rejecting her or feel isolated by her actions. This all came to head in the summer when I started going out with one of her friends and I had to feel like I was breaking up with her, both when she was upset and when she tried to pretend everything was fine.

Despite this, I feel we have built up a strong friendship since we first met. It came as a surprise to me when I found out that she was autistic several months after I knew her. She always came across as a hugely friendly and popular person, albeit a little strange, and despite some quite hilarious failures in logic I have never seen her as anyone different. She pays attention to those she is close to and values as important and demands it from anyone who she feels isn't paying her enough. This means she will always be there for you but can isolate you or bug you in conversations if she thinks you aren't paying her enough attention. She's got on my nerves and got me drunk, both cried and laughed with me, but she will always be Maddie. The most unique Drama student I know.

After meeting this man, I realised that my obsessive behaviour was a problem that needed resolving and so it was I sought help from my university's counselling system.

COUNSELLING AND TYPES OF SUPPORT AVAILABLE

There are support systems available at university if you know how to access them. I found support available from the university's counselling service, the university's disability service, the Royal Literary Fellows scheme and, in wider London, the National Autistic Society. I'll talk a bit about each of these in turn.

THE UNIVERSITY'S COUNSELLING SERVICE

I contacted my university's counselling service via email, because I'd found the address on the university website. Even though their service is to provide support in general rather than support tailored specifically for someone with a learning difference, I found them useful. I felt very low at times during my second year at university and so I took advantage of the university's counselling system to try to boost my self-esteem and figure out why I became so attached to people. They were really helpful and it was nice knowing that I had someone there to talk to if I needed it. I started a course of cognitive behavioural therapy which was incredibly helpful to me. During my break-up with my boyfriend and my experience with my colleague I had started to cut my wrists and self-harm a lot, and going to the university counsellor helped to improve my mental health dramatically – so much so that I felt able to share my experience with others and help other students on the spectrum when they needed it.

THE UNIVERSITY'S DISABILITY SERVICE

I didn't know that the service existed until the head of the department sent me an email. I could apply for learning aids such as a new laptop and printer. I got a chair delivered to me, because of my bad back, and a foot rest. I also got my internet paid for me for the last two years of university.

Every university has a disability department or support service and the first thing I'd advise a new student on the spectrum to do is to find out about your university's service and pay them a visit – even if it is just having a friendly face, or somewhere to sit when you need peace, the disability services at university always have some form of support to provide. They are always a helpful first point of contact.

In my case, I managed to get a job with the university's disability service as a Peer Mentor, which turned out to be a very rewarding experience. I mentored other students who had Asperger's. Most often they needed help with organising their work and sometimes meeting new people and joining societies on campus to better their social lives. I found the job so very rewarding because the girl who I mentored changed my life. She was the only person I knew with Asperger's at university at the time. She made me feel ok to be myself and proud to have autism. She was interviewed earlier on in the book and spoke with you about her cultural experiences and how being on the spectrum affects her job as a school teacher. We're very similar and I felt that I was not alone in the world when we met for sessions. She's an amazing woman and I wish that she could see for herself how amazing she is.

My boss changed my life too; if it weren't for him, I don't think I'd have ever begun writing this book. He wrote this about his first impressions of me.

Peer-mentoring boss: *I first met Maddy in the context of an informal interview for the post of a Peer Mentor with our department. She surprised me in lots of different ways not least because for some reason, probably the name, I'd expected her to be French and quite taciturn, but instead I found myself greeting an amiable Brummy with a proud interest in heavy metal (I recall a Slipknot badge on her bag).*

It was refreshing to hear someone speak so openly about the difficulties connected with Asperger syndrome and also her determination to master them. She might have a preference for solitude, and a convincing argument about her fellow man's ability to irritate and annoy, but it was also abundantly clear to me that Maddy cares very strongly about other people – her friends, family and other people who might be facing similar challenges to her, and the value of nurturing and supporting each other. This has become even clearer as Maddy has set about writing this book; rather than solely climbing the walls of her own memory, she's used it as an opportunity to start interesting conversations with family, and to go and renew old friendships.

Maddy has helped to remind me that autism is indeed a spectrum with an infinite sweep of different shades, hues and personalities. There are common traits, but the person will always be impossibly and, in today's increasing homogeneous world, refreshingly unique.

THE ROYAL LITERARY FELLOWS

The Royal Literary Fund run a scheme that places professional writers in universities to offer writing support to students. Our university offered support from such Royal Literary Fellows. They helped with grammar and essay-writing skills such as structure and the tone of academic writing.

The scheme operates in a lot of universities, and if your university offers it, it is good to invest in booking an appointment with them. There are sessions for an hour, and no matter what subject you study they are really helpful. My grades improved drastically when I took the time to go and see them. I'd advise anyone studying at university to do it whether they are on the spectrum or not.

THE NATIONAL AUTISTIC SOCIETY

I visited the National Autistic Society in order to start to write this book and in order to understand myself better. They are an organisation that helps young children and adults on the spectrum. Their head office, which I visited, is in Angel, London, but they have many local branches too. They have loads of resource books and videos to help with projects. They supported me to figure out many of my behaviours. No matter which country you live in, if you are autistic, you should send them an email because they are really helpful and you can find out anything that you wish to know. It was the National Autistic Society who helped me discover my hypersensitivity to sound and after this the doctors confirmed it.

MORE THOUGHTS ON THE ISSUE OF DIAGNOSIS

As well as sharing his first impressions of me, my peer-mentoring boss also had a few words to say about the issue of diagnosis. Here's what he said.

Peer-mentoring boss: The official purpose of a diagnosis is to identify the nature and cause of something. The official consequence of a diagnosis isn't always so clear, and with the bit in between purpose and consequence often entailing a strange blend of isolation, happiness and confusion. It isn't always easy to make a case for every diagnosis of autism leading to instant karma; having said that, it's equally hard to make a long-term case for the promotion of burying one's head in the sand.

With this in mind, there is a case for recognising not only the importance of a diagnosis but also the process leading up to and following it, so that people are left with something more than a piece of paper confirming all of their character weaknesses. A diagnosis shouldn't be expected to lead to a cure, but it doesn't seem too ambitious to suggest that it should help someone get a bit closer towards figuring out how their brain works – something which most of us could benefit from a bit of help with. On top of that, diagnosis should open the door to support – not patronising, annoying support that follows you round the room and asks you if you've remembered to go to the toilet but empowering collaboration that makes a difference.

My dad also contributed his thoughts on diagnosis.

Dad: *Although there are many who oppose diagnostic systems, the concept is useful if it is used to assist the person being diagnosed. Without the diagnosis of Asperger's the education system would have been quite happy to allow Madeleine to quietly fail, despite the fact that, with the right help, she has flourished and is a proud graduate from a very respectable London university!*

Unfortunately, the people who hold power in this country (both bureaucrats and politicians) will use any excuse to withdraw funding and look after the majority at the expense of minorities. As the saying goes, "Those who can do... those who can't teach... and those who cannot do or teach become politicians or government managers!"

There are countless examples where ignorance has resulted in serious misunderstanding about children. For example, children with mild epilepsy were often scolded and chastised for "daydreaming" or failing to concentrate in class. It was only when we understood that these children might be suffering from neurological difficulties that resulted in their absences that we could do something to assist them. The same is true for mild autism. Because a conventional educational system that is designed for the majority fails these children so badly, it does not mean that they do not have the potential to achieve great things.

Diagnosis helps us to understand what we are dealing with and then modify our educational responses to bring the best out in those who have been identified. So long as diagnosis points to the way forward, I will remain an ardent supporter of it!

Even though my father and boss were in support of diagnostic systems, I am not so sure myself even now.

KNOCKING OVER THE CHAIR

In February 2010 the university theatre company decided to put on a festival for new theatre writings. After much encouragement from a friend, I submitted the play I had written *Knocking Over the Chair* and it was accepted for the festival after a gruelling pitch night. For the pitch night you had to stand up and say why your play should be accepted for the festival. I'd spoken in the oratory contest in primary school, but nothing like this before, so I was terrified, but once my performance got accepted I celebrated with friends. Then the audition process began. Forty people auditioned for my play and I had a cast of 14; I had to decide my cast within a week of auditioning people, so I had some difficult decisions to make quickly.

Once I had my cast, I could rehearse and I had a very enthusiastic, energetic bunch of students working with me. The rehearsal process was probably one of the toughest things I have done in my career. I had no experience of directing at all, so another friend decided to help me out. I am very grateful to him for everything he did.

For the first rehearsal we had a line run-through and completed Act I, Scene 1, which was amazing, and we worked faster than the other directors who were performing their plays. However, towards the end we had some terrible run-throughs and there were a couple of times when I'd leave a rehearsal in tears. On the other hand, there were many times when I'd be elevated by my experience of rehearsing and that was because of how wonderful my cast were. I had a few problems with cast members bitching about each other and even me, but you get that in every company.

The dress rehearsal was a day that I will never forget. Everything that could possibly go wrong did. Two cast members were late and all the technology messed up. People forgot their props and we'd still not completely staged everything. Some people were not sure if we were going to pull it off at all. The head of the theatre company gave us some harsh words and said he didn't put his name to things that failed, so we had to have extra hours of rehearsal to get the play to the standard of performance that it should be. Some of the girls cried and I was utterly embarrassed because the lead male had brought his friends to watch. We'd had a good run-through a few days before. I cried because I was totally stressed and it was the first time I'd ever truly needed a cigarette, but we worked for hours on the day of the performance and we re-did the lighting and sound cues.

Sensory stimulus such as lighting and sound were challenging, but if the production needed it we did it. It did not matter about my hypersensitivity and one scene was based in a club and we had to dance to loud music in rehearsal. At the time, noise-cancelling headphones were not advertised as being useful to individuals on the spectrum, else I would have probably used them at every rehearsal.

The night of the performance was electric and we opened the New Writer's Festival with a bang. The audience laughed in all the right places and I was complemented on my ability to write. We had an amazing after-show party at my house once the production had ended, of which I need not go into details. However, the experience of putting the play on was one of the toughest things I've ever had to face, because being on the spectrum churned out all sorts of obstacles and anxieties. At that time I could barely organise myself let alone a cast of 14 actors.

I entered the world of booking rooms and of making sure that everyone was in the right place at the right time, which was something that I myself struggled to do. I also truly understood qualities of leadership for the first time, where if you are in charge of something you have to be a role model and your behaviour has to be respected by everyone in your team, else whatever you are trying to work on is doomed to fail. The general public do not understand how much effort goes into creating a show, and we had a period of approximately three months to rehearse, which sounds like a lot, but we were only meeting twice a week, so we really had to work hard in those sessions. And then once you perform the show, you have no evidence it ever happened unless it is filmed. So, it really is a challenging process. It was a bit of a nightmare but a fun nightmare, nonetheless.

DEPRESSION AND ATTEMPTED SUICIDE

My second year at university was coming to an end in June 2010, and one particular date around then is etched in my memory. On Monday, 28th June 2010, I had extremely powerful suicidal thoughts and I took myself off to the tube station to throw myself in front of a train. I was unsure what was happening to my body a lot of the time and the doctors still hadn't discovered my hypersensitivity to sound then. As I've said, I was using alcohol to combat social anxiety, and I wondered who would miss me? Who would care if this annoying autistic person was dead? I am very lucky that some lads pulled me from the tracks and called the police. The police in turn sent me to A&E and asked me if I wanted to contact my parents. I was embarrassed and did not want them to know, so I walked back to my shared accommodation alone from the hospital and never spoke of it again for a long while afterwards.

My mum was very supportive of me when I came home from university for the summer holidays. Even though she did not know exactly what happened, she must have known there was something wrong with me. I came home to sort my head out. I needed to learn to love myself, and I do think that there were a number of factors contributing to my depression. I had not really got over splitting up with my boyfriend in 2009 and the drinking had become worse after that point. I was stressed because of exams and course work and I found living with other people in shared accommodation challenging. I took some time to myself in summer 2010 and I found that it did me the world of good. I became a new person that summer and I was ready to focus on my final year of university, with less alcohol.

WHAT WOULD HAVE HELPED?

I think that if I were able to spot the signs of depression sooner then I might not have attempted suicide. The constant drinking and low self-esteem should have triggered alarm bells, but when I was young I did not have the ability to reflect and I just continued to make the same mistakes. The only thing I can think of that might have helped is if the university would have incorporated a mental health awareness course with lectures – not a course which would stereotype and label conditions but a course that would deal with issues faced by current students, such as depression and anxiety, and signpost where to get support from. If I had been more aware of what those things were, I think I might have got help quicker.

Also, if universities advertised more clearly where to go to get the help, then that would be beneficial. For example, there are the Samaritans, who will speak with you if you are feeling suicidal, and other charities such as MIND give useful information and guidance on mental health issues. Some universities offer advice leaflets in their health services departments and I think these are very useful. Some students do not know much about mental health issues and may not understand what the feelings they are experiencing are.

Having an awareness of what it is that you are feeling is incredibly helpful, and it is useful to have information available to you to help you through the difficult times.

TURKEY HOLIDAY 2010

That summer Mum took me and my sisters on holiday to Turkey. Now, I was just talking to you about learning to love yourself, and this holiday was the first time I did just that. I am in no way saying that all you need to stop being depressed is an expensive holiday; what I am saying is that self-care is very important – and that's what I did a lot of.

As she had retired in the March, Mum decided to spend a lot of money on going on a holiday. We stayed at the Mardan Palace hotel in Antalya. It was a five-star hotel and very luxurious. Upon arrival at the hotel, everyone's mouths fell open and I nearly cried at the beauty of the place. I felt that I wasn't worthy of such luxury and found it very hard to deal with. When we got into the hotel itself, the first thing we noticed were the chandeliers on the ceiling in the lobby that were more expensive than our house. The second thing we noticed was that we were being handed warm towels to wipe down our faces, on golden plates with golden tongs. We were then handed drinks of punch in tall glasses, and I couldn't take it all in. Next, we were told that we could put an extra £200 on our room cards so that we didn't have to take any money out of the hotel, but Mum declined because she didn't want to use it. Our suitcases were taken to our rooms on a golden baggage carrier.

For my whole life, I've felt as if I had to look after other people, and I'd never felt that it was ok for others to look after me until this particular holiday. By the end of the holiday, I was waiting for the ushers to open the door for me. I did a lot of soul searching that holiday, and it was the first time for many years that I'd been truly happy with my lot in life. I realised that I was lucky to have the opportunities that I've had and that there will always be someone in life who is worse off. I learnt to be grateful for everything that I've got – including my Asperger's. I learnt to like myself that holiday and I decided that my purpose in life was to have fun and find happiness. I taught myself how to turn negative thoughts into positive ones, and every time I'm sad now I just think of how beautiful Mardan Palace was. I decided that my self-worth was in my degree and in my friends and family and that I should be looking to the future rather than living in the past. On top of being proud to be autistic, that holiday made me quite a happy individual.

I saw how the rich children treated the ushers at the hotel and it made me angry. At one point, the children clicked their fingers and an usher came running with a towel. Those children just expected everything to be given to them and they were six or seven years old. They knew no different, so they couldn't be blamed for their behaviour – but if only they knew what it was like to be penniless; if only they knew what it was like for their mother to have to sell the sewing machine to be able to buy food for the week. That experience was what made me treasure every damned thing that I owned or had worked for and I was glad that things weren't handed to me. I learnt to appreciate everything!

The restaurant for breakfast was really extravagant. There was everything that you could ever hope for. There was even a substantial stand for different types of chocolate muffin. Everything in the hotel was extravagant. There was a pillow menu and the drawers were lined with velvet. Different types of cushions were laid out on the bed by the maids every day. Everything that you could ever need they'd thought of at that hotel, and the family and I could not believe that we had managed to achieve going somewhere so magnificent.

My Drama and French student friend came along with us on the holiday. I'd chosen to take her there as my friend because I thought that she truly deserved it. She'd been a good friend to me at university and had been through a lot that academic year.

We did some amazing things that holiday. We drank sambuca on balconies overlooking the pool. We sunbathed and swam most days. We went into the city to go shopping. We drove jet skis and went white-water rafting. We went on a jeep safari and a boat trip. We ate at loads of really nice restaurants and we went to an open-air club in the middle of the sea called Cecilia. We went in saunas and I went scuba diving. We went in a gondola around the hotel pool and watched fireworks on the balcony in the middle of August. We went on a Turkish spa day, which really helped my skin, and because I was only eating two meals a day I lost a load of weight that I'd put on from eating Weatherspoon's food in July. We went to a water park and we went on a blow-up chair driven by a boat around the ocean. That holiday I also learnt that I didn't need a man to make me happy, because I can enjoy the beautiful things in life that are already there that I didn't need to find. I was no longer jealous when I saw couples kissing because I was happy with what I had.

My little sister found the holiday challenging. Her friend that she'd taken with her was horrid and ungrateful. My sister didn't enjoy the holiday as much as she could have done. She flew home at the end of the first week because she couldn't enjoy being forced to be with people all of the time and not in her own space with her own familiar things.

Parents, consider siblings needs. One sibling may not need a diagnosis of autism but may still exhibit autistic traits and need support with other things. Try to pay attention to the individual needs of each child. If you feel that you cannot do that, then don't have so many children. Each child needs special focus, love and attention. Dad stayed with my sister in the house in Birmingham and none of us could understand how something that we thought was so beautiful could be so bad for someone else.

However, for me, I needed the break away from London and I sorted out my mental health massively. We all cried when we had to go home, and the staff at the hotel sent us a really nice message on Facebook which made us all really sad. Later Mum bought sunflowers to remind her of the hotel because it was their trademark. She also got really sad when she'd managed to make some vegetables look the way that they had in the hotel. Everyone laughed when we got off the plane after being told it was 13 degrees outside when we were used to it being 35. After the holiday, I stayed at my mum's for two weeks because I realised that home was important. I'd never really valued Birmingham much before, but I appreciated my mother and being around my family, so I went back to London for my third and final year as an undergraduate bearing this in mind.

STARTING FINAL YEAR

After my holiday, I welcomed my final year with open arms. Well, until the classes started again that is! In my final year freshers' week was a different experience entirely. It seemed to go on forever, but everyone was sad when it was over because it was the last one that some of us would do at university. As soon as I came back to London after the summer holiday, I went onto campus for the first time in ages. I collected my course packs and I went to a meeting to answer questions new students on the spectrum might have about university life. The event was a really positive experience. The new students could ask questions to people who had already experienced university life and were on the spectrum themselves. Afterwards, students at the event told me that they felt as if they were not alone on campus, and I stayed in touch with a few of them after I finished university.

I found out that I was on a 59 point average at the start of final year, so I knew the year was going to be tough if I wanted a 2:1 degree.

By the time I started my first lecture I'd completed a lot of reading beforehand. I read more than necessary because I was anxious about starting academic work again. We were given our course packs the Wednesday before and were only allowed a week to read before classes. I thought that was rather mean of the department, considering some of us had been off since April and were dying for some intellectual stimulus. I managed to read the entirety of my Madness and Theatricality course pack in an hour and I really enjoyed the Greek theatre that we were going to be studying. I didn't enter the class feeling like I couldn't remember anything, and I didn't feel overwhelmed, because I had chosen to specialise in that area of performance. The class was very physical and with a bout of fresher's flu I was very tired by the time we got to Hail Mary at the students union.

When I had my second class I was relieved to be able to sleep a little before the class – because I hadn't had much of it that particular month. Everyone had a lot of trouble in finding the lecture building and the room we were in. I was glad I wasn't the only one, because being on the spectrum makes me panic about things in an extreme way. Whilst I was really panicking about being late and getting my breath back when I sat down in the classroom, my colleague came strolling in ten minutes later in a calm fashion which suggested he hadn't been as worried as I was about finding the room. I will take this opportunity to demonstrate the contrast in thought process. Ten minutes before the class was due to start, I was panicking, anxious and upset. I knew that I wasn't late yet, but I also knew that I didn't know where to go. After much wandering around I found the room and once inside I had to calm myself down before I could concentrate. That was thought process number one. In contrast, my colleague clearly decided that as he was going to be late anyway he wasn't going to worry, which was the more rational response, and so he strolled into class with no distress and was able to get straight on with the work. I don't know if it helps at all to point out that some people on the spectrum have less rational minds than their neurotypical peers, but I just felt the need to show you that particular example.

I found the class exhilarating and I spoke to my adviser about my dissertation after the class. I hadn't always found academic writing easy and it was something I'd always struggled with, and at university it was worse because I had a habit of comparing myself to everyone else. There were many times where I found the work so hard that I nearly gave it all up, especially during my second year. (It was thanks to the lead male in *Knocking Over the Chair* that I didn't quit. He gave me the strength I needed to carry on.) However, there is a certain technique to writing academic assignments, and once you've got it you never forget it. It just took me a lot longer than most to figure out exactly what the technique was. And it turned out that I really enjoyed writing my dissertation – it was the one piece that I enjoyed writing most at university. It gave me a feeling of self-worth, because not many people are as knowledgeable as I am about audience catharsis and representation of Shakespearean ghosts in performances of 16th century literature.

SHARED LIVING: THE FINAL YEAR

My final year in shared accommodation had its pros and cons as everything does. I enjoyed living with four girls more than I thought that I would and the house was always tidy. My Law housemate helped me out with the bills so that I felt that I wasn't doing everything alone, and we did group online shops and we sometimes went to the pub on a Sunday evening for one quick drink before going back to working. The only thing that bothered me was that sometimes I felt bullied in the house, like whenever anything went wrong, I was always the first to get the blame, and the girls thought of an idea for the Halloween costumes which basically was a dig at me, calling me a failure for studying a Drama degree. They thought it was funny because they always joked about it, but I didn't find it amusing. Then there was the time they stuck a swastika symbol on my bedroom door. Also, there was one particular girl that I didn't see eye to eye with towards the end of the year. I found that living in a house full of girls was a lot bitchier than when we lived with a male. I felt like I didn't know who to trust when I told them something, because they'd go and tell the person that I was talking about. Other than these things, though, I loved my shared house in the final year. In fact, that final year at university was a great experience in many respects and I'll never forget it for as long as I live.

My Biomed housemate's boyfriend turned 22 in October and we gave him his presents at midnight. His surprise party went really well. I got up at 8am to finish my university work for the week and then I vacuumed the staircase. He got given breakfast by the other housemates; then his girlfriend took him out shopping. Whilst they were out, I bought party food and warned the neighbours that we were having a party. Afterwards, I went to campus for 4pm because I had to meet the Royal Literary Fellows. Once the meeting with them was over, I had to watch a film screening for Drama and do a bit of a rehearsal for class next day. When I'd done everything that I had to do on campus, I went to meet one of his ex-girlfriend's – they were still good friends – to show her where our house was. Everyone started arriving around 9.15pm and I just resigned myself to the fact that I probably wasn't going to sleep that night.

People on the spectrum can find it hard to change their daily routine and thinking about other people's needs isn't necessarily an easy thing to do. For example, I know someone who is so rigid in his routines that he will not change where he usually eats lunch or usually parks his car on campus. I decided not to be rigid about my working routine and that I could carry on working another time when it wasn't my colleague's birthday. If I hadn't made that decision, I think the party may have made me very anxious and upset.

My colleague had no idea that we were throwing a party for him and he was emotional when he came through the door at 9.30pm and we shouted surprise. We hired an entertainer called Mr Glamtastic and he was amazing. We hired him because we knew that my colleague had liked his music on a night out. Everyone got on really well, had a lot of fun and took tons of pictures. When Mr Glamtastic had finished his act we played drinking games until 4am. My colleague thanked me for his presents and he was smiling all evening. I was happy because he was happy.

The reason for me relating this experience so fully here is that there is an assumption that people on the spectrum cannot see things from others' points of view. I've included the above paragraphs to demonstrate that this is clearly not the case, as I understood how important someone's birthday could be for them and their partner and I was flexible in my routines and supportive of the party that was happening in my space. If I had been unable to see others' viewpoints, I would have continued to work and refused to participate in the party, which would have made my housemates sad. I also considered my colleague's likes and dislikes and organised a party that I knew he would enjoy. If I could not see others' viewpoints, I would not have been able to do this. So, I hope that including this has helped to dispel that myth a little.

As the final year advanced everyone got more serious about work. The late nights stopped and the music was usually off before ten, because we all had more important things to be getting on with.

APPLYING TO DO A MASTER'S DEGREE

The first semester of my final year was a really busy time for me. I remember having a number of essays to write, an exam (Madness and Theatricality) and an exam statement to get done all in a short period of weeks, on top of which the time to start writing up my dissertation was looming and I was initially terrified about that.

Nevertheless, I'd already decided that I'd like to do a master's degree, because my grandma worried me about what I'd like to do with my future when I stopped over at her house. In the second week of semester one I spoke with our M.A. course leader about how to apply for a master's degree. She told me that you applied to universities directly rather than through UCAS, like before, and that you should look for a course that supports the areas that you specialise in. I only applied for one university because I wanted to live at home rather than commuting. I hadn't the money to stay in London.

MADNESS AND THEATRICALITY

Madness and Theatricality was a module which I studied in my final year at university. It looked at how to portray mental health on stage and, looking back, I think the module informed a lot of my life choices after university. We had to work as a group for the Madness and Theatricality exam and stage a performance. The group I was in was all girls, so I thought that if anything the group would be organised. But our group experienced problems from the word go, because one of the girls refused to compromise with me and use techniques from the Greek theatre to inform our work about the contemporary. We had to go to see our professor in her office hour and she said that we would have to work together. I respected this woman a lot because she helped me progress at university.

Madness and Theatricality tutor*: My first clear memory of Madeleine was of a welcome event we held for new first year students in the Drama department... Perhaps I am mixing two memories here but I think Madeleine turned up to it to help welcome them, when she was in her second year. She seemed determinedly individual and forthright. And I think she might have been the only student from another year group there. If I'm remembering this wrongly, it still seems like the kind of thing Madeleine might do – decide that people needed* *welcoming and if no one else from her year group was going to help, well, tough, she'd turn up anyway.*

I got to know her better on the second-year course Performance Studies and Interdisciplinarity. This is a difficult course for some students; it deals with a range of tough theoretical work from disciplines other than drama and performance. I set up a lot of small group discussion in that class and my strongest memory of Madeleine is of her sitting with another student in the session that dealt with Gender Studies and teasing him into responding, when it seemed he was suggesting that all this gender stuff was a bit obvious. "So, tell me what you think gender is then..." I remember her saying. And, in a forthright but friendly way, she forced him to engage with the material.

So, I was surprised when Madeleine told me she was autistic. I have worked with students who have been labelled as having "Asperger's Syndrome" – though I gather that this is now a contested term – and they have seemed much less socially inclined than Madeleine. And I read a fair amount about people on the severer end of the autistic spectrum and have had two colleagues with autistic children – children who seem never to sleep and whose speech mainly consists of echoing others. I know that these severely affected young people are nothing like the "Asperger's students"; nevertheless, the idea of an "autistic spectrum" has made sense to me in the past, with the very high-functioning students demonstrating mild versions of the difficulties severely autistic children seem to have: difficulties reading what I'm asking of them – seeming to listen but not taking in what I'm saying. Madeleine seems very different from this. She responds to questions thoughtfully and clearly has a nuanced understanding of what's being discussed in a class. This is now sounding like a reference! But I am writing what I have experienced – one gets the impression there wouldn't be any point in flattering Madeleine falsely.

Now that she has told me she is autistic, I guess I can put some ways of behaving, some aspects of her social being, down to that. I'm now teaching her on a practical class and she's very forthright in group practice, more openly critical of what's happening in a rehearsal than other students might be. Perhaps some students find that hard to take?

She sometimes sounds abrupt – but to me, this seems useful; practical work can take a long time to get off the ground when students are too busy being polite about one another's ideas to move on from something that doesn't work. She's also very clear with me about what her worries are, about things she might find difficult to deal with in this class (the current practical class deals with issues around mental health). One particular play – Sarah Kane's 4.48 Psychosis *– she found profoundly upsetting. I asked the students to respond to it using a particular task and Madeleine sent me hers but didn't want to read it out in front of the group. I was happy to accept this. In fact, I was happy for anyone in the group to keep their work to themselves in this case as the play deals with such a painful subject. But In Madeleine's case, she has clearly put a lot of thought and a lot of herself into a piece that wasn't going to get a public hearing. I was impressed by that.*

On the other hand, might her determination and forthrightness lead to inflexibility when she likes an idea and doesn't want to let it go? I hope not. She is very keen to do well this year – 3rd year grades count for most in the calculation of our degree – but I hope she can also continue to just enjoy experimenting. She is willing to "put herself out there" and take real risks, whether in discussion or performance. There's no danger of a horrible silence when Madeleine's around – she just doesn't waste time being self-conscious. But given that I could be saying this kind of thing about someone who hadn't been diagnosed as autistic – I'm not sure how useful the term is, though she says accepting her diagnosis has helped her, which is obviously great. In the end, she seems determined to get everything she can from university and not to let self-doubt and self-consciousness get in the way. That seems to me to be something to learn from rather than to label.

I'll explain a bit more about the Madness and Theatricality exam as it's another good example of how much work goes into one performance.

I think most people have a tendency to view exams as something that is revised for, for months and then sat at the end in a large hall where you have to write about topics or do multiple choice questions. Drama exams are not like that and, in a way, I think they are harder because they rely on five or six people getting together in a group to do the work. It does not matter who puts in more effort, you all still get the same grade at the end of the performance, and if your performance does not work then you fail and get no grade at all. I get really cross with people who think Drama is a doss subject. It is hard to control your emotions and portray different characters day after day, even on demand sometimes, and people really take for granted how much work actually goes in to creating an event, only to have it disappear once the show has ended.

As someone with autism I found the preparation for the performance stressful and anxiety-provoking, especially when people didn't do things that they said they would, for example, not turning up to rehearse on the correct day.

My professor suggested allocating a separate time to worry about things and then just getting on with the work. This is a technique that I use in my everyday life today. Seeing as I was worried right that instant, I allocated 8.30pm–9pm as my time to worry about things and so I did a brainstorm for myself.

Ultimately, I adapted to the way of working with the group and we achieved something marvellous in the end. During the first week of December, the group had a run-through scheduled for 11am one morning. Our lighting states were very simple, so tech only took 15 minutes. We then did two runs and felt that there was nothing else that we could do to prepare for the exam. I went home for my lunch, because I couldn't afford to eat out and then I went to fencing to get some adrenaline running through me.

The session was helpful and afterwards I went to the Arts building flooded with nerves and fear. Some good friends of mine had come to support me and I was grateful to them. I sat and watched the two performances that were before mine and they were of a very high standard. Then it was time to perform and in the interval I was worried because my throat seized up. I thought that I wasn't going to be able to speak during the performance due to nerves. Everything went well, however, and it was over before I'd even really begun to enjoy it.

My friend and I walked home, and I tried to suppress the tears because I knew that I was never going to perform a practical exam as an undergraduate again. Later, over Christmas, I found out that I had scored 80% for that piece of work and I was happy because I'd never scored so highly at university before. I felt it was a nice Christmas present from my professor.

SOCIETIES: THE FINAL YEAR

You would think that being a final year student all you would have time for is work. That, surprisingly, isn't true; it's just that everything is a lot more intense than in previous years. You work like there's no tomorrow and you party in exactly the same manner, so sleep becomes a very rare experience.

I re-joined the fencing society and the film society in my final year, making me a member of five societies in total – including of course the theatre company which was voted the best society by the student union in 2010. I think societies are wonderful things, because you get to meet people with the same interests as yourself. I'd recommend it to anyone. I took my sports societies very seriously in the final year, because I couldn't afford to join the gym. I lost quite a bit of weight and got quicker with my fencing, but after the first week of doing it I began to feel horrendous pains in my knees and decided to go to the doctor. I'd had problems with my left leg for a while because my left knee would lock into place, but that winter my knees hurt so badly that I'd cry and need pain killers. I had X-rays done and blood tests, which revealed that I had a vitamin D deficiency. This could have been due to my repetitive diet, and the fact that I did not go outside much except to go to lectures and pubs. It was the deficiency that was hurting my legs, so I was prescribed tablets and I was just relieved that it wasn't anything more serious like arthritis or MS. If I hadn't been in my fencing team, it would have taken me a lot longer to figure out there was something wrong with my knees.

INTERVIEW 8: DANIEL

I will now interview a young man on the spectrum who also views university societies as being incredibly important.

Introduce yourself

Hi! I'm Daniel and I am 20 years old. Bit of a general nerd of all sorts of things.

What is your diagnosis?

Asperger's syndrome, but these days I use "high-functioning autism" or "autistic spectrum disorder" to describe myself.

What age were you when you were diagnosed?

I don't recall, but I believe I was diagnosed age four. I only really knew of my diagnosis when I was about eleven.

What are you studying at the moment?

Biological Sciences.

Do you have any special interests?

I am an 11th to 13th–century re-enactor, as well as a LARPer and tabletop gamer.

Do you have any sensory difficulties?

Yes. Overcrowding and loud noises are overwhelming.

How do you cope with your sensory difficulties whilst at university?

I have a short "battery life". Once I run out of energy, I understand that I need to rest, and forcing myself to continue to do things on an "empty battery" will not be productive.

What do you enjoy most about university?

The battle re-enactment society. I have been doing it for two years now, and it's what keeps me grounded while at uni (and physically fit).

What do you find most challenging about university?

Finding the motivation to keep academic attendance up, as well as completing course work. When things become overwhelming, my academics are one of the first things to begin to slip out of my routine.

What do you think could be done to make university better for people on the spectrum?

Offering dedicated quiet spaces on campus, outside of the library which can become overcrowded, dedicated to people with sensory issues to "recharge". This would help keep these students on campus and fulfilling their academic obligations.

What are your ambitions for the future?

Currently my focus is on graduating. After that, I would be happy with any job working in a laboratory, be that leading research or work as a technician. Most important to me is maintain[ing] the friendships I have made with people. I have found that these relationships are essential to my wellbeing.

Dan's answers demonstrate how important it is to have likeminded friends, and I too have tried to maintain the relationships that I have developed at various institutions.

CHRISTMAS AND NEW YEAR

I liked the Christmases at my university because it was always a really nice atmosphere. They put the tree up in the square on campus around the 2nd of December and there was always a Christmas concert for choir where we sang carols. For Christmas our seminar leaders brought in chocolates and it was always really nice on the last session. Each of the three years, I bought presents for my housemates and it was a lovely experience. Although we never had a Christmas tree in our shared house because we could not afford it, we'd do things like hanging up stockings outside my housemates' bedroom doors and covering the house in tinsel. The atmosphere was always really festive with Christmas music and cooking happening in the house. It was always odd when everyone went home, though, because campus was dead and very lonely.

On 16th December 2010, I auditioned for the mid-seasonal festival that the theatre company ran. I spent the day handing out presents and having meetings about essays and dissertations. I couldn't believe that semester one had ended and I was sad that I only had one more semester left at university, but I was very excited because my dad was finally coming to London to see my house and university.

When Dad came, he had forgotten how large London was and he didn't like having to walk everywhere. We walked from Mile End Station to my house and the snow was starting to fall. When we got to my house Dad met my housemates and he said that they seemed like very nice people. Afterwards, we explored my university's campus and I took him to the Arts building; he saw the Pinter studio, and then we went to the union and got some lunch. Dad gave me some money to buy new shoes, because my other ones had holes in them. After I'd shown Dad the campus, we met my housemates in the coffee shop and Dad got on well with my Biomed housemate, because they discussed science and looked at photographs from Finland. Once Dad had gone, I bought new shoes from Oxford Circus and then I went out for a meal with my English course mates.

Christmas Day felt strange, because I couldn't actually believe it was there. I'd be graduating in five months and had no idea what to do with my life. I couldn't quite believe that it'd be 2011 the next week and so the whole of Christmas was very surreal to me. I was going to finish my education, unless I did a master's degree, which I was still unsure of, because I was having difficulty locating two people to do references for me.

I spent most of Christmas Day 2010 putting my photographs into albums in order by date. I needed to give myself a task in order to cope with socialising with my family. Now that could sound quite harsh to some people, to use the term "cope with", but allow me to explain. My family are not a particularly close family, but we get together once every year in the name of Christmas. We then spend three days together when the rest of the year we only communicate via the internet or the occasional visit or phone call, so I find that quite challenging due to the fact that I believe that we do not really know or understand one another. We watch the same Christmas films each year and we sit at the table Christmas Eve together, but I still do not believe that we know each other as a family.

All I wanted for Christmas was photos of my university experience, but the trouble was that I printed 5,000 of them and I only had six photo albums. We finished opening presents at 1pm, because we had a breakfast break at 11am, and so I spent the next five hours arranging my photographs. Once I'd finished that task, I tidied my room so that I had space for my new presents and then I came down for dinner because my eldest sister's boyfriend was over. We were having steak and chips. It wasn't a traditional Christmas meal, but my family always ate ours the night before, because Mum used to always work Christmas night and when Mum and Dad divorced my aunty came to stay with us every Christmas, which was also a new tradition.

I find certain aspects of Christmas difficult, but I enjoy it overall. I do not like the fact that consumerist culture forces Christmas preparation to begin in September due to competing to sell the most stuff. I find society's complete lack of regard for people who are poor or struggling with mental health issues difficult. For example, someone could be missing a loved one who has died and gets told, "Cheer up, it's Christmas." I also cannot bear the religious ambiguities that surround Christmas. We do it to celebrate the birth of Christ. Sure, but we are not a Christian family and there is no record of Christ's actual birth date. I believe that as a country we just actually enjoy having gifts, singing and overindulging but we have to dress it up as a religious ceremony to make ourselves feel better about it.

WHAT WOULD HAVE HELPED?

It can be said that people on the spectrum, particularly youngsters, might find Christmas upsetting. It only happens once a year. It is a change in their routine, and if their family are not religious they might find the reasons behind it difficult to understand. If they find it hard to socialise, then making small talk with family members, about topics that don't interest them, could be incredibly difficult. (I have also heard of children who are scared of Father Christmas.) The National Autistic Society states that, "People with autism may become confused or distressed by all the new activity." The society also suggests parents talk with their child about what Christmas means to the family and preparing them with an activities schedule that parents and child create together.

For me, I find it is a change in my routine, but I have simply created a Christmas routine which I can now cope with.

Young people on the spectrum, it is ok if you do not like Christmas. You may feel that you need your own space and that is fine. However, I would suggest that you try to ask for this in a positive way that will not hurt your family's feelings. Try to see things from their perspective. If they enjoy Christmas, then that is fine too. If they want to sing Christmas carols, then let them. Don't tell them, "Christmas music is dumb and annoying," even if you think that is the case. You can go upstairs to your room and you won't have to listen to it, but try not to invalidate the fun and experiences that others are having. You can tell them what your needs are in an honest way without being hurtful. In my opinion, being with family is special regardless of the fact that you may not be close to them because they are the first people that you will meet once you are born into this world.

Parents, all I can suggest is to see what works for your child and your family. If your child does not want to spend too much time with the family socialising, then allow them to go to their bedroom if they need too. Christmas should be a time which is enjoyed by all, and your child may enjoy the holiday in a different way to yourself. If they enjoy sitting in the gift boxes instead of playing with their new toys, then let them; do not scold or mock them for it. I feel this paragraph is important because many young people on the spectrum and parents alike struggle with Christmas, and it is not an unusual occurrence or something to be mocked. Everyone, autistic or not, just try to see things from all perspectives and Christmas can still be an enjoyable experience. The food is great and so is the music, when it is not forced down your throat by shopping centres and radio stations from September, and Christmas is a time for community and a time to be grateful for what you have.

EARLY 2011 AND MY 21ST BIRTHDAY

After the students came back to the university in the new year (2011) it was all systems go with the work as we knew graduation was in July. I felt like I was not myself as I always seemed to be in my room working instead of going out with my friends like I wanted to. My housemates started to say I was becoming reclusive, and perhaps I was, but I was just so anxious about finishing my work. I did not really socialise until my 21st birthday in March.

The final reading week in my final year fell just before my birthday. Reading weeks occurred twice a year for the three years and you did exactly what the name suggests that you do. You spent the week reading to catch up with all the work you are behind on. A lot of students spend this time doing very little, sleeping and going to protest events like I did. In final year, though, reading week was a much more serious affair because everything you did counted towards your overall degree score. The final reading week of my university career was tough and a lot of hard work. I was sad because it was my last reading week at university. I was happy as it was my birthday party the next week, but sad because I only had three months left to finish my university work. I worked solidly for four days but then I hit a setback because I really wasn't interested in the reading that I had to do and so it became a battle to get motivated. I managed to motivate myself by taking a break and having lunch with some friends, but it took me so long to read one particular article that it really put me behind again. When reading week ended I was terrified, because everything was starting to come together and I knew that 2011 was a really important year in my life.

On 9th March 2011 I got a conditional offer to study for a master's degree and I was so happy that I cried. I couldn't believe that I got accepted onto the course, because all my life I'd had to cope with feelings of inadequacy. Students, reading week taught me that preparation is the most important thing. This lesson does not just have to be for university work but for anything in life, such as job interviews, group sessions or plays. Planning and preparatory work is very important, and even if you do not decide to go to university and the only thing you take away from this chapter is that planning is important, then I will have done the job I set out to do.

I pretty much had a week-long celebration for my birthday. As 21 is a big birthday I was really quite emotional throughout. On previous birthdays I had been depressed because I had hated being me due to low self-esteem or I was unable to see the wonderful things that I did have in my life. When I was 21, I finally acquired a new outlook from somewhere and I began to practise being grateful for the things that I had.

I had several parties – such as a party at the pub where my friends told me they weren't coming because they had too much work to do and then surprised me at the pub with cake. Also, there was the house party that they threw me which was Rocky Horror–themed fancy dress. Finally, there was a party in Birmingham where I had a pink limo take me to an adult wacky warehouse. I started to enjoy things in the moment and stop worrying about the past or future when I turned 21. I was able to look forward to the future and wondered what adventures life would take me on. My birthday usually fell around reading week in semester two and at that point in 2011 we only had three weeks left on campus.

EDINBURGH PITCH NIGHT

During my final year, it was announced that the Edinburgh pitch night would be on Tuesday, 22nd March 2011. If you're not familiar with it, the Edinburgh Fringe Festival is a month-long festival in Scotland which takes place in August every year. Artists go there to showcase their work with the hope of being discovered by talent scouts. They go there to make themselves a reputation in the theatre industry. Edinburgh pitch night was an audition process that gave the winning students the opportunity to take a show to

Edinburgh. I'd taken part in my second year and had been devastated when my play didn't get into the Edinburgh Fringe Festival then. I knew that it was all part of the theatre business, but I couldn't shake the feeling of inadequacy. I got very depressed about it, became unwell for a while and nearly stopped doing Drama altogether. However, my final year saw me more determined than ever because I knew that it was my last chance to go to Edinburgh unless I created my own theatre company.

So, it was my final year of university and my final attempt to take a show to the Edinburgh Fringe Festival. I was really nervous and resolved to conclude that my play wasn't going to get accepted so that I wouldn't be disappointed on the night. I practised my losing face and knew that if I did lose I was going to go straight home to drink in my room. I practised my pitch a lot in my room. I met with a member of my cast at 5pm to practise the pitch one more time, because the night didn't start until 6pm. We sat in the New Globe pub and I had a glass of white wine for Dutch courage. There were seventeen pitches and only four got accepted, so I lost again, but that year I was happy because I knew that I had done my best and I did not mess up the pitch. I was free from my nightmares about the second year where I lost my bottle and went home to cut myself in my room. I went to bed tipsy with a smile on my face, happy, because I'd been invited to perform my poetry live in Peterborough for another competition. I was grateful to everybody who supported me that night, particularly my Biomed housemate and her boyfriend. They'd helped me sort out my presentation, printed off a load of handouts for me and given me courage. I was still hopeful because there were auditions for the plays left before I told myself to give up on my dream for another year. Now, though, I had exam term to focus on and one final presentation left to give. Instead of giving up on my dreams, I turned a negative situation into a positive and recovered my confidence after having been knocked back the previous year.

MY FINAL WEEK ON CAMPUS

The final week of teaching on campus was at the end of March too. The first thing of concern was to finish all of my essays, and so I booked many writing workshops with the Literary Fellows and office hours with my tutors throughout the week. I went to seven of them in total and I was still very anxious that my writing wasn't good enough to get me the 2:1 that I so desperately wanted. The second thing of concern was that I barely had enough money to live until the next loan, so I applied for the Access to Learning Fund. The Access to Learning Fund is a non-repayable grant which helps students who struggle financially. Each university has a different system, so when you apply to your institution ask about it during freshers' week.

I was also desperately upset to be leaving uni. It was the first institution where I ever cried about leaving. When it was time for me to leave primary school, secondary school and sixth form, in each case I was ready to move on by the end of my time there, but I wanted to be a student, at university, forever.

One Monday I had meetings about my dissertation structure all day. In the evening we went to Nando's to celebrate, because the Law students had finished their undergraduate classes. I didn't like the idea of all the goodbyes that I was going to have to say all week. The hardest goodbye to say was to my fencing team. I knew I was going to cry and couldn't bear the thought of not seeing some of them every week.

I went to my final Children's Literature lecture and was sad to be saying goodbye to friends of mine who had their last day that day. At the end of the lecture everyone clapped, and I found out I got 70% for a previous assignment, so I cried, because I'd never got a 70 for written work before. After the seminar I ran home to get changed for the colours and honours ceremony. I wore the nicest purple dress that I could find and went to meet my fencing team at

Mile End Station. The boys looked lovely in their suits and I felt very proud to be a part of their team. We got to the venue and I took my team captain's arm and I knew I was going to cry again, because I didn't want to leave them ever. I was awarded half colours, which was basically an award for effort within the team. It meant a lot to me because I'd not won anything in sports since my judo trophies in 2000 and it meant that my team captain obviously thought that I could do it because he was in charge of the nominations. I knew that every time I looked at my award badge that I'd think of him. He was the only one who ever said that I could do it in a sport, and now when I fence I can hear him cheering me on in the back of my head. After the ceremony we went on to a boat party and it was a wonderful evening.

I felt that I had to go to my final Shakespeare lecture. Some people didn't go because it was just a paperwork class, but I felt compelled to go as to me it was a significant ending. Afterwards we had a boys vs. girls fencing match. The girls lost and I felt sad because it was the last ever match I'd fence as part of that team. In the evening we went to the last Hail Mary and I cried on the way home because I didn't want to leave uni.

HANDING IN MY DISSERTATION

I handed in my dissertation on 17th May 2011 two days before the official hand-in date, and it was a very surreal experience. I'd started to panic on 1st May and I'd had sleepless nights right up until the hand-in.

You see the trouble was that I didn't believe that any of my essays were good enough to hand in and was fighting a large urge to delete everything and start again. I'd gone back home for a week during the Easter period and learnt to adjust to the way life would be when I came home for real. It wasn't that bad an occurrence. I printed out three copies of my dissertation: two for the markers and one for me – my copy had a hardback cover so that I could display the largest piece of writing I'd ever completed. When the day came, it felt as if a weight had been lifted from my shoulders – although I was still a bit wary because my Biomed housemate hadn't finished her exams and still had two more to go, so I didn't want to rub it in her face that I'd finished and she hadn't. After I'd handed my dissertation in, I went for a drink in Weatherspoon's (or 'spoons as we'd call it) with my course mates, but everyone was so exhausted that we didn't stay out for very long, so it was anti-climactic. By the time the official hand-in day happened I'd already been free for two days and so it didn't seem like a very big deal to me. I'd been sad the night before, because of some horrible things said about me in the University of London fencing club. I stayed up all night trying to sort things out and worrying, so I was very tired when I got to the drinks reception at 4pm. I'd gone to say goodbye and thank you to my adviser, my Drama professor and my boss, because without them I'd not have a degree at all. I drank a lot of wine and my colleague, the one who I'd dumped my boyfriend for due to being obsessed with, and I spoke for the first time in two months. He wasn't unpleasant – just it seemed very forced and uncomfortable, so when my friend wanted to leave I left to go to 'spoons and drink with the film society. I'd rather stay with them than some of my course mates. A group of us went to Brick Lane and we had an enjoyable evening. However, I was sad because I wanted to mark handing in my dissertation in a memorable way, but it hadn't been possible due to anxiety and everyone finishing at different times. However, I needn't have worried because our celebration of the end of my contract at our student house was big enough for the two occasions.

GOODBYE SHARED LIVING

Our contract ended on 5th July 2011 and I was desperately upset to be leaving. One month before I was due to move out, I started to get upset about it. My Biomed housemate cried one night and I was extremely touched by her strong show of affection towards me. I looked at the photos from my three years at university and I felt sadness in my heart, but I knew I had to move on. London had been my home for over two years and I couldn't imagine what life would be like studying for an MSc. Even though the friends in Birmingham were still the same and I'd never had any strict rules placed on me at my mum's house, I liked having the ability to say that my student house was my own. I was excited about all the opportunities that lay before me, but I couldn't bring myself to let go of student life so easily. One of my friends at the time came in his van to take the majority of my stuff and once he'd gone the house felt empty, because there was hardly anything that belonged to me left in it.

On 1st July we had a house party for my Biomed housemate's birthday. That day I spent the day preparing the house for the party. Mum came to collect the last of my stuff that I couldn't fit in my friend's van and she dropped my friend Ginge off at our house. The party was amazing, we sang happy birthday to my Biomed housemate at midnight, and I would relive that party again in a heartbeat if I could. I was sad when we closed the door of the house and I left my keys on my desk next day. My Law housemate cried, and because she was crying it made me upset too, so I had to compose myself before Ginge and I travelled back to Birmingham. I wasn't too devastated, however, because I knew I was coming back to London for graduation, and so when I got home I just curled up in bed and slept off the final hangover of my undergraduate days.

GRADUATION

I graduated from university on 19th July 2011 and the ceremony started at 2.30pm. I'd been agitated because the university admin was awful and they took an incredibly long time to send our invitations out. I was also shocked that it cost £50 for two guests to come and watch my graduation ceremony. I'd already paid £25 for a yearbook and I had to measure my head and chest to get robes that fitted correctly. Once I'd paid for everything, though, I couldn't believe it was happening. Three years previously in my first week as a student the headmaster had shown us photographs of other ceremonies and I'd been sad because it seemed like an impossible goal and that the day was so far away. Now it was here.

The night before the ceremony I stopped at Dad's and his partner made me a roast dinner. I'd had nightmares most nights leading up to the ceremony. There were dreams about falling over on stage or my anxiety about seeing my colleague again. I'd spent two hours searching for my student I.D. card and getting agitated with the people I was speaking to on Facebook because I couldn't find it. However, the morning of the ceremony I woke up at 9am and for the first time in my life understood why some women feel the need to spend half an hour in the bathroom getting ready. At 9.30am Dad was trying to get me out of the door, but I was still putting my foundation on. Dad drove to Stanmore Underground Station and parked there, and then we got the Jubilee Line to Westminster. One thing I do not miss about London is the tubes. I did not eat a thing until Dad bought me some chocolate buttons at Westminster Station, because we'd not had any time beforehand.

The ceremony was really badly organised and we had to queue for ages to get our tickets and gowns. I saw my Biomed housemate's boyfriend in his gown and he looked very handsome. Then in the queue to collect the robes I saw my colleague who I'd fallen in love with. The first time I did not say a word to him, but I knew I'd regret it for the rest of my life if I were a coward and did not apologise for my strange behaviour towards him, and so the next time I saw him I apologised to him and congratulated him. He said, "Thank you, it's ok man, it's ok," but I could see in his eyes that for him it'd never be ok and so I turned my back. When he collected his degree I was proud of him. I was glad that I knew him, even for a little while and even after everything, because without him I'd never have written *Knocking Over the Chair* and I'd not have discovered my passion for writing play scripts. I hope that one day he will find it in his heart to truly forgive me – because all human beings make mistakes. Fine, mine was a pretty large one, but he was not completely innocent either. He never understood why our short friendship meant so much to me, and it was because without realising he showed me how unhappy I was and that things had to change. He was the inspiration for so many of my poems, lyrics and performances, and so I wished him all the best for the future and clapped until my palms were red when he shook the principal's hand and walked well and truly out of my life.

When I had my time on stage I felt relief – relief that it was all over; my battle to prove to the world of education that I was not a lost cause or a failure had ended. However, when I sat back in my seat I faced a new fight, the unemployment fight, and trust me it was a very long war which saw lots of hard work, effort and preparing continued professional development folders. I was happy and honoured that we graduated with Dr Bruce Dickinson from Iron Maiden, who was being awarded an honorary music doctorate. I was happier still that I won an award for being able to hold down the most pints in the yearbook. Dad took a lot of photos and the drinks reception was really nice. I got to introduce Dad to more of my friends and my favourite professors. At 6pm everything died down and I handed my gown back and collected my bags from the cloakroom. I was going to stay with my housemates from the shared house for three days, because I missed them all desperately.

INTERVIEW 9: VICKI

I will now interview one final lady, who is currently studying her PhD. She is very similar to me in many ways but also very different too. Here is what she had to say.

Introduce yourself

My name is Vicki Taylor and I am a 32-year-old, Birmingham-based actor, poet and academic. I have multiple disabilities and I love rainbows!

What is your diagnosis?

I have multiple diagnoses including classic autism, ADHD, learning disability, physical disabilities and long-term mental health diagnoses, amongst other medical labels.

What age were you when you were diagnosed?

I can't remember.

What are you studying at the moment?

I am doing my PhD on the impact of theatre on the neurodiverse population at the University of Birmingham.

Do you have any special interests?

I have special interests in rainbows, acting, and advocating for autism.

Do you have any sensory difficulties?

I have many sensory sensitivities including being hypersensitive to light, sound, smell and taste – and hyposensitive to touch. This means that I find it very difficult to process sight, sound, smell and taste, and so I find these senses painful and uncomfortable. However, I require touch in order to process, which means that I process friendships through physical contact like hugging.

How do you cope with your sensory difficulties whilst at university?

I do not attend lectures as I find them too difficult. I do most of my university studying independently through distance learning. I also have an autism-specialist mentor who accompanies me to seminars or talks or supervisions.

What do you enjoy most about university?

The best thing about university is the learning – I love learning. I love achieving things that are beyond my potential and beyond all expectations. I want to prove that people with neurodiverse conditions can achieve anything – even high standard academia – if they want to.

What do you find most challenging about university?

My biggest challenge at university is that there are too many people, and I also struggle with information overload! I learn in my own way, which I am writing a book about.

What do you think could be done to make university better for people on the spectrum?

I think distance learning should be more widely accepted as a strategy for people on the spectrum. I think that all students on the spectrum should have access to an autism-specialist mentor and one- to-one tutorials if and when required by the student. Also, all learning materials should be offered in multiple formats to comply with the different sensory sensitivities – such as visual presentations, audio recordings, and text lists.

What are your ambitions for the future?

I want to be a neurodiverse actor and an advocate for neurodiverse individuals. My aim in life is to be an inspiration to other people.

Vicki's answers demonstrate that people on the spectrum can achieve highly in academic settings and that everyone has their own unique way of learning and coping with situations.

FINAL THOUGHTS AND MY REASONS FOR WRITING THIS BOOK

"You yourself, as much as anybody in the entire universe, deserve your love and affection."

John Amodeo, *The Authentic Heart*

"Never be bullied into silence. Never allow yourself to be made a victim. Accept no one's definition of your life, but define yourself."

Harvey Firestein

As one door closes another opens. I fondly waved goodbye to my undergraduate education but would soon be starting study for my master's degree. And here too ends the main narrative of my book. I had, as I say, succeeded in proving that I was not a lost cause or a failure – far from it. I would like to point out that because of determination, hard work, graft, supportive friends and family I have achieved the best I can today. Someone on the spectrum, without the support, may struggle more than I did, and that is why I think that it is so important that the correct support is needed from the start, so that people on the spectrum can flourish in the way that they are capable of. But I'd also like to say one final time that what worked for me may not work for someone else on the spectrum – as human beings we are all different. It may be you just have to keep trying to find out what works for you through trial and error, but don't ever give up or think yourself worthless. You are not.

The job situation worries me. In a capitalist world where most people are underpaid for the work that they do and it is acceptable to encourage apprenticeships for working in fish and chip shops where young staff are only paid £4.30 per hour, I am surprised that there is support and encouragement for young people with autism who want to work. But believe me it is there. It may be few and far between but you can find it in the form of Autism West Midlands, the National Autistic Society, Grapevine in Coventry and, if your passion is theatre, the Open Theatre Company in Birmingham. The help is there if you search for it and if you ask for it. It may feel like looking for a needle in a haystack, but once you find the correct support it cares for you and encourages you to be your best.

I feel sorry for the youth of today who have to stay at school until they are 18, because there are no job opportunities for them and once they get out there they get told they need a year's experience, so they are forced into apprenticeships who can pay as little as they like or they have to work voluntarily to make up the experience. I can only pray that with enough activism and everyone being the change that they want to see in the world that the world will indeed change even if the progress is slow.

Of course, the adjustment from school or university into the working world is another transitional period that individuals on the spectrum might find more challenging to cope with than others. The working world is competitive and cruel and if you have been having support all the way through your education and then it just stops because you are an adult it can be hard.

The Personal Independence Payment (PIP) is an allowance that you can get if your disability causes you difficulties. It is available for anyone between 16 and 64 years old and is paid into your account monthly if you are successful in claiming the funds. It has specific assessment criteria and a long application form, so support might be useful when applying for the funds. The process can be quite daunting, particularly the idea of being seen by an assessor, but try not to worry and gain as much support as you can from family, friends or carers.

The National Autistic Society have an advice about work page, which offers useful tips and advice about work, and Autism West Midlands in Birmingham employ individuals on the spectrum to work on their reception desk. There are a growing number of companies – albeit most so American companies – that are seen as autism-friendly employers. Companies like Microsoft, Ford, Freddie Mac, SAP and Chevron have recruitment programmes that actively recognise the value of hiring neurodiverse individuals. I personally believe that occupational therapy can be a rewarding career for someone on the spectrum because it is about adapting the environment to suit the individual and supporting the individual to develop in their environment. However, it can be quite challenging as it involves speaking with lots of strangers and is a separate degree.

Sadly, finding a job does involve a lot of research about finding out who the most non-discriminatory companies are, and applying for support funds is a tough and long process, but it is worth doing because working has enabled me to feel empowered and valued in society. On their website the National Autistic Society quote a jobseeker with autism as saying, "Autistic people have some very valuable skills which can be applied in the workplace. They might have very good attention to detail, or be really good at sticking to routines and timetables. Therefore, they are likely to be very punctual and reliable. Everyone has different skills but there will always be something." I am a firm believer in this too, and also that if you persevere you will succeed. I wish you all the very best in the future.

My main aim for writing this book has been to give a voice to people on the spectrum who are so often written about by experts but silenced in their daily lives. I wished to demonstrate that, although many of us exhibit similar symptoms, a one-size-fits-all model simply does not work when caring for individuals on the spectrum.

I also wanted to bang the drum for individualised care in schools. I think that all young people should have individualised education plans based on abilities and interests and that all children should be supported and collaborated with to understand what their needs are. Focus should no longer be on how well individuals do in exams but on how to best utilise their skills and passions to support them in the world of work. The education system has to change and this book aims to rally educators and call for action for changes to be made which better improve accessibility for individuals with learning differences.

So, my aim is to influence people and to highlight the dire need for change within the education system regarding how to support individuals on the spectrum. I want to inspire people to work hard, and I want children and young people on the spectrum to have a bit of hope for the future. I don't want to be some kind of martyr and say look at me, look at how much I've suffered. I want to say I'm happier now. I'm the happiest I've ever been in my life, since accepting that autism is a wonderful part of who I am. I only wish that people could feel and experience some of the things that I have.

I hope that by interviewing individuals on the spectrum I have demonstrated a few things including:

Firstly, that yes, we all have similar signs and symptoms such as sensory processing difficulties, but that does not mean that we should all be looked after in exactly the same fashion or in a one-size-fits-all sort of way.

Secondly, that we are all as valid and capable as neurotypical individuals are and that our opinions are worthy despite coming from someone with an autistic brain. Just because we are on the spectrum, it does not somehow invalidate our opinions or beliefs because we are different to you.

And thirdly, that people on the spectrum can achieve great things if given the right encouragement and a supportive environment to figure out life in.

Acceptance of oneself is what brings true happiness. Once that is achieved then that is the biggest part of the battle over.

My family always said, "Respect yourself and then others will respect you," and my Biomed housemate always said to me, "Be proud of and accept your autism."

I wish to thank everyone who I knew at university, because they made me into the person who I am today. I want to thank all of my helpers and teachers across all the institutions I've been a part of. I particularly want to thank the men and women whom I have felt connected with – you know who you are. Because of you I have grown and changed as a person and learnt how to love appropriately.

I want to leave you all with something to consider. Think of a time in your life when you were at your lowest point. Think how it made you feel and then consider what you did to make yourself smile again. Did you give up, look to the ground and say, "I'm not worth fighting for!" or did you stand up and fight, saying, "I'm going to be the best that I can possibly be and learn to love and accept myself so that others can appreciate how wonderful I am"?

MY CURRENT AMBITIONS

1) To live past 36

2) To pass my driving test and have my own car to drive

3) To own my own property

4) To take a play that I have written to the Edinburgh Fringe Festival

5) To qualify as an occupational therapist and get a job in that field

6) To have a year off from education before going into work to go on tour with Open Theatre Company and to support refugees or underprivileged children in a foreign country who need provision from occupational therapy personnel

7) To have a book published of my plays and poems

8) To go to Drama school and work with my theatre company Alternative Voices

9) To meet Danny Filth and Corey Taylor again – my favourite musicians ever!

10) To pass the advanced display test in my historical re-enactment society

11) To maintain a healthy weight of 67kg

12) To get better at Spanish, History and reading music

13) To learn to burlesque dance

14) To complete a Maths GCSE

15) To continue to nourish my spirituality and learn along my religious path

16) To be hand-fasted and have children, maybe?

NOTABLE PEOPLE

Hans Asperger – the Austrian paediatrician from whom Asperger's syndrome is named and who in 1938 discovered a group of children with distinct psychological characteristics

Simon Baron-Cohen – Director of the Autism Research Centre at the University of Cambridge

David Eastham – the first autistic author of a poetry book, *Understand* in 1985

Mary Temple Grandin – an American professor of animal science consultant to the livestock industry. Her book *Thinking in Pictures* provides valuable insight into her experiences living with autism.

Anne Hegertey – an English television quiz personality appearing on *The Chase* and 2018's *I'm a Celebrity Get Me Out of Here*. Anne has Asperger's and positively promotes Asperger's in the media.

Leo Kanner – Ukrainian-American psychiatrist who published a landmark paper on autism in 1943, "Autistic disturbances of affective contact"

Gary Mackinnon – Scottish systems administrator with Asperger's accused of hacking American defence systems

Rudy Simone – American author, self-diagnosed as Aspergic

Donald Triplett – the first person in the world to be diagnosed with autism. Donald was "Case 1" in Leo Kanner's 1943 paper.

RESOURCES

Autism West Midlands – the leading charity in the West Midlands for people on the autism spectrum

The National Autistic Society – the UK's leading charity for people on the autism spectrum and their families

Mind – the leading mental health charity in England and Wales

Samaritans – the long-established charity that offers support to anyone in emotional distress or contemplating suicide throughout the UK and Ireland

KEY REFERENCES

"10 tips to beat insomnia" NHS website article 2019

"Always Someone Else's Problem" report by the Office of the Children's Commissioner 2013

Aspergirls: Empowering Females with Asperger Syndrome by Rudy Simone (Jessica Kingsley Publishers 2010)

"Autism and bereavement: a guide for parents and carers" Autism West Midlands downloadable pdf 2020

"Autism and education in England 2017" report by the All Party Parliamentary Group on Autism 2017

Autism and Asperger Syndrome by Uta Frith (Cambridge University Press 1992)

Changing the Course of Autism by Bryan Jepson (Sentient Publications 2007)

Diagnostic and Statistical Manual of Mental Disorders (5th ed.; DSM–5; American Psychiatric Association 2013)

"Encouraging good sleep habits in children with learning disabilities" booklet by Paul Montgomery and Luci Wiggs (Oxford Health NHS Foundation Trust 2014)

Stigma: Notes on the Management of Spoiled Identity by Erving Goffman (Prentice-Hall 1963)

That's Not Right! My Life Living with Asperger's by Alex Manners (Cavalcade Books 2019)

AUTHOR CONTACT DETAILS

If you'd like to contact me with questions, concerns, comments or queries or with any suggestions on how to make the book more accessible, my email address is alternativevoices123@gmail.com

Lightning Source UK Ltd.
Milton Keynes UK
UKHW020628121121
393845UK00002B/2

9 781838 149000